BLACK&DECKER®

THE COMPLETE GUIDE TO

OUTDOOR CARPENTRY

More than 40 Projects Including:
- **Furnishings**
- **Accessories**
- **Pergolas**
- **Fences**
- **Planters**

Creative Publishing
international

MINNEAPOLIS, MINNESOTA
www.creativepub.com

Creative Publishing international

Copyright © 2009
Creative Publishing international, Inc.
400 First Avenue North, Suite 300
Minneapolis, Minnesota 55401
1-800-328-0590
www.creativepub.com

Printed in Singapore

10 9 8 7 6 5 4 3 2 1

Library of Congress Cataloging-in-Publication Data

The complete guide to outdoor carpentry : more than 40 projects
including furnishing, accessories, pergolas, fences, planters.
    p. cm.
  At head of title: Black & Decker.
  Includes index.
  Summary: "Features more than 40 projects that easily can be built in a
weekend with ordinary power hand tools and materials available at any
local home center or hardware store"--Provided by publisher.
  ISBN-13: 978-1-58923-458-1 (soft cover)
  ISBN-10: 1-58923-458-8 (soft cover)
  1. Garden structures--Amateurs' manuals. 2. Outdoor
furniture--Amateurs' manuals. 3. Carpentry--Amateurs' manuals.
I.Black & Decker Corporation (Towson, Md.)

TH4961.C6543 2009
684.1'8--dc22

2009010733

President/CEO: Ken Fund
VP for Sales & Marketing: Kevin Hamric

Home Improvement Group

Publisher: Bryan Trandem
Managing Editor: Tracy Stanley
Senior Editor: Mark Johanson
Editor: Jennifer Gehlhar

Creative Director: Michele Lanci-Altomare
Senior Design Managers: Jon Simpson, Brad Springer
Design Managers: James Kegley

Lead Photographer: Joel Schnell
Shop Manager: Bryan McLain
Shop Assistant: Cesar Fernandez Rodriguez
Production Assistants: Jessica Elsenpeter, Michelle Lee,
  Nicole Rosenbloom, Nichole Schiele, Katie Yokiel

Production Managers: Linda Halls, Laura Hokkanen

Project Design: Dan Cary
Page Layout Artist: Whitney Stofflet

The Complete Guide to Outdoor Carpentry
Created by: The Editors of Creative Publishing international, Inc., in cooperation with Black & Decker.
Black & Decker® is a trademark of The Black & Decker Corporation and is used under license.

NOTICE TO READERS

For safety, use caution, care, and good judgment when following the procedures described in this book. The publisher and Black & Decker cannot assume responsibility for any damage to property or injury to persons as a result of misuse of the information provided.

The techniques shown in this book are general techniques for various applications. In some instances, additional techniques not shown in this book may be required. Always follow manufacturers' instructions included with products, since deviating from the directions may void warranties. The projects in this book vary widely as to skill levels required: some may not be appropriate for all do-it-yourselfers, and some may require professional help.

Consult your local building department for information on building permits, codes, and other laws as they apply to your project.

Contents

The Complete Guide to
Outdoor Carpentry

Introduction

Ask any experienced woodworker or carpenter to tell you about his or her first woodworking project and the chances are pretty good that it was built for the outdoors: a birdhouse, doghouse, picnic table, or perhaps an Adirondack chair from a kit. For a number of reasons most of us are more comfortable with building exterior projects. The tolerances are not as tiny as they are for indoor furniture. The joinery tends to be simpler. The materials are easy to find and fairly inexpensive. But none of these reasons takes anything away from the appeal of outdoor carpentry. The fact is, the things we build for our outdoor living are almost always fun to use and very rewarding to make.

In *The Complete Guide to Outdoor Carpentry* you will find plans, step-by-step pictures, and instructions for 41 shop-tested projects built from wood. They cover a wide range of skill levels, styles, materials, and functions. Although several of the projects might be easier and faster to build if you have a workshop equipped with stationary tools, every bench, table, fence, and gate in this book can be crafted using only common handheld power tools.

Although outdoor carpentry presumes that you will be working with wood, you'll find a few interesting ideas for working other materials into your projects. You'll find a trestle-style picnic table where the traditional wood seat boards and tabletop are replaced with composite decking for a low-maintenance furnishing that's also a great conversation piece (pages 78 to 85). For the backyard cook who is looking for a safe spot to store fuel and grilling accessories, check out the locker with an aluminum angle iron frame and cedar plywood panels (pages 112 to 115). For the more experienced carpenter or woodworker, you'll find projects featuring traditional hardwoods and woodworking joinery, such as the mahogany sun lounger (pages 68 to 75) and the white oak Adirondack chair with canvas sling seat (pages 20 to 25).

Outdoor carpentry is a much bigger category than simply "furnishings." For the gardener in the family it means potting tables, planters, and yard carts. You'll find clever plans for several of these practical projects as well as decorative garden accessories like bridges, water pumps, and lanterns. If you're thinking big, look for the gates, fences, arbors, trellises, and portable garden shed. Whatever your preference is when it comes to outdoor living, you'll find a project or two (or more) that's just for you in this book.

Seating Projects

You'll never fully enjoy your backyard without comfortable seating. Chairs, benches, and swings are mainstays of outdoor living. In this chapter you'll find a dozen seating projects that range from fanciful to simple, classic to retro, and nautical to Eastern-inspired.

Each design in this chapter has been carefully shop-tested for comfort. A couple of degrees of slant in a seatback might not appear to make much difference when you're drawing up a plan, but your body can tell immediately. And if your seating is not comfortable, what use is it? You can be confident that the benches and chairs that follow have been subjected to hands-on (well, not hands exactly) testing from sitters of all sizes.

If you are a relative newcomer to carpentry, consider starting with one of the simpler projects, such as the Knockdown Garden Bench or the Slatted Garden Bench. If your skills are a bit more advanced, think about tackling the Porch Swing and Porch Swing Stand or perhaps the Luxury Sun Lounger that's crafted from mahogany and features stainless steel brightwork.

In this chapter:

- Side-by-side Patio Chair
- Knockdown Garden Bench
- Sling-back Adirondack
- Classic Adirondack Chair
- Porch Swing
- Porch Swing Stand
- Tiled Garden Bench
- Slatted Garden Bench
- Trellis Seat
- Rose Bench
- Storage Bench
- Luxury Sun Lounger

Side-by-side Patio Chair

You can share a view, some shade, and a table for snacks and a beverage with a friend when you've got this side-by-side patio chair in your backyard. You might recognize the design, as it was inspired by the side-by-side chairs that were often included in the ubiquitous redwood patio sets popular in the '50s and '60s. Those sets typically included a lounge chair, some small tables, a patio table with an umbrella holder, and a side-by-side table and chair similar to the one shown here.

You'll find that these seats are most comfortable when they're appointed with cushions, but they're still easy to enjoy when left bare. And just about any patio table umbrella can be used with this set—simply size the umbrella post hole to fit. The optional umbrella should also be secured in a weighted base that is placed under the table.

Even a beginner can build this side-by-side chair in a day using less than $100 in materials. It's easiest to build if you have a table saw, miter saw, jigsaw, and router. If you don't have a table saw, then you can use a circular saw to rip the 2 × 4 frame pieces down to 3" widths. The purpose for these parts being 3" wide is to give the set a more refined appearance, but you can simplify the design and avoid rip cuts by using full width 2 × 4s. If you choose to use full-width 2 × 4s, then you must move the front rail notch up ½" and the seats will end up being a ½" higher.

Materials ▶

5 1 × 4" × 8 ft. boards	Deck screws (2", 2½")
5 2 × 4" × 8 ft. boards	Exterior-rated glue
1 2 × 6" × 8 ft. board	Finishing materials
1 ¾ × 12 ft. deck board	

This lounge chair built for two offers comfortable seating separated by shared table space. It is a perfect furnishing for intimate conversations or for quiet leisure time spent sharing a bowl of snacks and an occasional sidelong glance.

Side-by-side Patio Chair

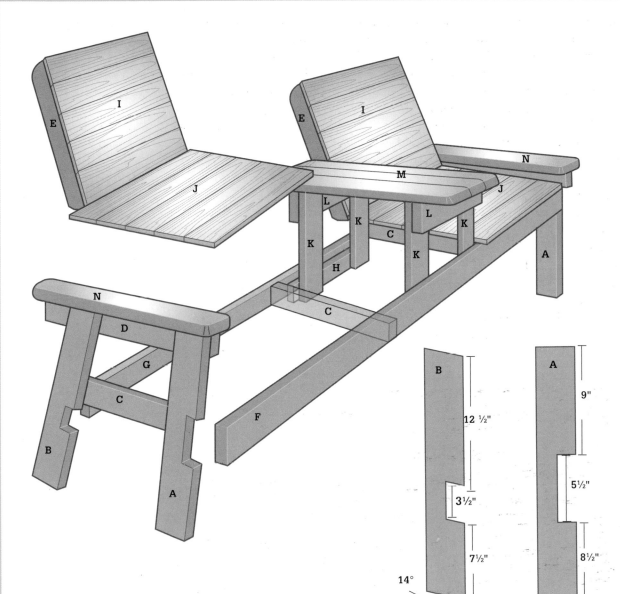

Cutting List

Key	Part	Dimension	Pcs.	Material
A	Front legs	1½ × 3 × 23"	2	PT Pine
B	Back legs	1½ × 3 × 23½"	2	PT Pine
C	Seat supports	1½ × 3 × 18⅝"	4	PT Pine
D	Arm supports	1½ × 3 × 22½"	2	PT Pine
E	Back supports	1½ × 3 × 21¾"	4	PT Pine
F	Front rail	1½ × 5½ × 60¾"	1	PT Pine
G	Back rail	1½ × 3½ × 60¾"	1	PT Pine

Key	Part	Dimension	Pcs.	Material
H	Table bottom crosspiece	1½ × 3 × 19¾"	1	PT Pine
I	Back slats	¾ × 3½ × 19"	10	PT Pine
J	Seat slats	¾ × 3½ × 20½"	10	PT Pine
K	Table posts	¾ × 1½ × 13½"	4	PT Pine
L	Table supports	1½ × 3 × 16¾"	2	PT Pine
M	Tabletop planks	1¼ × 5½ × 24"	3	PT Pine
N	Armrest	1¼ × 5½ × 24"	2	PT Pine

Side-by-side Patio Chair

BUILD THE FRAME

Cut 2 × 4 boards to make the legs, back supports, and seat supports. These parts must be rip-cut down to 3" wide to conceal their telltale 2 × 4 look (for best results, rip ¼" off each edge to get rid of the bullnose profile milled into most 2 × 4s). Use a table saw or a circular saw and edge guide to make the rip cuts. It is often easier to cut the parts to length first and then rip them to width because the shorter boards are more manageable.

Use the construction drawings (see page 9) to lay out the notches, miters, and radius-curve profiles on each piece. These details must be correctly noted onto the parts. Lay out the notches that will hold the front rail in between the front legs and the back rail in between the back legs. Drill a ⅜" blade access hole in the inside corners of each notch and then cut the notches out with a jigsaw. Clean up cuts with a chisel or small profile sander.

Miter-cut the ends of the back legs at 14° angles. Be careful to cut the miters in the correct direction so that the notch is on the front edge of the back legs. Miter-cut one end of each seat support to 14° **(photo 1)**. *Note: Parallel angled cuts on the ends of a workpiece are called "plumb cuts."* Miter-cut the bottom

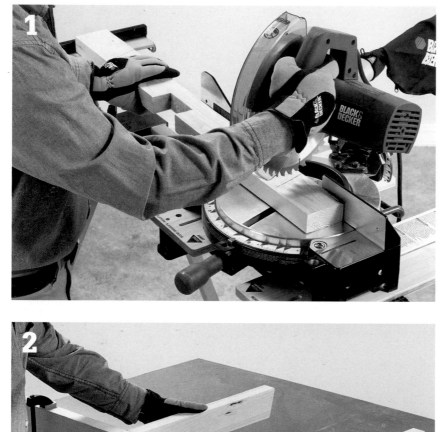

Make plumb cuts on legs. Set the miter saw table to 14° (orient the blade to the right side of the 90° mark). Position each back leg so the notch is facing away from the saw fence and trim off the right end of the back leg. Make a parallel 14° miter cut on the other end.

Attach the seat supports. The seat supports should be attached to the front rail using exterior wood glue and 2½" deck screws.

end of the back support to 14° and cut a 3" radius in the top back corner.

Cut the front and back rail to length. Mark the locations along the back face of the front rail where each seat support will be attached. Attach the seat supports to the front rail with 2½" screws (**photo 2**). Rails should be located 1½" and 19" in front of each end.

Apply exterior-rated wood glue to the bottom face of each notch. Place the front rail in the front leg notches and the back rail in the back leg notches. Keep the ends of the rails flush with the outside faces of the legs. Attach the rails to the legs with screws (**photo 3**).

Adjust the positions of the parts so that the front leg is plumb and the arm support is level. Then attach the back legs to the outside seat supports and the arm support to the front and back legs (**photo 4**).

Cut the table bottom crosspiece to length and width. Attach the back supports to the seat supports with 2½" screws (**photo 5**). In addition, attach the two outside back supports to the arm supports. This completes the assembly of the chair frame.

ATTACH THE SEAT & BACK SLATS

The appearance of your side-by-side chair is greatly influenced by the uniformity and spacing of the back slats and seat slats. The best way to achieve uniform

Attach the legs. The front rails should be attached to the front legs and the back rails are attached to the back legs. Use exterior wood glue and 2½" deck screws.

Attach the supports and legs. Temporarily clamp the parts together in the correct orientation and then drive 2½" screws through the inside faces of the arm supports and seat supports to attach them to the legs.

lengths for the slats is to set a stop block for your power miter saw. Use spacers between the slats to ensure regular gaps. For the 1/8" gaps required here, you can use 16d common nails as spacers.

Cut all of the back slats and seat slats to length **(photo 6)**. Sand the ends prior to installation while you still have unrestricted access. Place the slats on the back supports, leaving a 1/8" space between slats. Drill two 1/8"- dia. pilot holes and countersinks through each slat end, centering the holes over the back support. Attach the slats to the supports with 2" screws **(photo 7).** Attach the seat slats to the seat supports, again leaving a 1/8" gap in between the slats.

ATTACH THE TABLE & ARMREST
Cut the table posts, table supports, tabletop planks, and armrests to length. Use a coping saw or jigsaw (an oscillating jigsaw is best) to round the front corners of the outside tabletop planks and armrest. Cut each corner to a 1"-radius (roughly the same as a can of tomato paste). Sand the edges smooth with a power sander. Also use

Attach the back supports to the arm supports using 2½" deck screws. Make sure all screw heads are recessed slightly.

Cut the slats. Set the stop-block attachment on your power miter saw or stand for the correct length. Measure the first slat to make sure the length is correct.

the jigsaw to round the back outside corners of the armrests to a 4" radius. Use a compass to mark the 4" radius (slightly larger than a 1-gallon paint can).

Round over the outside edges of the tabletop and armrests with a router and ¼" piloted roundover bit. Attach the crosspiece between the two middle seat supports. Attach the table posts to the inside face of the front rail and front face of the table bottom crosspiece with 2" deck screws. Attach the table supports to the table posts with 2" screws. Finally, attach the tabletop planks to the

table supports with 2" screws, leaving a ⅛" space between the planks, and attach the armrests to the arm supports with 2" screws. Center the pilot and countersink holes over the supports.

Optional: Drill an umbrella posthole through the middle plank (**photo 8**). The typical patio umbrella pole diameter is 1½". For increased comfort, order back cushions and seat cushions. A good size for a back cushion is 3" thick × 19" square. The seat cushions should be around 3" deep × 17" long × 19" wide.

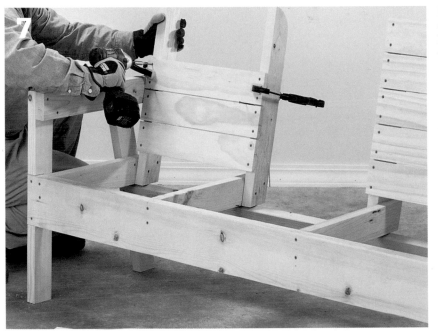

Fasten the slats. Use 16d nails as spacers for a ⅛" gap. If you're using a cordless drill/driver with adjustable torque, set the clutch at a very low setting to prevent overdriving the screws. Drive two 2" screws through each end of the slat and into the back support. Use framing nails or scraps of wood as spacers between the slats.

Drill a hole for the optional umbrella post. Here, the 1½"-dia. posthole is located 8¾" from the back edge of the tabletop (on center) and is centered across the middle plank. A 1½"-dia. hole saw chucked into your drill is the best tool for making the pole hole.

Knockdown Garden Bench

Snoopy shoppers at your local home center will never guess you're building a garden bench when they spot your cart full of materials for this project. That's because the materials for this garden bench are more typical for a backyard deck. Concrete foundation blocks and beefy dimensional lumber may suggest decks, but here they are combined to create a contemporary, Eastern-influenced garden bench. Featuring interlocking joinery (in the finest Asian tradition) and minimal use of metal fasteners, this bench is reminiscent of the post-and-beam construction featured in many ancient Japanese timberframe structures.

The precast concrete piers, designed to hold a deck undercarriage, are dressed up with stain to function as tapered concrete bench legs. The seat is made from deck posts and typical joist lumber (4 × 4s and 2 × 10s). You only need a few power tools to build this bench—a circular saw, jigsaw, and drill/driver. A couple of additional tools can speed up the construction: a 12" miter saw, because of its capacity to cut 4 × 4s in a single pass, and a router to round over the cut edges.

The sturdy combination of crossing half joints and hefty parts creates a very solid bench. But it's also a very heavy bench. Fortunately, this type of joinery also eliminated the need for many fasteners, making it easy to disassemble the bench into pieces so you can move it around your yard as you please and reassemble it quickly and easily.

Materials ▸

1	2 × 6" × 8 ft. cedar	2½" exterior-rated
2	2 × 8" × 8 ft. cedar	screws
1	2 × 10" × 8 ft. cedar	Exterior wood stain
4	4 × 4" × 8 ft. cedar	Concrete stain
4	Precast concrete deck piers	

Because the principal parts of this unique garden bench fit together with no mechanical fasteners, it can be disassembled and moved around your yard with little effort.

Knockdown Garden Bench

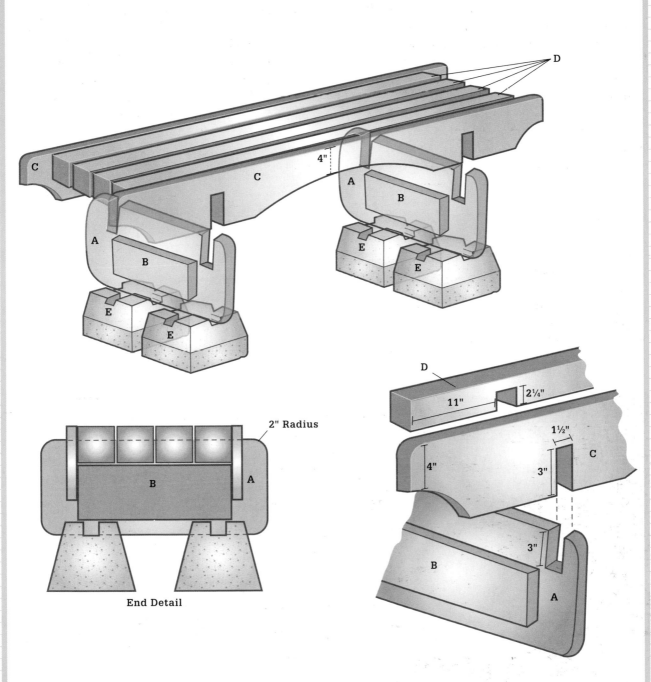

2" Radius

End Detail

4"

D

11"   2¼"

1½"

4"   3"   C

3"

B   A

Key	Part	Dimension	Pcs.	Material
A	Cross supports	1½ × 9¼ × 22"	2	Cedar
B	Cross support braces	1½ × 5½ × 14"	4	Cedar
C	Seat front and back	1½ × 7¼ × 72"	2	Cedar
D	Seat beams	3½ × 3½ × 70"	4	Cedar
E	Base piers	6½ × 10½ × 10½"	4	Concrete

Knockdown Garden Bench

MAKE THE CROSS SUPPORTS

The cross supports are the notched end pieces that support the seat beams. Cut them to length from 2 × 10 stock. Also cut the cross support braces to length from 2 × 6 stock (these sandwich the cross supports, to prevent the cross supports from rocking). Outline the notches that will hold the front and back onto the cross supports. Drill ⅜"-dia. starter holes for the jigsaw blade, located inside one corner of each notch area. Cut out the notches with a jigsaw (**photo 1**). Scribe 2" radius lines on the outside corners of the cross supports, and cut along the radius lines with a jigsaw. Sand the corner radius cuts smooth and round over the outside edges of the cross supports with a router and ¼"-radius piloted roundover bit (**photo 2**).

MAKE THE SEAT FRONT & BACK

Cut the seat front and back pieces to length and width from 2 × 8 stock. These parts need to be cut with multiple profiles, including roundovers on the top, scallops on the bottom, and notches to mate with the notches in the cross supports. First, mark the outlines of the notches that will fit over the cross supports. Drill ⅜"-dia. jigsaw blade starter holes at an inside corner of each notch. Next, cut out the notches with a jigsaw.

Draw a concave, 6" radius line on each bottom corner of each front and back part to create cutting lines for decorative scallops with refined profiles. Draw a 2"-radius roundover line (convex) at each top corner. Sand the cuts smooth and round over the outside edges of the seat front and back pieces with a router and ¼"-radius roundover bit.

The front and back parts also have shallow arcs cut into the bottoms. To lay out these arcs, mark a center point (end to end) 4" down from the top of each workpiece and then drive a screw halfway into each center point. Mark the end points of the arc (19½" from each end) and then bend a 40" long flexible piece of scrap wood or metal over the screw to form the arc profile. Trace the arc profile (**photo 3**). Next, cut along the radius and arc profile lines, and then sand the arcs smooth. Ease the edges with your router and roundover bit.

Cut the notches in the cross supports. Drill a starter hole for your jigsaw blade in one corner of each notch. Clean up the edges of the notch with a chisel, if necessary.

Round over the part edges. Ease the outside edges of the cross supports with a router and ¼" roundover bit. Leave the edges of the cross-support notches square.

3

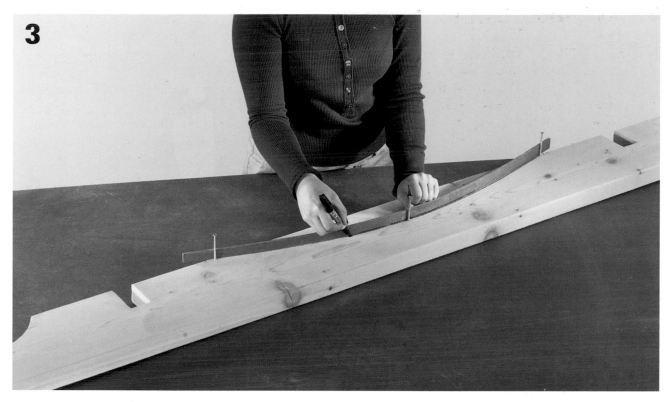

Draw the bottom profile arcs. Bend a scrap piece of wood or metal across a screw or nail to form the arc profile along the bottom edges of the front and back. Trace the arc with a marker.

Precast Concrete Piers ▸

Precast concrete piers are designed for use with platform-style decks that are not attached to a structure. Individual piers measure roughly 8" high and are 11" square at the base. They weigh 45 pounds each. The cast top channels are sized to accept standard 2× dimensional lumber. If you will not be moving the bench around, it's a good idea to prepare a few inches of compactable gravel as a base for each pier to help with stability and drainage.

MAKE THE SEAT BEAMS

The space between the seat front and back is filled with seat beams cut from 4 × 4 stock. This helps keep the weight (and cost) of the project down, compared to using solid 2 × 8s all the way across. Cut the seat beams to length and width. Clamp the seat beams together and mark the notch edge lines across the tops of all four beams. Set your circular saw blade depth to 2¼" and make several crosscuts between the notch layout lines to remove waste material (**photo 4**). Smooth the saw kerf edges remaining in the notch bottoms (**photo 5**) with a chisel and wood mallet (don't use a hammer).

STAIN THE BENCH PARTS

Apply exterior-rated wood stain to all of the wood parts. Redwood and cedar tones are traditional colors, but for a look that's more appropriate to the design, try using a dark stain color. A penetrating, semi-transparent wood stain is easy to apply and gives the wood a durable finish.

The concrete piers can also be stained with concrete stain to blend in better with the wood bench parts. Apply a concrete stain to all surfaces of each of the concrete base piers (**photo 6**).

ASSEMBLE THE BENCH

Position the top edge of each cross support brace between the cross support notches and 2¼" below the top edge of the cross support. Attach the cross support braces with 2½" exterior screws (**photo 7**). These are the only mechanical connections you need to make.

Place the four concrete piers in the location where the bench will be set up. Position the piers in pairs that are approximately 3 ft. apart. Place one support brace across each side pair of concrete piers. Place the seat front and back on the cross supports. Shift the concrete piers and cross supports until the notches align. Place the seat beams between the front and back pieces (**photo 8**). Adjust the parts so that all notches seat fully on the adjoining parts.

Cut notches into the seat beams. Remove waste material from the notch area by making multiple kerf cuts with a circular saw set to 2¼" cutting depth.

Smooth out the notches. Use a sharp wood chisel and mallet to clean up the ridges and edges left in the notch bottom after cutting the kerf.

6

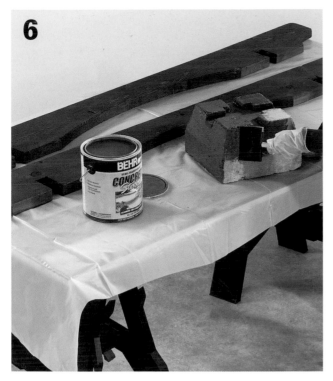

Color the parts. Apply a coat of dark concrete stain to the precast concrete piers. Follow the stain manufacturer's instructions for application and dry time. Stain the wood parts a matching or complementary dark wood tone with exterior wood stain.

7

Make the cross support assemblies. Attach the cross support braces on each side of the cross support using 2½" deck screws. Drill ⅛" pilot holes for the screws to minimize the chance of wood splitting.

8

Assemble the bench. Transport the parts to the location where the bench will be installed. Set the supports onto the piers and then position the bench into the notches in the supports. Adjust the component positions until all of the notches are fully seated.

Sling-back Adirondack

Named for the region of New York State where this classic design originated about 100 years ago, the Adirondack chair is an iconic piece of American outdoor furniture. Through the years countless Adirondack variations have been built, all featuring the trademark wide arms, slanted seat, and slanted backrest that define the style. The version shown here combines those tried-and-true frame proportions with the laid-back comfort of a sling-back canvas beach chair to create an Adirondack chair that borrows from multiple design sources.

The parts are fastened with stainless steel screws. Stainless steel is an excellent material for outdoor use because it does not corrode or stain wood, but it is softer than hardened steel so it's necessary to drill a pilot hole for every screw to prevent stripping the head or breaking the shaft. Stainless steel finish washers (sometimes referred to as decorative washers) are used under the heads of all exposed screws.

The most unique feature of this chair is the canvas seat. Select a material that is weather resistant and will not stretch. The top and bottom edges of the canvas are exposed, so they must be hemmed (a custom tailor or interior designer can do this for you). A simple straight-stitch hem is all that is required. The hemmed canvas is secured between two wood rails and can be easily removed for storage, cleaning, or replacing.

Materials ▸

Lumber (white oak)	2 ¼"-dia. × 3½"
4 ¾" × 5" × 8 ft.	machine screws
1 60" × 50" canvas	14 ¼"-dia. finish
(10 ounce)	washers
Wood screws (1¼", 2")	14 ¼"-dia. washers
No. 10 finish washers	14 ¼"-dia. locknuts
12 ¼"-dia. × 3"	
machine screws	

Adirondack chairs are classic backyard furnishings. No two designs are exactly alike, but the form is instantly recognizable even when it has a unique feature like the canvas seat on this interpretation.

Sling-back Adirondack

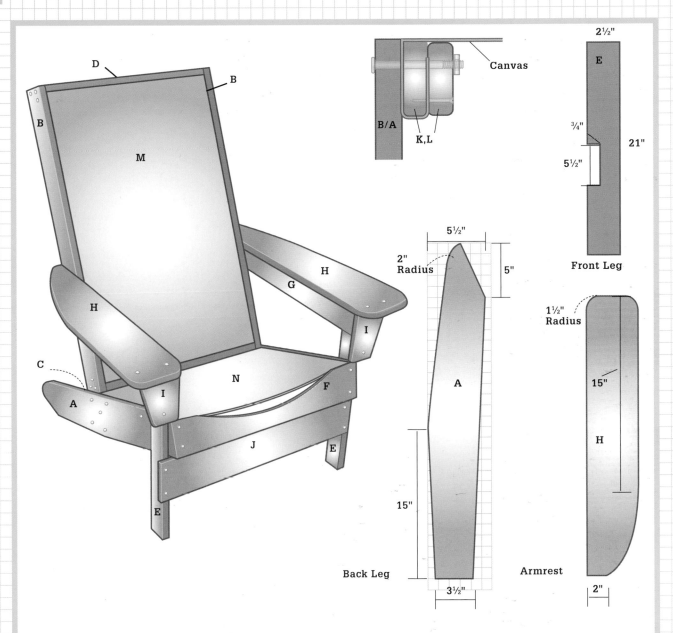

Canvas

B/A

K,L

2½"

E

¾"

21"

5½"

Front Leg

5½"

2"
Radius

5"

A

15"

Back Leg

3½"

1½"
Radius

15"

H

2"

Armrest

Cutting List

Key	Part	Dimension	Pcs.	Material
A	Back legs	¾ × 5 × 36"	2	White oak
B	Backrests	¾ × 4 × 40"	2	White oak
C	Back leg braces	¾ × 2½ × 22½"	2	White oak
D	Backrest braces	¾ × 2½ × 21"	2	White oak
E	Front legs	¾ × 2½ × 21"	2	White oak
F	Front leg brace	¾ × 5½ × 25½"	1	White oak
G	Armrest supports	¾ × 2½ × 26"	2	White oak

Key	Part	Dimension	Pcs.	Material
H	Armrest	¾ × 5½ × 28"	2	White oak
I	Corbels	¾ × 4 × 7"	2	White oak
J	Front Rail	¾ × 5½ × 24"	1	White oak
K	Back canvas rails	¾ × 2 × 33¾"	4	White oak
L	Seat canvas rails	¾ × 2 × 16"	4	White oak
M	Back canvas	33½ W × 37¾ L	1	Canvas (10 ounce)
N	Seat canvas	32W × 17L	1	Canvas (10 ounce)

Sling-back Adirondack Chair

CUT THE PARTS

Cut all of the wood chair parts to length first and then rip-cut them to width on a table saw or with a circular saw and straightedge cutting guide (**photo 1**). If you are using random-width, rough-sawn hardwood, square it and plane it to thickness before cutting it to length. Rip-cut all parts that share the same width at the same time: the armrests and front rails are 5½" wide; the back leg is 5" wide; the backrests and corbels are 4" wide; the back leg braces, backrest braces, front legs, and armrest supports are all 2½" wide; and the back and seat canvas rails are 2" wide. Draw the back leg outline on each back leg blank (**photo 2**). Use the construction drawing (page 21). Cut along the back leg layout lines with a jigsaw.

Clamp the front legs together face-to-face and use a router and ½"-dia. straight bit to cross-cut the notch that holds the front rail in the front leg (**photo 3**). Clamp stop blocks to the legs at a distance from the notch edges equal to the distance from the edge of the router bit to the edge of the router base plate.

Draw the armrest shape on the armrests (see drawing, page 21). The arc runs from a point on the back edge that is 2" from the inside edge to a point on the outside edge that is 15" from the front edge. The front corners are 1½"-radius. Use a jigsaw to cut along the armrest layout lines. Miter-cut the back end of the armrest supports to 27°.

The final frame parts to cut are the corbels that support the outside edge of the armrest. Cut the two corbels to length and then draw the arc profile on each corbel and cut along the arc line with a jigsaw.

ASSEMBLE THE FRAME

Sand all faces of every workpiece smooth before beginning the assembly process. Attach the backrests to the back legs with 1¼" stainless steel screws (**photo 4**). The backrest should be square with the top edge of the back half of the back leg. Attach the backrest braces to the backrests with 2" stainless steel screws and finish washers (**photo 5**).

Clamp the front leg brace to the front legs, keeping both legs perpendicular to the brace. Drill two countersunk pilot holes through each side of the brace and into the legs. Attach the brace to the legs with 2" stainless steel screws and finish washers. Clamp the

Dimension your lumber. If you purchased sanded-four-side (S4S) stock, you will only need to rip it to the correct widths after you cut the parts to length.

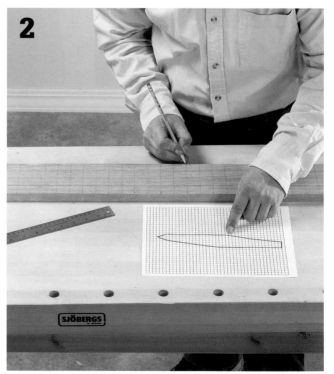

Lay out the parts. Use the back leg layout pattern on the construction drawing as a reference for marking the outline of the back legs on the back leg blanks.

armrest supports to the front legs. The front and top edges of the front brace are flush with the front and top edges of the front legs. Drill two countersunk pilot holes and attach the parts with 1¼" stainless steel screws and finish washers. Hold the front leg assembly upright and place the back legs on the front leg brace. Adjust the back leg assembly until the angled back edge of the arm support is flush with the back edge of the backrest and the front leg is plumb. Clamp the armrest support to the backrest and attach the leg assemblies with 1¼" stainless screws (**photo 6**). Attach the back leg braces to the back legs with 2" stainless steel screws and finish washers. Drill two countersunk pilot holes through each back leg and into each brace.

Clamp the corbel to the front of the front leg and armrest support. Align the top and inside edges of the three parts. Drill one countersunk pilot hole through the corbel and into the front leg. Drill a second countersunk pilot hole through the corbel and into the end of the armrest support. Attach each corbel with two 2" stainless steel screws and finish nails. Attach the armrests to the armrest supports with three 2" screws (**photo 7**). Attach the front rail to the front edges of the back legs with 2" screws. Apply an exterior wood finish to the frame.

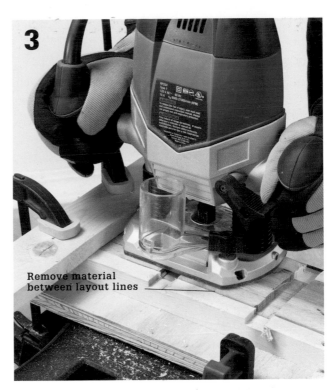

Remove material between layout lines

Cut the leg notches. Clamp a straightedge to each side of the front leg notch layout lines to function as stops for your router. Cut the front leg notch in several passes with a router, lowering the bit with each pass.

Join the legs and backrest. First, clamp the backrests and the back legs together. Drill two pilot holes through the backrest and into each back leg. Drive 1¼" stainless steel screws with finish washers.

Install the backrest braces. Space the backrest braces 33¾" apart with the top backrest brace flush with the top of the backrests and the backs flush.

ATTACH THE CANVAS SEAT & BACK

The sling-style seat and back canvas panels are secured to the frame by rolling one side of the canvas around one rail and then sandwiching that rail between a second rail and the backrest. Machine screws secure the rails to the backrest. Cut the seat and back canvas rails to length if you have not already cut them. Cut the canvas seat and back to size, keeping the factory-seamed edges in the exposed position when possible. With the right side on a table, fold up ¼" of material along one long side of the canvas and then press. Fold the fabric over again ½" and press for a finished, straight edge. Hand- or machine-stitch a ⅜" hem. Repeat for the other side. With the seat canvas still right side down on a table, align one of the seat canvas rails on top

of the canvas so the canvas top edge is centered lengthwise under the rail. Roll the rail and canvas back onto the fabric two full turns (**photo 8**). Clamp another seat canvas rail on top of the fabric with edges flush. Connect the rails with three 1¼" screws (**photo 9**). Repeat the process of rolling the canvas and attaching the second rail for the other lower edge of the seat canvas.

Clamp the seat canvas rails and canvas to the back legs with the fronts of the canvas rails flush against the front rail. Drill ¼"-dia. pilot holes through the front legs, back legs, and seat canvas rails. Attach the canvas rails with ¼"-dia. machine screws, finish washers, and lock nuts (**photo 10**). Repeat the same process to attach the back canvas to the back canvas rails and then to the backrests (**photo 11**).

Attach the armrest supports. Drive two 1¼" screws through the inside faces of the back legs and two 1¼" screws through the inside faces of the backrests. Locate these screws 1" from the bottom edge of the back legs and 1" from the back edge of the backrests.

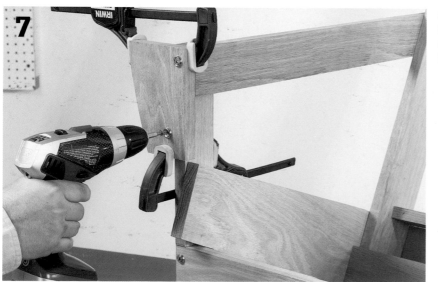

Attach the corbels. Drive two 2" screws through the top of the corbel and into the armrest support. Drill a pilot hole for each screw.

8

Wrap the seat rail by rolling the top and bottom edges of the seat canvas around one of the seat canvas rails. The canvas sides should be hemmed by this point if they are not factory edges.

9

Secure canvas between rails. Sandwich the canvas between the two rails and fasten the rails together with screws. Drill pilot holes and countersinks for each screw.

10

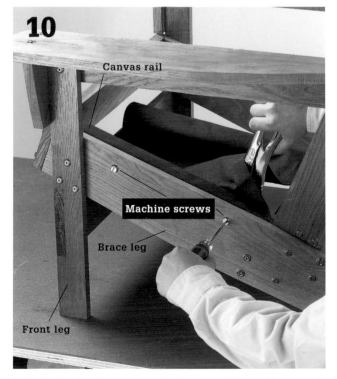

Canvas rail

Machine screws

Brace leg

Front leg

Attach the front canvas rails. Run one 3½" machine screw through the front leg, back leg, and seat canvas rails. Run two 3" machine screws through the back leg and canvas rails.

11

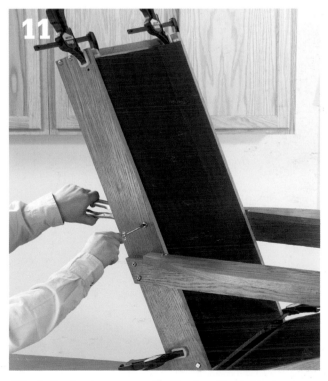

Attach the back canvas rails. Use four 3" machine screws per side to attach the back canvas rails to the backrest.

Classic Adirondack Chair

Adirondack furniture has become a standard on decks, porches, and patios throughout the world. It's no mystery that this distinctive furniture style has become so popular. Attractive but rugged design and unmatched stability are just two of the reasons for its timeless appeal, and our Adirondack chair offers these benefits and more.

Unlike most of the Adirondack chair designs you're likely to run across, this one is very easy to build. There are no complex compound angles to cut, no intricate details in the back and seat slats, and no complicated joints. It can be built with basic tools and simple techniques. And because this design features all of the classic Adirondack chair elements, your guests and neighbors may never guess that you built it yourself (but you'll be proud to tell them you did).

We made our Adirondack chair out of cedar and finished it with clear wood sealer. But you may prefer to build your version from pine (a traditional wood for Adirondack furniture), especially if you plan to paint the chair. White, battleship gray, and forest green are popular color choices for Adirondack furniture. Be sure to use quality exterior paint with a glossy or enamel finish.

Materials ▸

1 2 × 6" × 8 ft. cedar	Deck screws (1¼",
1 2 × 4" × 12 ft. cedar	1½", 2", 3")
1 1 × 6" × 14 ft. cedar	⅜ × 2½" lag screws
1 1 × 4" × 8 ft. cedar	with washers
1 1 × 2" × 12 ft. cedar	Finishing materials
Moisture-resistant glue	

This straightforward example of an Adirondack chair design is nicely proportioned and very easy to build from dimensional cedar lumber.

Classic Adirondack Chair

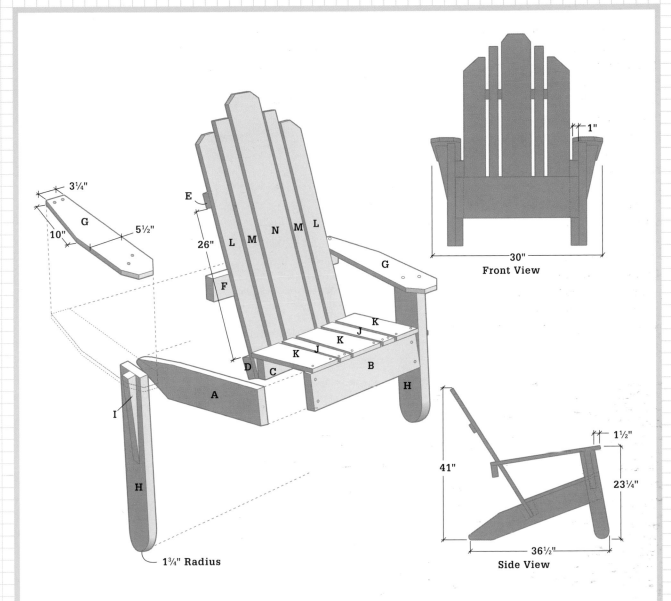

3¼"

G

5½"

10"

E

26"

L M N M L

F

G

K
J K
J K
D C K J
B

A

I

H

1¾" Radius

1"

30"

Front View

41"

1½"

23¼"

36½"

Side View

Cutting List

Key	Part	Dimension	Pcs.	Material
A	Leg	1½ × 5½ × 34½"	2	Cedar
B	Apron	1½ × 5½ × 21"	1	Cedar
C	Seat support	1½ × 3½ × 18"	1	Cedar
D	Low back brace	1½ × 3½ × 18"	1	Cedar
E	High back brace	¾ × 1½ × 18"	1	Cedar
F	Arm cleat	1½ × 3½ × 24"	1	Cedar
G	Arm	¾ × 5½ × 28"	2	Cedar

Key	Part	Dimension	Pcs.	Material
H	Post	1½ × 3½ × 22"	2	Cedar
I	Arm brace	1½ × 2¼ × 10"	2	Cedar
J	Narrow seat slat	¾ × 1½ × 20¼"	2	Cedar
K	Wide seat slat	¾ × 5½ × 20¼"	3	Cedar
L	End back slat	¾ × 3½ × 36"	2	Cedar
M	Narrow back slat	¾ × 1½ × 38"	2	Cedar
N	Center back slat	¾ × 5½ × 40"	1	Cedar

Classic Adirondack Chair

MAKE THE LEGS

Sprawling back legs that support the seat slats and stretch to the ground on a near-horizontal plane are signature features of the Adirondack style. Start by cutting the legs to length. To cut the tapers, mark a point 2" from the edge on one end of the board. Then, mark another point 6" from the end on the adjacent edge. Connect the points with a straightedge. On the same end, mark a point 2¼" from the other edge. Then, on that edge mark a point 10" from the end. Connect these points to make a cutting line for the other taper. Cut the two taper cuts with a circular saw. Use the tapered leg as a template to mark and cut identical tapers on the other leg of the chair (**photo 1**).

BUILD THE SEAT

The legs form the sides of the box frame, which supports the seat slats. Where the text calls for deck screw counterbores, drill holes ⅛" deep with a counterbore bit. Cut the apron and seat support to size. Attach the apron to the front ends of the legs with glue and 3" deck screws.

Position the seat support so the inside face is 16½" from the inside edge of the apron. Attach the seat support between the legs, making sure the part tops are flush. Cut the seat slats to length, and sand the ends smooth. Arrange the slats on top of the seat box, and use wood scraps to set ⅝" spaces between the slats. The slats should overhang the front of the seat box by ¾".

Fasten the seat slats by drilling counterbored pilot holes and driving 2" deck screws through the holes and into the tops of the apron and seat support. Keep the counterbores aligned so the cedar plugs used to fill the counterbores form straight lines across the front and back of the seat. Once the slats are

Cut tapers into the back edges of the legs with a circular saw or jigsaw.

Round the sharp slat edges with a router and roundover bit or simply break the edges by sanding with a power sander.

installed, use a router with a ¼" roundover bit (or a power sander) to smooth the outside edges and ends of the slats (**photo 2**).

MAKE THE BACK SLATS

The back slats are made from three sizes of dimension lumber: 1 × 2, 1 × 4, and 1 × 6. Cut the back slats to length. Trim off the corners on the widest (1 × 6) slat. First, mark points 1" in from the outside top corners. Then, mark points 1" down from the corners on the outside edges. Connect the points and trim along the lines with a saw. Mark the 1 × 4 slats 2" from one top corner in both directions. Draw cutting lines and trim the same way (these are the outer slats on the back).

ATTACH THE BACK SLATS

Cut the low back brace and the high back brace and set them on a flat surface. Slip ¾"-thick spacers under the high brace so the tops of the braces are level. Then, arrange the back slats on top of the braces with

⅝" spacing between slats. The untrimmed ends of the slats should be flush with the bottom edge of the low back brace. The bottom of the high back brace should be 26" above the top of the low brace. The braces must be perpendicular to the slats.

Drill pilot holes in the low brace and counterbore the holes. Then, attach the slats to the low brace by driving 2" deck screws through the holes. Follow the same steps for the high brace and attach the slats with 1¼" deck screws.

MAKE THE ARMS

The broad arms of the chair, cut from 1 x 6 material, are supported by posts in front and the arm cleat attached to the backs of the chair slats. Cut the arms to length. To create decorative angles at the outer end of each arm, mark points 1" from each corner along both edges. Use the points to draw a pair of 1½" cutting lines on each arm. Cut along the lines using a jigsaw or circular saw (**photo 3**).

Make corner cuts on the fronts of the arms (shown) and the tops of the back slats using a jigsaw.

Attach the square ends of the posts to the undersides of the arms, being careful to position the part correctly.

Mark points for cutting a tapered cut on the inside back edge of each arm (see Diagram). First, mark points 3¼" in from each inside edge on the back of each arm. Next, mark the outside edges 10" from the back. Then, connect the points and cut along the cutting line with a circular saw or jigsaw. Sand the edges smooth.

ASSEMBLE THE ARMS, CLEATS & POSTS

Cut the arm cleat and make a mark 2½" in from each end of the cleat. Set the cleat on edge on your work surface. Position the arms on the cleat top edge so the arm back ends are flush with the cleat back, and the untapered edge of each arm is aligned with the 2½" mark. Fasten the arms to the cleats with glue. Drill pilot holes in the arms and counterbore the holes. Drive 3" deck screws through the holes and into the cleat.

Cut the posts to size. Then, use a compass to mark a 1¾"-radius roundover cut on each bottom post corner (the roundovers improve stability). Position the arms on top of the square ends of the posts. The posts should be set back 1½" from the front ends of the arm and 1" from the inside edge of the arm. Fasten the arms to the posts with glue. Drill pilot holes in the arms and counterbore the holes. Then, drive 3" deck screws through the arms and into the posts (**photo 4**).

Cut tapered arm braces from wood scraps, making sure the wood grain runs lengthwise. Position an arm brace at the outside of each arm/post joint, centered side to side on the post. Attach each brace with glue.

Drill counterbored pilot holes in the inside face of the post near the top . Then, drive deck screws through the holes and into the brace (**photo 5**). Drive a 2" deck screw down through each arm and into the top of the brace.

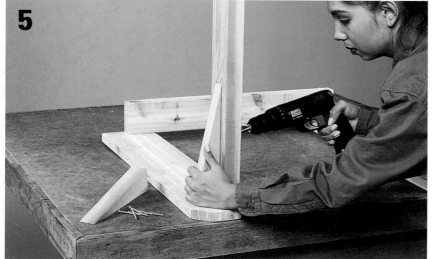

Drive screws through each post and into an arm brace to stabilize the arm/post joint.

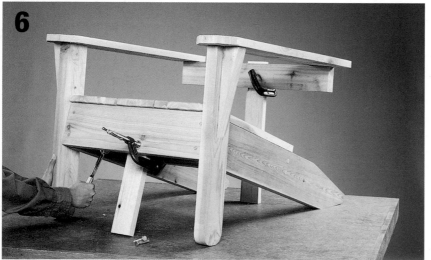

Clamp wood braces to the parts of the chair to hold them in position while you fasten the parts together.

ASSEMBLE THE CHAIR

To complete the construction, join the back, seat/leg assembly, and arm/post assembly. Before you start, gather scrap wood to brace the parts while you fasten them.

Set the seat/leg assembly on your work surface, clamping a piece of scrap wood to the front apron to raise the assembly front until the leg bottoms are flush on the surface (about 10"). Use a similar technique to brace the arm/post assembly so the back cleat bottom is 20" above the work surface. Arrange the assembly so the posts fit around the front of the seat/leg assembly and the bottom edge of the apron is flush with the front edges of the posts.

Drill a ¼"-dia. pilot hole through the inside of each leg and partway into the post. Drive a ⅜ × 2½" lag screw and washer through each hole, but do not tighten completely (**photo 6**). Remove the braces. Position the back so the low back brace is between the legs and the slats are resting against the front of the arm cleat. Clamp the back to the seat support with a C-clamp, making sure the low brace top edge is flush with the tops of the legs.

Tighten the lag screws at the post/leg joints. Then, add a second lag screw at each joint. Drill three evenly spaced pilot holes near the top edge of the arm cleat and drive 1½" deck screws through the holes and into the back slats (**photo 7**). Drive 3" deck screws through the legs and into the ends of the low back brace.

APPLY FINISHING TOUCHES

Cut or buy ¼"-thick, ⅜"-dia. cedar wood plugs and glue them into visible counterbores (**photo 8**). After the glue dries, sand the plugs even with the surrounding surface. Finish-sand all exposed surfaces with 120-grit sandpaper. Finish the chair as desired; we simply applied a coat of clear wood sealer.

Drive screws through counterbored pilot holes in the arm cleat, near the top and into the slats. Check to make sure they did not penetrate the back slats on the seat side.

Glue cedar plugs into the counterbores to conceal the screw holes.

Porch Swing

A beautiful evening outdoors gets a little better when you're sitting and enjoying it from a porch swing. The gentle, rhythmic motion of the swing is a relaxing coda to any stressful day.

Essentially, a porch swing is a garden bench with chains instead of legs. Like garden benches, swings can be built to suit just about any style. Also like garden benches, too often the style of a porch swing comes at the expense of comfort. In fact, if you were to test each of the thousands of porch swing designs in existence, you might be amazed to discover how many are simply not comfortable. This porch swing was designed with both style and comfort in mind. It sits a bit deeper than many other versions and the back is pitched at just the right angle. Another key to its comfort is that the back rails don't extend all the way down to the seat slats, creating open space that is ergonomically important.

Despite the custom appearance of this porch swing, it is actually built from common ⅞" cedar boards, ¼" cedar deck boards, and cedar 2× lumber.

This porch swing can be hung from eyehooks in a porch ceiling that features sufficient structural framing, including joists that are no smaller than 2 × 8. Or, you can hang it in a variety of locations from a freestanding porch swing stand. The swing stand shown on pages 40 to 45 is designed to complement this swing.

Materials ▸

2 1 × 6" × 8 ft. cedar boards	Eyebolts (exterior):
1 ¾" × 12 ft. cedar deck board	2 @ ⅜ × 3½"
	2 @ ⅜ × 6½"
4 2 × 4" × 8 ft. cedar	8 ⅜"-dia. washers
Deck screws (2½", 3")	Finishing materials
	4 ⅜"-dia. locknuts

This cedar swing is roomy enough for two but compact enough to hang from either a stand or a front porch ceiling. Made of cedar, it is lightweight yet durable and moisture-resistant.

Porch Swing

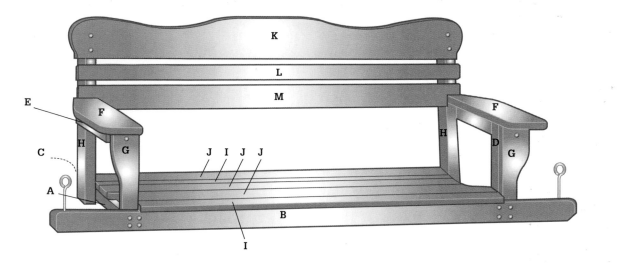

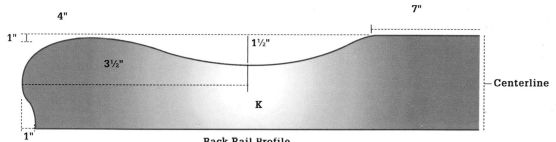

4"
7"
1"
1½"
3½"
Centerline
K
1"

Back Rail Profile

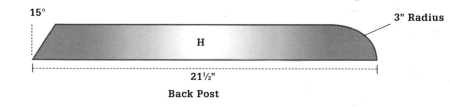

15°
3" Radius
H
21½"

Back Post

Cutting List

Key	Part	Dimension	Pcs.	Material	Key	Part	Dimension	Pcs.	Material
A	Seat supports	1½ × 3¼ × 17½"	3	Cedar	H	Back posts	1½ × 3 × 21½"	2	Cedar
B	Front rail	1½ × 3 × 68"	1	Cedar	I	Seat slats	⅞ × 2⅜ × 48"	2	Cedar
C	Back rail	1½ × 2½ × 48"	1	Cedar	J	Seat slats	⅞ × 5 × 48"	3	Cedar
D	Front posts	1½ × 2½ × 11¾"	2	Cedar	K	Top back rail	⅞ × 5½ × 54"	1	Cedar
E	Arm support	1¼ × 2 × 22"	2	Cedar	L	Middle back rail	⅞ × 2 × 52"	1	Cedar
F	Armrest	1¼ × 5½ × 24¼"	2	Cedar	M	Bottom back rail	⅞ × 3 × 52"	1	Cedar
G	Arm front	1¼ × 3¼ × 9¼"	2	Cedar					

Porch Swing

BUILD THE SEAT FRAME

Make the workpieces for the seat supports by cutting three 17½" lengths of 2 × 4. Cedar is shown here; you can also use treated pine if you want a natural wood finish or untreated SPF-(spruce, pine, or fir) if you plan to paint the swing. Lay out the seat support profile on one of the seat support pieces (**photo 1**) using the diagram on page 33 as a reference. The seat support is scooped on the top edge so the seat slats follow a comfortable flow. At the low point in the middle of each support, the thickness of the part drops to 1¾". At the back end the part should be 2½" from top to bottom and at the front end it should peak at 3¼" and then drop down slightly over the last inch. Plot the profile so the tops of the part follow straight lines that conform to the width of the slats that will rest on them. The back edge of the part should be mitered at 15° to follow the backrest angle. Cut along the layout line with a jigsaw and then use the first seat support as a template to trace the profile onto the remaining

Lay out the parts. Plot the seat support profile onto one of the seat support workpieces using the dimensions given on page 33 as a reference.

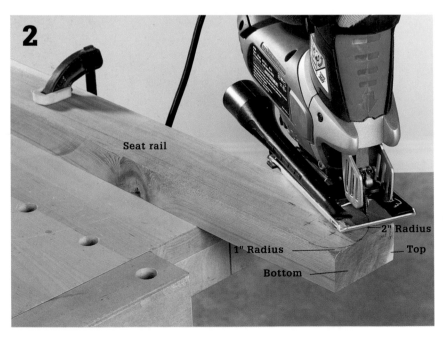

Seat rail

2" Radius

1" Radius — — Top

Bottom

Cut the end profiles. Use a compass to draw the front rail end radius and cut along these lines with a jigsaw. Sand the cuts smooth.

two seat supports. Also use the jigsaw to cut out the second and third seat supports. Gang the seat supports together with clamps and sand the profiles all at the same time so they are exactly the same.

Make the seat front rail by cutting a 2 × 4 to 68" long and rip-cutting ¼" off each edge to remove the rounded edges, leaving a workpiece that's 3" wide. On the front face of the front rail first mark a 2" radius on the bottom corners and then draw a 1" radius on the top corners. Cut along the corner radius lines with a jigsaw (**photo 2**). Make the seat back rail by cutting a 2 × 4 to 48" in length and then rip-cutting it down

to 2½" wide. Attach the seat supports to the seat front and back rails with 3" deck screws (**photo 3**).

ATTACH THE BACK & ARM SUPPORTS

Cut a pair of 11¾" lengths of cedar 2 × 4 and rip-cut these pieces to 2½" wide to make the front posts. Drill counterbored pilot holes and attach the front posts to the front rail and outside seat supports with 2½" deck screws (**photo 4**). *NOTE: Counterbore pilot holes for all structural joints.* If you're looking to save a bit of time, consider attaching the seat slats with screws driven through pilot holes that are countersunk only.

Join rails and seat supports. Drive two 3" deck screws through the front rail and into the front ends of the seat supports. Also drive one 3" screw through the back rail and into the back end of each seat support. Apply exterior glue to the mating parts first to reinforce the joints.

Attach the front posts. Drive two 2½" deck screws through the side of the front post and into the outside seat supports. Drive two 2½" deck screws through the front rail and into the front posts.

Next, cut two 21½" lengths of 2 × 4 and rip them to 3" wide, and then miter-cut the bottom ends to 15° to make the back posts. Next, draw a 3" radius on the back top corners of each back post and cut along the radius line with a jigsaw. Attach the back posts to the outside seat supports with 2½" screws (**photo 5**).

Cut one 22" length from a ¾ deck board (actual thickness is 1" to 1¼") and rip-cut that piece into two 2"-wide pieces to make the two arm supports. Attach the arm supports to the front and back posts with 2½" screws (**photo 6**). Cut two 9¼" pieces of the ¾ deck board to

make the arm fronts. Lay out the arm front profile on each piece and cut the profiles with a jigsaw. Attach the arm fronts to the front posts with 2½" deck screws.

ATTACH THE BACK RAILS & SEAT SLATS

Cut two 24¼" pieces of ¾ deck boards to make the armrests. Lay out the armrest profile on each deck board and cut the boards using a jigsaw. The backside edge should have a curved taper of 1" starting 7" from the end. The armrests should be rounded at a 1" radius on both front corners. Cut four 48" long pieces of ⅞ × 5½"

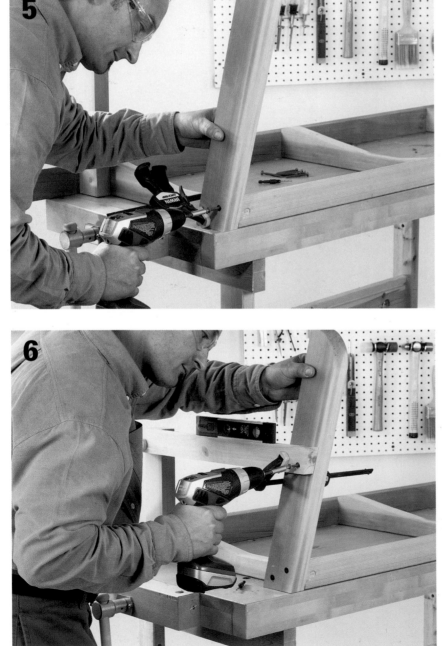

Attach the back posts. Drive two 2½" deck screws through each back post and into the outside seat supports.

Attach the arm supports. Drive two 2½" deck screws through each end of the arm supports and into the front and back posts. Then attach the arm front with two 2½" deck screws.

(nominal 1 × 6) boards to make the seat slats. Rip-cut three of the boards to 5" wide and then rip-cut the fourth deck board into two 2⅝" wide pieces.

Cut a 54" piece of ¾ deck board to make the top back rail. Make a template of one-half of the top back rail on a piece of cardboard according to the profile drawing on page 33. Cut the template out with scissors or an X-acto knife. Trace the template onto each half of the top back rail (**photo 7**). Then, cut along the layout line with a jigsaw. Sand smooth. Cut a 52" piece of ¾ deck board to make the middle

and bottom rails. Rip-cut this piece into one 2" wide board and one 3" wide board. Use a router and ¼" roundover bit to ease the edges of the armrests, seat slats, and back rails (**photo 8**). Attach the armrests, seat slats, and back rails with 2½" deck screws (**photo 9**).

FINISH THE SWING

Although you may choose to leave the swing unfinished if it is made of a good exterior wood, such as cedar or redwood, most people prefer to apply a top coat or even

7

Lay out the back rail profile. Use the information on page 33 to make a cardboard template of half of the top back rail. Use this template to lay out the first half of the top back rail profile and then flip the template to lay out the second half.

an exterior wood stain and a top coat. Protecting the wood not only allows the wood tone to retain its color, it also minimizes the raised wood grain effect that occurs when water soaks into unprotected wood. The raised grain is not uncomfortable in and of itself, but it can lead to splintering.

Before applying your finish of choice, sand all of the wood surfaces up to 150 grit using a pad sander. Do not use an aggressive sander, such as a belt sander. Cut or buy wood plugs from the same species as the swing wood. Glue the plugs into the counterbored holes at screw locations. Once the glue has set, trim the plugs flush with the wood surface using a flush-cutting saw, or simply sand the tops down so they are even with the surrounding wood surface. Then, wipe down the entire project with a rag dipped in mineral spirits or rubbing alcohol, wait for the wood to dry, and then apply your finish. If you have access to an HVLP sprayer, it is an excellent choice for applying the finish smoothly and quickly. Two or three light coats will yield much better results than one or two heavier coats.

Ease the edges. Round over all edges of the armrests, back rails, and the top edges (smooth face) of the seat slats. Use a router with a ¼" radius roundover bit to make these profile cuts.

Finish the assembly. Attach the armrests, seat slats, and back rails with 2½" deck screws.

HANGING THE SWING

Install the four ⅜"-dia. eyebolts that will be fastened to the hanging chains or ropes (**photo 10**). Of these two options, chains take a bit longer to install but they won't need adjusting once they're set, and you don't have to tie and retie knots. Porch swing chains can be purchased as kits from hardware stores and from online sellers. Each kit contains a pair of chain assemblies with two swing chains, which consist of a Y-fitting that connects to an S-hook at the end of a single chain dropping from the ceiling or stand. Make sure the chain you buy is of sufficient strength and rated for outdoor usage. If you are using rope, choose rope that won't shrink or stretch (such as ⅝"-dia. nylon rope).

Two bolts are attached through the front rail and two bolts are attached through the back edges of the armrests and back posts. Hang the porch swing from chains or ropes so that the front edge is approximately 16" off the ground. The back edge of the swing should be level with the front edge or slightly lower. Adjust the hanging height to suit the primary users.

Prepare for hangers. Drill ⁷⁄₁₆"-dia. guide holes for each ⅜" eyebolt. Fasten the eyebolts with washers and locknuts.

Porch Swing Stand

What good is a porch swing if you don't have a place to hang it? Porch swings originally hung from the ceilings of covered porches, but you don't need a porch to enjoy a porch swing in your outdoor living space. Instead, you can build this attractive porch swing stand to hold your swing. It will look great in a garden, yard, or on a deck. And the total height is low enough to fit under most raised porches or decks. In fact, unless you're sure that your ceiling has the structural strength to handle a swing, this stand is probably a better option.

This swing stand is designed to hold up to a 4-foot-wide porch swing. The only tools you need to build it are a power miter saw or circular saw, jigsaw, and drill/driver. The design is simple enough to build in a day, but the speed of construction doesn't result in any lack of strength. The cross braces and gussets that reinforce the 4 × 4 legs and 4 × 6 top beam give this stand more than enough strength to hold two adults

(do not exceed). The only modification you may need to make to the plan is to match the distance between the eyebolts in the stand to the dimension between your porch swing's hanging chains or ropes.

Materials ▸

1 2 × 6" × 10 ft. cedar	20 ⅜" lock washers
1 2 × 8" × 12 ft. cedar	20 ⅜" nuts
4 4 × 4" × 8 ft. cedar	2 ½" × 6" eyebolts
1 4 × 6" × 8 ft. cedar	

3" deck screws
Lag bolts (hot dipped
  or stainless steel):
  8 @ ⅜" × 5
  12 @ ⅜" × 6½"

This sturdy stand made from cedar timbers is designed to support the swing project shown on pages 32 to 39. But if you like the stand, its design is neutral enough to support any other swing or seat that you buy, build, or already own.

Porch Swing Stand

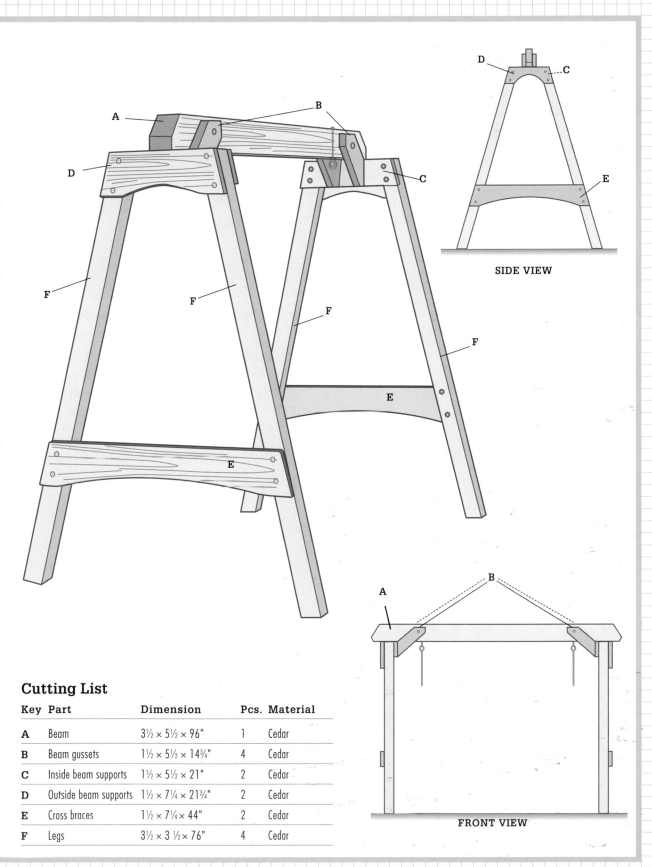

SIDE VIEW

FRONT VIEW

Cutting List

Key	Part	Dimension	Pcs.	Material
A	Beam	3½ × 5½ × 96"	1	Cedar
B	Beam gussets	1½ × 5½ × 14¾"	4	Cedar
C	Inside beam supports	1½ × 5½ × 21"	2	Cedar
D	Outside beam supports	1½ × 7¼ × 21¾"	2	Cedar
E	Cross braces	1½ × 7¼ × 44"	2	Cedar
F	Legs	3½ × 3 ½ × 76"	4	Cedar

Porch Swing Stand

CUT THE PARTS

Cut each 76"-long 4 × 4 leg with parallel 14° miters at the ends (**photo 1**). You need a 10" or 12" power miter saw for enough capacity to cut the legs in a single pass. Be sure to provide ample support for the workpiece, including the cutoff portion. If you don't have a miter saw, mark the angled cutting lines with a protractor or speed square, and cut them with a circular saw or handsaw. Cut the two 44" long cross braces from a piece of 2 × 8. Miter-cut each end to 14°.

The bottom edge of the cross brace features a decorative arc profile. Draw this arc using a flexible strip of wood (such as 1"-wide strip of ¼" lauan plywood) as a gauge. Mark points on the workpiece that are 4" from the outside edges of the long side of the cross brace. At each mark, tap two small nails into the face of the cross brace near the edge. Tap a third rail centered across the length of the brace and 2" up from the bottom to mark the apex of the arc. Flex a thin scrap of wood against the nails to create a smooth

Cut the stand legs to length. If you have a 10" or 12" power miter saw, you should be able to make the 14° end cuts in one pass. Be sure the end of the workpiece is supported.

Trace the cross-brace arcs. Flex a thin piece of wood or metal against two nails to act as a template for laying out the arc profile on the leg cross braces.

arc profile. Trace the arc with a pencil (photo 2) and then remove the nails and cut along the line with a jigsaw.

Miter-cut the 14° ends of the two 21"-long 2 × 6 inside beam supports to length. Miter-cut the 14° of the two 21¾"-long 2 × 8 outside beam supports. Use the same method that you used to create the arc on the cross braces to create an arc along the bottom edge of the outside beam supports.

Cut the beam gussets 14¾" long. Make two marks 3½" in from each end along the top edge of each gusset, and draw a 45° line from each mark to the outside end of the gusset. Then, draw a second 45° line from the outside edge down to the bottom edge of the gusset (photo 3). Cut off the corners of each gusset on these marked cutting lines.

The top beam is an 8-foot long 4 × 6 timber. Miter-cut the top corners of the beam to 45°, starting 3½" in from each end of the beam.

ASSEMBLE THE STAND

To attach the gussets to the inside beam supports, first mark the center of each beam support and then measure out 1¾" from the center to designate the

Make the gussets. Draw 45° cutting lines at ends of the beam gussets using a try square as a guide. Trim along the cutting lines.

Attach the gussets. Bore counterbore holes and guide holes for bolts, washers, and nuts through the beam supports, cross braces and legs. Drive ⅜" × 6½" lag screws with washers to secure the gussets.

positions of the inside edges of the gussets. Draw alignment lines on these marks, perpendicular to the top and bottom edges of the beam supports. Position your drill ¾" to the outside of these lines and bore ³⁄₁₆"-dia. guide holes through the beam supports. Hold the gussets in position and drill ⅛" pilot holes in the ends of the gussets using the beam pilot holes as a guide. Attach the gussets to the beam supports with 3" deck screws.

Lay the legs on a flat surface. Position the outside beam support and cross brace under the legs. Then, position the inside beam support and gusset assembly on top of the legs. Clamp the legs between the beam supports and clamp the cross brace to the legs. Drill two 1⅛"-dia. × ½" deep counterbore holes and ⁷⁄₁₆"-dia. guide holes through each joint and attach the parts with ⅜"-dia. × 5" and ⅜"-dia. × 6½" bolts (**photo 4**).

Raise the leg assembly. Position the beam on the beam supports so it fits in between the gussets. Clamp the beam in place and then drill counterbores and guide holes through the joints, just as you did for the leg assembly. Fasten the beam with ⅜"-dia. × 6½" bolts secured by washers and locknuts (**photo 5**).

The chain or rope that supports the swing will be fastened to an eyebolt that runs down through the beam. Drill two ⁹⁄₁₆"-dia. vertical pilot holes through the center of the beam, spaced the same measured distance as there is between your swing's hanging chains or ropes. To avoid creating a place for water to pool, a counterbore hole is not drilled for the nuts that fasten the eyebolts. Fasten two ½"-dia. × 6" eyebolts with lock washers and nuts to the beam (**photo 6**).

INSTALL THE STAND & HANG THE SWING

The swing stand should be placed on level ground. A porch swing is not intended to swing fast or in a long arc, like a play swing does, so there is no need under normal use to anchor the stand to the ground. Hang the porch swing so the top front edge of the seat is approximately 16" off the ground (**photo 7**). The back edge of the swing should be level with the front edge or slightly lower. Adjust the hanging height to suit the primary users.

Attach the beam. Drill counterbores for washers on both gussets and drill guide holes for ⅜"-dia. x 6½"-long lag bolts. Insert the bolts and secure with lock washers and nuts.

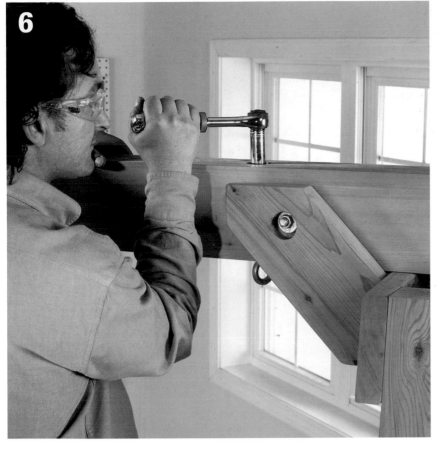

Install eyebolts on the beam. Fasten ½"-dia. eyebolts to the beam with washers and locknuts.

Hang the swing. Use chains (preferred) or rope to hang the porch swing from the eyebolts in the swing stand beam. The front edge of the swing seat should be roughly 16" off the ground, and the swing should be level or tilted slightly backwards when at rest.

Tiled Garden Bench

Unique materials make for unique outdoor carpentry projects. On this creative garden bench, an assortment of ceramic tiles and accent tiles are set onto the bench top and produce quite an impact. In fact, those accents and a few dozen 4 × 4" tiles transform a plain cedar bench into a special garden ornament. And you can easily accomplish the whole project over one weekend.

In addition to the standard carpentry tools, you need some specialized but inexpensive tile setting tools. A notched trowel, grout float, and sponge are necessary for setting the tiles. Snap-style tile cutters are fairly inexpensive but don't do a very good job cutting floor tiles like the ones used in this project. You'll have much better luck with a wet saw. Wet saws are more expensive than snap cutters, though they have become more affordable in recent years. They are readily available from rental centers and tile retailers. Because you will be charged an hourly rate (or by half-days in some cases), have all of your tiles premarked

for cutting so you can get right to work once you get the wet saw home.

If you have never set tile before or feel at all unsure of your skills, many home centers and tile retailers offer free classes on tiling techniques.

Materials ▶

2 2 × 4" × 10 ft. cedar	1¼" Cementboard
1 2 × 6" × 8 ft. cedar	screws
1 4 × 4" × 8 ft. cedar	Clear wood sealer
1 ¾ × 4" × 4 ft.	Field and accent
exterior plywood	tiles
1 ½ × 3" × 5 ft.	Thinset mortar
Cement board	Tile spacers
Plastic sheeting	Grout
Deck screws (2", 3")	Grout sealer

A ceramic tile arrangement creates a decorative bench top that stands up well to the elements.

Tiled Garden Bench

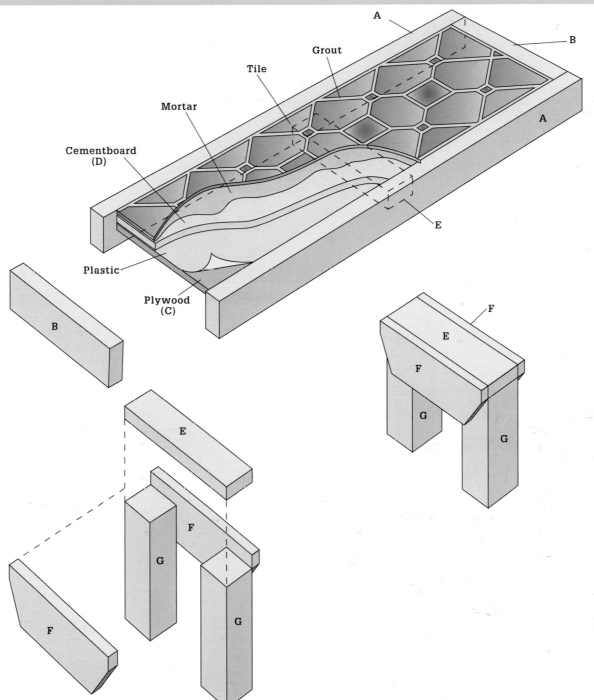

Cutting List

Key	Part	Dimension	Pcs.	Material
A	Sides	1½ × 3½ × 51"	2	Cedar
B	Ends	1½ × 3½ × 16"	2	Cedar
C	Subbase	¾ × 15 × 48"	1	Ext. Plywood
D	Underlayment	½ × 15 × 48"	1	Cementboard

Key	Part	Dimension	Pcs.	Material
E	Stretchers	1½ × 3½ × 16"	3	Cedar
F	Braces	1½ × 5½ × 16"	4	Cedar
G	Legs	3½ × 3½ × 13"	4	Cedar

Tiled Garden Bench

BUILD THE FRAME

Cut two sides and two ends, then position the ends between the sides so the edges are flush. Make sure the frame is square. Drill ⅛"-dia. pilot holes through the sides and into the ends and then drive 3" screws through the pilot holes.

Cut three stretchers. Mark the sides 4½" from the inside of each end. Using 1½" blocks as spacers beneath the stretchers, position each stretcher and make sure they're all level. Drill pilot holes and fasten the stretchers to the sides with 3" screws (**photo 1**).

MAKE THE TILE BASE

Cut the subbase from ¾" exterior-grade plywood. Cut the tile underlayment from cementboard. Staple plastic sheeting over the plywood, draping it over the edges. Lay the cementboard rough-side up on the plywood and attach it with 1¼" cementboard screws driven every 6". Make sure the screw heads are flush with or slightly below the surface. Position the bench frame upside down on the underside

of the subbase and attach it with 2" deck screws driven through the stretchers and into the plywood (**photo 2**).

BUILD THE LEGS

The braces are angled to be more aesthetically pleasing. Cut four braces from a cedar 2 × 6. Mark the angle on each end of each brace by measuring down 1½" from the top edge and 1½" along the bottom edge. Draw a line between the two points and cut along that line using a circular saw.

On each brace, measure down ¾" from the top edge and draw a reference line across the stretcher for the screw positions. Drill ⅛"-dia. pilot holes along the reference line. Position a brace on each side of the end stretchers and fasten with 3" deck screws driven through the braces and into the stretchers.

Cut four 13" legs from a 4 × 4. Position each leg between a set of braces and against the sides of the bench frame. Drill pilot holes through each brace and attach the leg to the braces by driving 3" screws through the braces

Assemble the frame. Use 1½" blocks to support the stretchers. Drill pilot holes and fasten the stretchers to the sides with 3" deck screws.

Position the frame over the subbase and fasten it by driving 2" deck screws through the stretchers and into the plywood. Also drive some screws down through the cementboard underlayment and plywood and into the stretchers.

Position each leg between a set of braces and against the sides of the bench frame. Drill pilot holes through each brace and attach the leg to the braces.

Dry-fit the field tiles using tile spacers to set consistent gaps. Set the accent tiles in place and mark the field tiles for cutting.

and into the leg (**photo 3**). Repeat the process for each leg. Sand all surfaces with 150-grit sandpaper, then seal all wood surfaces with clear wood sealer.

SET THE TILE

Field tiles are the main tiles in any given design. In this project, square field tiles are cut to fit around four decorative picture tiles and bright blue accent tiles. Snap perpendicular reference lines to mark the center of the length and width of the bench. Beginning at the center of the bench, dry-fit the field tiles using tile spacers to set consistent gaps. Set the accent tiles in place and mark the field tile for cutting (**photo 4**). Cut the tiles as necessary and continue dry-fitting the bench top, including the accent and border tiles.

Mix the thinset mortar, starting with the dry powder and gradually adding water. Stir the mixture to achieve a creamy consistency. The mortar should be wet enough to stick to the tiles and the cementboard, but stiff enough to hold the ridges made when applied with the notched trowel. Remove the tiles from the bench and apply thinset mortar over the cementboard using a notched trowel (**photo 5**). Apply only as much mortar as you can use in ten minutes.

Set the tile into the thinset mortar using a slight twisting motion as you press down. Do not press too hard—the goal is to seat the tile, not to displace the mortar. Continue adding thinset and setting the tiles until the bench top is covered (**photo 6**). Remove the tile spacers using a needlenose pliers, and allow the mortar to set up and dry.

GROUT THE TILE

Grout fills the gaps between the tiles. Apply masking tape around the wood frame to prevent the grout from staining the wood. Mix the grout and latex grout additive according to package instructions. Use a grout float to force the grout into the joints surrounding the tile, holding the float at an angle (**photo 7**). Do not apply grout to the joint between the tile and the wood frame.

Wipe the excess grout from the tiles with a damp sponge. Rinse the sponge between each wipe. When the grout has dried slightly, polish the tiles with a clean, dry cloth to remove the slight haze of grout. Seal the grout.

Apply a setting bed of thinset mortar onto the cementboard using a notched trowel.

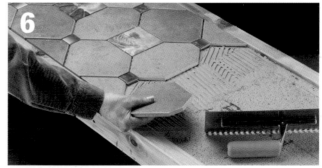

Set the tiles into the thinset mortar using a slight twisting motion as you press down.

Mix a batch of grout and use a grout float to force it into the joints between tiles. Buff off the excess once the grout sets up.

Slatted Garden Bench

Casual seating is a welcome addition to any outdoor setting. This lovely garden bench sits comfortably around the borders of any porch, patio, or deck. With a compact footprint, it creates a pleasant resting spot for up to three adults without taking up a lot of space. Station it near your home's rear entry for a convenient place to remove shoes or set down grocery bags while you unlock the door.

The straightforward, slatted design of this bench lends itself to accessorizing. Station a rustic cedar planter next to the bench for a lovely effect. Or, add a framed lattice trellis to one side of the bench to cut down on wind and direct sun. You can apply exterior stain or a clear wood sealer with UV protectant to keep the bench looking fresh and new. Or, leave it unfinished and let it weather naturally to a silvery hue.

Materials ▸

1	2 × 8" × 6 ft. cedar	Moisture-resistant glue
4	2 × 2" × 10 ft. cedar	Wood sealer or stain
1	2 × 4" × 6 ft. cedar	Deck screws (1½",
1	2 × 6" × 10 ft. cedar	2½")
1	2 × 2" × 6 ft. cedar	
1	1 × 4" × 12 ft. cedar	

Graceful lines and trestle construction make this bench a charming furnishing for any garden as well as porches, patios, and decks.

Slatted Garden Bench

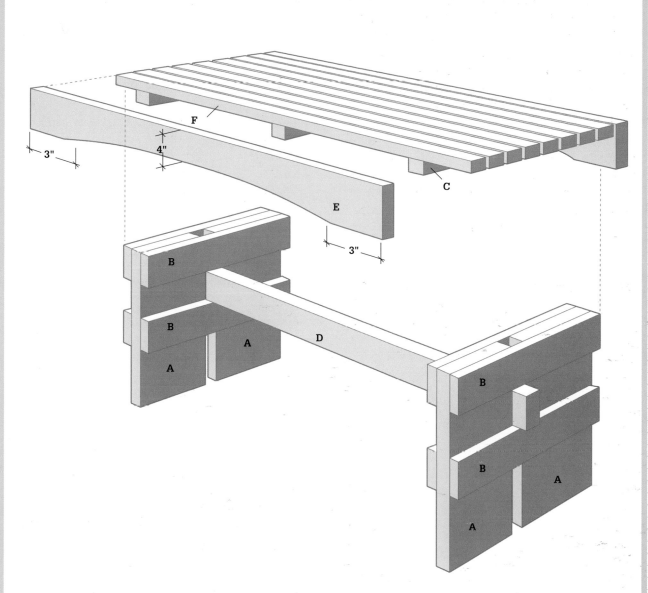

Cutting List

Key	Part	Dimension	Pcs.	Material
A	Leg half	1½ × 7¼ × 14½"	4	Cedar
B	Cleat	¾ × 3½ × 16"	8	Cedar
C	Brace	1½ × 1½ × 16"	3	Cedar
D	Trestle	1½ × 3½ × 60"	1	Cedar
E	Apron	1½ × 5½ × 60"	2	Cedar
F	Slat	1½ × 1½ × 60"	8	Cedar

Slatted Garden Bench

BUILD THE BASE

Cut the leg halves, cleats, and trestle to length. Sandwich one leg half between two cleats so the cleats are flush with the top and the outside edge of the leg half. Then, join the parts by driving four 1½" deck screws through each cleat and into the leg half. Assemble two more cleats with a leg half in the same fashion.

Stand the two assemblies on their sides, with the open ends of the cleats pointing upward. Arrange the assemblies so they are roughly 4 feet apart. Set the trestle onto the inner edges of the leg halves, pressed flush against the bottoms of the cleats. Adjust the position of the assemblies so the trestle overhangs the leg half by 1½" at each end. Fasten the trestle to each leg half with glue and 2½" deck screws (**photo 1**).

Attach another pair of cleats to each leg half directly below the first pair, positioned so each cleat is snug against the bottom of the trestle. Slide the other leg half between the cleats, keeping the top edge flush with the upper cleats. Join the leg halves

with the cleats using glue and 2½" deck screws (**photo 2**). Cut the braces to length. Fasten one brace to the inner top cleat on each leg assembly, so the tops are flush (**photo 3**).

MAKE THE APRONS

Cut the aprons to length. Lay out the arc profile onto one apron, starting 3" from each end. The peak of the arch, located over the midpoint of the apron, should be 1½" up from the bottom edge. Draw a smooth, even arc by driving a casing nail at the peak of the arc and at each of the starting points. Slip a flexible ruler or strip of thin plywood or hardboard behind the nails at the starting points and in front of the nail at the peak to create a smooth arc. Then, trace along the inside of the ruler to make a cutting line (**photo 4**). Cut along the line with a jigsaw and sand the cut smooth. Trace the profile of the arc onto the other apron and make the cut. Sand the cuts smooth.

Cut the slats to length. Attach a slat to the top inside edge of each apron with glue and deck screws (**photo 5**).

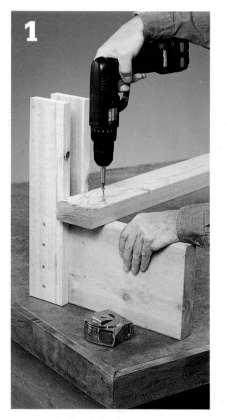

Attach the trestle to the legs, making sure it is positioned correctly against the top cleat bottoms.

Attach the remaining leg half to the cleats on both ends, sandwiching the trestle on all sides.

Attach the outer brace for the seat slats directly to the inside faces of the cleats.

Mark the profile cuts on the aprons. Use a flexible ruler pinned between casing nails to trace a smooth arc.

Attach a 2 x 2 slat to the top inside edge of each apron using 2½" deck screws and glue.

INSTALL THE APRONS & SLATS

Apply glue at each end on the bottom sides of the attached slats. Flip the leg and trestle assembly and position it flush with the aprons so that it rests on the glue of the two slatted bottoms. The aprons should extend 1½" beyond the legs at each end of the bench. Drive 2½" deck screws through the braces and into both slats.

Position the middle brace between the aprons, centered end-to-end on the project. Fasten it to the two side slats with deck screws. Position the six remaining slats on the braces using ½"-thick spacers to create equal gaps between them. Attach the slats with glue and drive 2½" deck screws up through the braces and into each slat (**photo 6**).

APPLY FINISHING TOUCHES

Sand the slats smooth with progressively finer sandpaper, up to 150-grit. Wipe away the sanding residue with a rag dipped in mineral spirits. Let the bench dry. Apply a finish of your choice—a clear wood sealer protects the cedar without altering the color.

Attach the seat slats with glue and 2½" deck screws. Insert ½"-thick spacers to set gaps between the slats.

Trellis Seat

Made of cedar lattice and cedar boards, this trellis seat is ideal for conversation or quiet moments of reading. The lattice creates just the right amount of privacy or shelter for a small garden or patio. It's an unobtrusive structure that is sure to add some warmth to your patio or deck. Position some outdoor plants along the top cap or around the frame sides to dress up the project and bring nature a little closer to home.

The warmth of the cedar contributes a great deal to the overall appearance of this project. The versatility of the design also allows it to fit into just about any backyard environment. If you have a more formal yard with classical elements or a Victoriana feel, a pristine white structure may be more to your liking. Fortunately, lattice panels are widely available in low-maintenance white PVC. The other wood elements of the design are easy enough to paint white, but if you've ever tried to paint lattice you'll be glad you used the PVC product.

For a cleaner appearance, conceal visible screw heads on the seat by counterboring the pilot holes for the screws

and inserting cedar plugs (available at most woodworking stores) into the counterbores.

Although the lattice panels provide some shading, wind blocking, and privacy, the effects are greatly enhanced if you plant climbing plants such as ivy or clematis at the base. You can put them in containers if you'd like to be able to move things around. Or you can plant them right in the ground if you have a permanent home for your trellis seat.

Materials ▸

1	4 × 4" × 6 ft. cedar	Moisture-resistant glue
2	2 × 8" × 8 ft. cedar	Deck screws (1¼", 2",
5	2 × 4" ×10 ft. cedar	2½", 3")
1	1 × 6" × 10 ft. cedar	4d galvanized casing
11	1 × 2" × 8 ft. cedar	nails
1	½" x 4 × 8 ft. cedar	Finishing materials
	lattice	

Spice up your patio or deck with this sheltered seating structure. Set it in a quiet corner to create a warm, inviting space for relaxation.

Trellis Seat

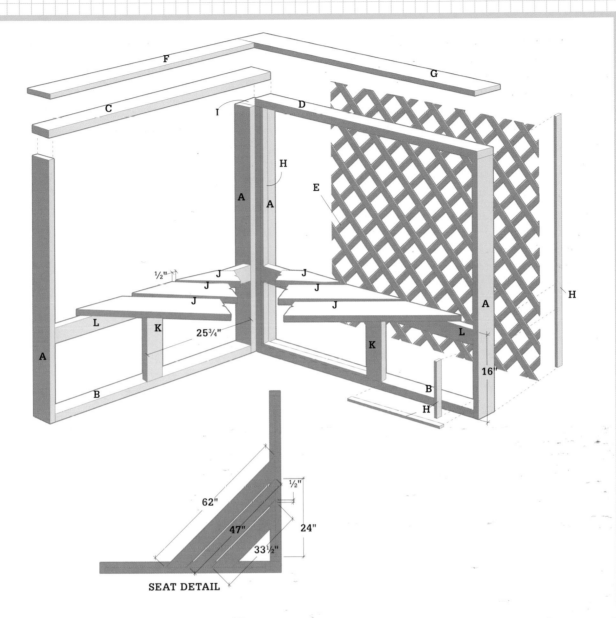

SEAT DETAIL

Cutting List

Key	Part	Dimension	Pcs.	Material
A	Frame side	$1\frac{1}{2} \times 3\frac{1}{2} \times 49\frac{1}{2}$"	4	Cedar
B	Frame bottom	$1\frac{1}{2} \times 3\frac{1}{2} \times 48$"	2	Cedar
C	Long rail	$1\frac{1}{2} \times 3\frac{1}{2} \times 56\frac{1}{2}$"	1	Cedar
D	Short rail	$1\frac{1}{2} \times 3\frac{1}{2} \times 51$"	1	Cedar
E	Lattice	$\frac{1}{2}$" $\times 4' \times 4'$	2	Cedar
F	Short cap	$\frac{3}{4} \times 5\frac{1}{2} \times 51$"	1	Cedar

Key	Part	Dimension	Pcs.	Material
G	Long cap	$\frac{3}{4} \times 5\frac{1}{2} \times 56\frac{1}{2}$"	1	Cedar
H	Retaining strip	$\frac{3}{4} \times 1\frac{1}{2}$" cut to fit	22	Cedar
I	Post	$3\frac{1}{2} \times 3\frac{1}{2} \times 49\frac{1}{2}$"	1	Cedar
J	Seat board	$1\frac{1}{2} \times 7\frac{1}{4} \times$ *	3	Cedar
K	Brace	$1\frac{1}{2} \times 3\frac{1}{2} \times 11$"	2	Cedar
L	Seat support	$1\frac{1}{2} \times 3\frac{1}{2} \times 48$"	2	Cedar

*Cut one each :35", 49", 63"

Trellis Seat

MAKE THE TRELLIS FRAME

Cut the frame sides, frame bottoms, long rail, short rail, braces, and seat supports to length. To attach the frame sides and frame bottoms, drill two evenly spaced ³⁄₁₆"-dia. pilot holes in the frame sides. Counterbore the holes to ¼" deep. Apply glue to the frame sides and bottoms, and then drive 2½" deck screws through the frame sides and into the bottoms.

Drill counterbored pilot holes in the top faces of the long and short rails. Attach the long and short rails to the tops of the frame sides with glue. Drive deck screws through the rails and into the ends of the frame sides. The long rail should extend 3½" past one end of the frame (**photo 1**).

Mark points 22¼" from each end on the frame bottoms to indicate the position for the braces. Turn the frame upside-down. Drill counterbored pilot holes in the frame bottoms where the braces will be attached. Position the braces flush with the inside frame bottom edges. Attach the pieces by driving 3" deck screws through the frame bottoms and into the ends of the braces.

Position the seat supports 16" up from the bottoms of the frame bottoms, resting on the braces. Make sure the supports are flush with the inside edges of the braces.

Attach with glue and 3" deck screws driven through the frame sides and into the ends of the seat supports. Attach the braces to the seat supports by drilling angled ³⁄₁₆"-dia. pilot holes through each brace edge. Drive 3" deck screws toe nail-style through the braces and into the top edges of the seat supports (**photo 2**).

JOIN THE TRELLIS FRAMES TO THE POST

Cut the post to length. Attach the two frame sections to the post. First, drill counterbored pilot holes in the frame sides. Drive evenly spaced 3" deck screws through the frame sides and into the post (**photo 3**). Make sure the overhang of the long rail fits snugly over the top of the post.

ATTACH THE LATTICE RETAINING STRIPS

Cut the lattice retaining strips to fit along the inside faces of the trellis frames (but not the seat supports or braces). Nail the strips to the frames, flush with the inside frame edges using 4d galvanized casing nails (**photo 4**).

CUT & INSTALL THE LATTICE PANELS

Since you will probably be cutting through some metal fasteners in the lattice, fit your circular saw with a remodeler's blade. Sandwich the lattice panel between

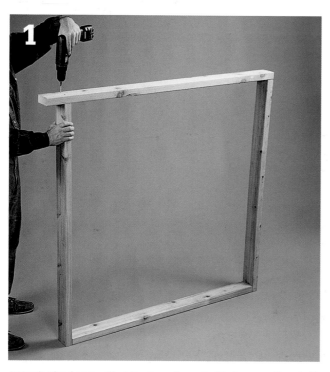

Attach the long rail at the top of one trellis frame with a 3½" overhang at one end to cover the post.

Drive deck screws toenail-style through the braces and into the seat supports.

two boards near the cutting line to prevent the lattice from separating. Clamp the boards and the panel together, and cut the lattice panels to size.

Position the panels into the frames against the retaining strips, and attach them to the seat supports with 1¼" deck screws (**photo 5**). Secure the panels by cutting retaining strips to fit along the outer edges of the inside faces of the trellis frame. Nail strips in place.

BUILD THE SEAT
Cut the seat boards to length. On a flat work surface, lay the seat boards together, edge to edge. Insert ½"-wide spacers between the boards. Draw cutting lines to lay out the seat shape onto the boards as if they were one board (see Seat Detail, page 55, for seat board dimensions). Gang-cut the seat boards to their finished size and shape with a circular saw. Attach the seat boards to the seat supports with evenly spaced deck screws, maintaining the ½"-wide gap. Smooth the seat board edges with a sander or router.

INSTALL THE TOP CAPS
Cut the short cap and long cap to length. Attach the caps to the tops of the long and short rails with deck screws (**photo 6**). Brush on a coat of clear wood sealer to help preserve the trellis seat.

Fasten the trellis frames to the post at right angles using deck screws.

Nail 1 x 2 retaining strips for the lattice panels to the inside faces of the trellis frames.

Fasten the lattice panels to the seat supports with 1¼" deck screws, and then attach outer retaining strips.

Attach the long and short caps to the tops of the trellis frames. The long cap overlaps the long rail and the post.

Rose Bench

Every gardener deserves a quiet, restful place to sit and contemplate the beauty of the blossoms. This bench, which is both quick and easy to build, is ideal for compact mounding rose varieties or miniature rose trees. It is constructed entirely from redwood, but you may use just about any exterior-rated wood.

A bench planter is a perfect starter project—all you need are simple construction skills and common carpentry tools. Allow a weekend to gather materials, cut pieces, and assemble the bench.

The keys to construction of this planter bench are the threaded rods that run through the slats from front to back, drawing them together. The rods have a nut and washer at each end, set into counterbore that are fitted with wood plugs to disguise them and then painted over. The rods run through each slat and through the spacer blocks that fit between the slats, so drilling the guide holes for the rods in perfect alignment is a critical step.

Materials ▸

9 2 × 4" × 8 ft. cedar	Deck screws
5 1 × 4" × 8 ft. cedar	½"-dia. threaded
6 1 × 3" × 8 ft. cedar	rods with nuts
6 1 × 6" × 8 ft. cedar	and washers
3 2 × 2" × 8 ft. cedar	
Galvanized finishing	
nails	

This lovely bench project combines comfortable seating with a pair of planter boxes for a unique effect.

Rose Bench

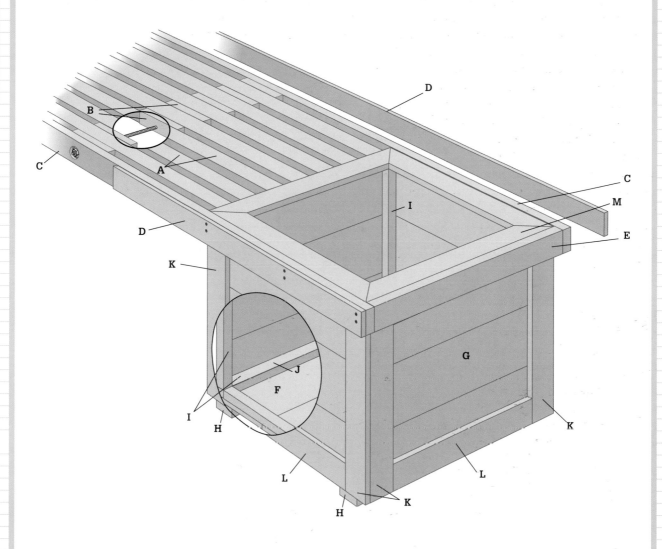

Cutting List

Key	Part	Dimension	Pcs.	Material
A	Inner Slat	1½ × 3½ × 61½"	7	Cedar
B	Filler	¾ × 3½ × 5"	16	Cedar
C	Outer slat	1½ × 3½ × 94½"	2	Cedar
D	Long rail	¾ × 3½ × 96"	2	Cedar
E	Short rail	¾ × 3½ × 16½"	2	Cedar
F	Base strip	¾ × 5½ × 16½"	6	Cedar
G	Side strip	¾ × 5½ × 16½"	24	Cedar

Key	Part	Dimension	Pcs.	Material
H	Foot	1½ × 3½ × 16½"	4	Cedar
I	Corner brace	1½ × 1½ × 15¾"	8	Cedar
J	Bottom brace	1½ × 1½ × 13½"	8	Cedar
K	Corner frame	¾ × 2½ × 13¾"	16	Cedar
L	Box trim	¾ × 2 × 13¼"	16	Cedar
M	Cap	¾ × 3½ × 16½"	8	Cedar

Rose Bench

ASSEMBLE THE SEAT

Cut the 2 × 4 inner slats, 1 × 4 filler pieces, and 2 × 4 outer slats to length from 2 × 4 stock. Make a drilling template from another piece of scrap 1 × 4 and drill ½" guide holes 15" from each end, centered top to bottom. Make another template for the filler strips with the ½" hole centered exactly top to bottom and end to end. Using the templates as guides, drill ½" holes in the inner slats and in the filler strips (**photo1**). Also drill ½" holes in the outer slats, making sure the distance from the template to each workpiece end is equal. Drill a 1"-dia. × ¾"-deep counterbore for each hole in the outside faces of the two outer slats (these will accommodate the nuts and washers that are threaded onto the threaded rods).

Lay out the inner slats, outer slats, and fillers as shown in the diagram on page 59. Thread a washer and nut onto one end of each threaded rod and insert the rods into the aligned guide holes. Thread a washer and nut onto the free ends of the threaded rods and tighten to draw the bench assembly together. Make sure the edges of all the parts stay flush as you work. Fully tighten the nuts on both ends and then trim any rod that extends past the face of an outer slat using a hacksaw. Check the ends of the assembly—if they are uneven, trim them with a circular saw so they form a straight line.

ASSEMBLE THE PLANTER BOXES

Cut all of the base strips and side strips to length from 1 × 6 stock. Cut the 2 × 4 feet to length and then position three base strips on top of each pair of feet. Attach the strips to the feet with 2" deck screws to form a platform for the box bottoms (**photo 2**). Drill three of four ½"-dia. deep holes in each platform.

Cut the corner braces and bottom braces to length from 2 × 2 stock. Fasten bottom braces between corner braces to create a pair of brace assemblies with four corner posts. Use 2½" deck screws driven into pilot holes to fasten the parts. Set each assembly on a platform so all edges are flush, and attach this assembly by driving 2" deck screws down through the bottom braces.

Attach side strips to the corner posts to make the side of the boxes (**photo 3**). Each side should have three strips with the bottom strip flush with the bottom of the platform.

Drill guide holes for the threaded rods in the rails and fillers using templates as guides.

Attach three base strips on top of a pair of feet to create platforms to use as the box bases.

TRIM THE PLANTER BOX SIDES

Cut the corner frame pieces to length from 1 × 3 stock (you may have to rip this to width yourself, or use 1 × 4 instead). Fasten a pair of trim boards so they butt together at each box corner. The bottoms of the trim boards should be flush with the bottoms of the box sides. The top should stop 2¾" short of the box tops to create ledges all around the box. Attach the boards with 6d galvanized finish nails (**photo 4**). Cut the box trim for the top and bottom of each box side by ripping a ½" strip off a piece of 1 × 3 and cutting to length. Attach with finish nails.

The tops of the boxes are trimmed with mitered 1 × 4 installed picture-frame style with the outside edges flush with the outsides of the boxes. Make 45° miter cuts at each end of the cap trim pieces. Fit the top trim to the top of each planter and fasten all trim with 6d galvanized finishing nails (**photo 5**).

FASTEN THE PLANTERS & SEAT

Align the assemblies so that the ends of the planters are flush with the ends of the seat's outer rails. Drill pilot holes and fasten the planters to the outer rails using four deck screws at the ends of each planter. Position the long rails so they are flush with the tops and edges of the outer slats, concealing the nuts and the ends of the threaded rods. Attach the long rails with 6d galvanized finish nails (**photo 6**). Fit the short rail between the ends of the long rails and attach to planter box tops with finish nails.

Attach the side strips to the corner braces with 2" deck screws to create the boxes.

Attach the corner trim boards and the top and bottom trim boards to each planter assembly.

Miter-cut the cap trim boards and nail them in place on the box tops.

Attach the planters to the outer rails of the seat using deck screws. Fasten the rail strips with finish nails to hide the bench top hardware and fasteners.

Storage Bench

Few areas in your home are better suited for a sturdy bench than porches, entryways, breezeways, and even patios and garages that are located next to an entry door. The reasons are pretty obvious: it's convenient to have a place to sit while removing shoes or boots, and a flat, raised surface is perfect for setting down groceries and packages while fumbling around for the house keys. This wood offers an expansive, sturdy top for accommodating these tasks, but it also has a bit of classical styling so it doesn't end up looking like just another plastic bin with a lid.

The principal design flair on this project is created by the scalloped rim rails and vertical columns running along the faces and sides. With a subtle Grecian architectural theme, the look imparts a bit of elegance to the sturdy wood box and lid. The parts also provide structural support, allowing for thin front and side panels that keep down the weight and cost while allowing slightly more interior storage space.

Because this bench is painted, it can be built with inexpensive construction-grade lumber even if it is destined for porch, patio, or some other exposed or partially exposed area. If you plan to use a two-tone painted finish like the one seen here, save yourself a lot of tricky work by prepainting the parts before assembly. As shown, the design does not include metal lid support hardware; if you plan to use the project as a boot bench where children may be fishing around for boots and shoes for an extended time, add lockable metal lid supports to minimize the possibility of the lid slamming down.

Materials ▸

4	1 × 4" × 8 ft. clear pine	1	¾" × 4 × 8 ft. AB plywood
2	1 × 2" × 8 ft. clear pine	3	2½" brass butt hinges
6	1 × 6" × 10 ft. clear pine		¼"-dia. dowels
			00 biscuits
			Deck screws

Indoor/outdoor benches that combine seating and storage are readily available for purchase today, but the typical model in stores has a bleak appearance that's much more about utility than design appeal. This storage bench employs some classical styling elements for an appearance that makes no concessions to utility.

Storage Bench

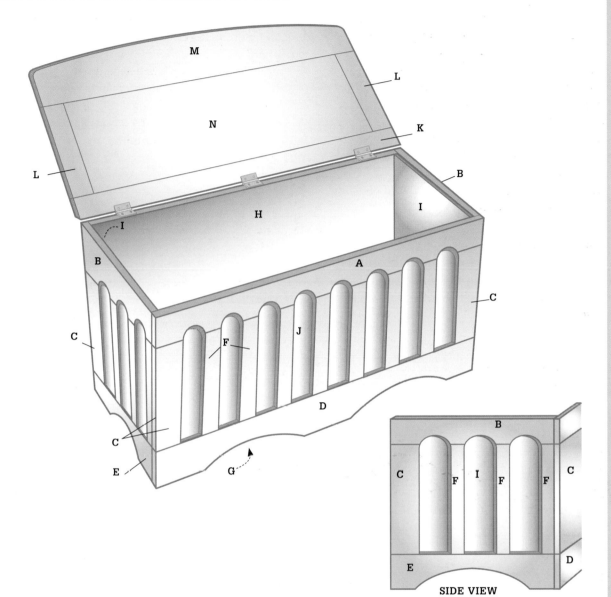

SIDE VIEW

Cutting List

Key	Part	Dimension	Pcs.	Material
A	Front Top Rail	$\frac{3}{4} \times 3\text{-}\frac{1}{2} \times 40\frac{1}{2}$"	1	Pine
B	Side Rail	$\frac{3}{4} \times 3\frac{1}{2} \times 16\frac{1}{2}$"	2	Pine
C	Corner Boards	$\frac{3}{4} \times 3 \times 12$"	4	Pine
D	Front Base Rail	$\frac{3}{4} \times 5\frac{1}{2} \times 40\frac{1}{2}$"	1	Pine
E	Side Base Rail	$\frac{3}{4} \times 5\frac{1}{2} \times 16\frac{1}{2}$"	2	Pine
F	Filler Stiles	$\frac{3}{4} \times 1\frac{1}{2} \times 12$"	13	Pine
G	Bottom Panel	$\frac{3}{4} \times 15\frac{3}{4} \times 39$"	1	AB plywood

Key	Part	Dimension	Pcs.	Material
H	Back Panel	$\frac{3}{4} \times 21 \times 39$"	1	AB plywood
I	Side Panel	$\frac{1}{4} \times 13 \times 12$"	2	AB plywood
J	Front Panel	$\frac{1}{4} \times 13 \times 38$"	1	AB plywood
K	Back Lid Rail	$\frac{3}{4} \times 3\frac{1}{2} \times 41$"	1	Pine
L	Side Lid Rail	$\frac{3}{4} \times 3\frac{1}{2} \times 10$"	2	Pine
M	Front Lid Rail	$\frac{3}{4} \times 5\frac{1}{2} \times 41$"	1	Pine
N	Lid Panel	$\frac{3}{4} \times 10 \times 34$"	1	AB plywood

Storage Bench

MAKE THE PROFILED RAILS

The top rails and base rails for this bench feature decorative cutouts and curves that should be cut before the bench frame is assembled. The top rails have a series of half-circles separated by 1½" of square-end material that mates with the tops of the 1 × 2 filler stiles. The best way to make the half-round cutouts is to cut full circles in a workpiece and then rip-cut that piece down the center. For the top rails, a piece of 1 × 8 SPF (spruce/pine/fir) is wide enough to make both the sides and the top. Cut a 1 × 8 to about 48" long and then draw a centerline from end to end. Lay out 3"-dia. circles along the centerline so the equators of the circles are 1½" apart on the centerline (start in the center and work out toward the ends, leaving slightly more than 3" of uncut wood at each end). Chuck a 3"-dia. hole saw in a drill and carefully cut the circles (**photo 1**). If you have a drill press, use it here.

After the holes are cut, set up a table saw to rip-cut the workpiece along the centerline. If you do not have a table saw, use a circular saw and a straightedge cutting guide. Cut along the centerline (**photo 2**). Then, trim the ends of one ripped workpiece so they are exactly 3" out from the outer edges of the circular cutouts. Cut the side top rails from the other half of the workpiece (**photo 3**). Each side rail should have 3" of uncut material at the back and 1½" at the front.

Cut the 1 × 6 stock for the base rails to length and lay out the arcs according to the dimensions on page 63. The arcs essentially create leg forms at the ends of each rail and in the middle of the front rail. Use a jigsaw to cut out the arcs (**photo 4**) and then sand them so they are smooth. Cut the corner boards and the filler stiles to length.

MAKE & JOIN THE PANEL ASSEMBLIES

Join the rails, corner boards, and stiles to create a front panel assembly and two side panel assemblies. Because of the width of the top and base rails, there are several better options than screws to connect the horizontal rails to the

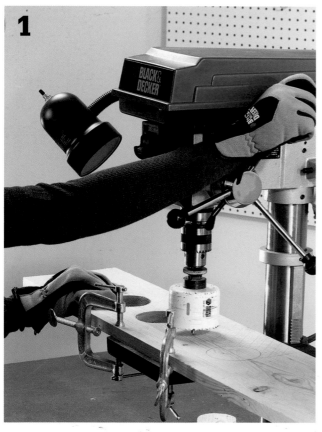

Cut out 3"-dia. circles along a centerline on a 1 × 8 workpiece to make the top rails. Use a 3" hole saw to cut the wood.

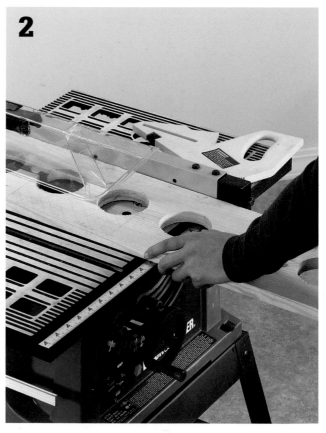

Rip-cut the rail workpiece along the centerline to create two workpieces with half-round cutouts. Use one for the front top rail and the other to make the side top rails.

vertical corner boards and filler stiles. If you own or have access to a pocket screw jig, pocket screws can be used to make the connections. Otherwise, use dowels to reinforce the joints. You can use a dowel jig or dowel points for this, or you can rely on math and marking.

To join the horizontal and vertical parts with dowels, start by using a drill press (if you have one) to drill ⅜"-dia. × ¾" deep dowel holes in the bottom edges of the top rails **(photo 5)**. Clamp a straightedge guide to your drill press table to ensure that the holes are a uniform distance in from the front edges of the workpieces. The holes should be centered on each 1½" shoulder where it will meet a spacer stile. Use a pair of evenly spaced dowels to secure each corner board. After the dowel holes are drilled into the rails, clamp all of the stiles and corner boards together edge-to-edge with the ends flush. Use the same drill press setup to drill dowel holes in the ends of the clamped parts **(photo 6)** making sure the dowel hole above each spacer stile location is centered. *TIP: If your drill press doesn't have enough throat capacity to drill these dowel holes, you may be able to do it by orienting the table so it is in a vertical position.*

Apply a small amount of exterior glue into each dowel hole, and make the dowel joints to complete the assembly. Use a bar clamp or pipe clamp to draw the parts together, if necessary. Once the glue has dried, join the front assembly to the side assembly with glue and 2½" countersunk wood screws. Make sure the top and bottom edges are flush. Cut the back panel to size from ¾" plywood and attach it to the backs of the side assemblies with glue and 2½" countersunk wood screws. Cut the bottom panel to size and install it in the base of the bench so the top of the panel is ¼" below the tops of the base rails using glue and countersunk 2½" wood screws **(photo 7)**. You could also use biscuits and a plate joiner or pocket screws to make these connections.

Cut the front panel and side panels to size from ¼"-thick plywood. If you are using a two-tone painting scheme, paint the frame and the panels separately using two or three thin coats of exterior trim paint. Once the paint has dried, apply a thin bead of exterior-rated adhesive to the backs of the filler stiles and corner boards and then position

Trim the scalloped rails to length so the correct amount of uncut materials is left at each end.

Make the 2"-deep arc cutouts on the bottoms of the rails to create the feet shapes.

the panels behind the front and side assemblies, centered so any reveals are even around the perimeters of the panels. Press on the panels to set them in the adhesive and then staple them or drive ¾" brads to reinforce the joints.

MAKE & ATTACH THE LID

The lid for this storage bench is made from ¾" plywood that's framed with solid wood. To make it this way, you need to employ either a plate joiner, a pocket screw jig, or a dowel jig. A simpler alternative is to cut the entire lid to the finished dimensions from ¾" exterior plywood, and fill the voids in the plywood edges with wood filler before painting.

Cut the lid frame parts from 1 × 4 and 1 × 6 stock. Trace the profile for the front edge into the 1 × 6 using the dimensions on page 63 as a guide. Cut the lid panel to size from ¾" AB plywood (or another high-quality grade). Join the back and side lid rails using dowels, biscuits, or pocket screws and glue; then attach the lid panel to the inside edges of the three-sided frame using the same joinery techniques. Attach the front lid rail to the front ends of the side rails and the front edge of the lid panel (**photo 8**). Sand the lid smooth after the glue dries and fill any holes or voids with wood filler. Paint the lid. Attach the lid with three 2½ × 2½" exterior-rated butt hinges (**photo 9**) or, if you prefer, a piano hinge. Add optional lid supports and other hardware as you see fit.

Drill dowel holes in the top and bottom rails to make dowel joints with the filler stiles and the corner boards..

Drill mating dowel holes in the top and bottom ends of the filler stiles and the corner boards. Gang the parts together edge to edge to ensure a uniform setback from the front faces.

7

Install the base panel using glue and counterbored screws. The top of the base panel should be ¼" below the tops of the bottom rails on all sides.

8

Make the bench lid by capturing the plywood lid panel between the back and side lid rails and then adding the front lid rail.

9

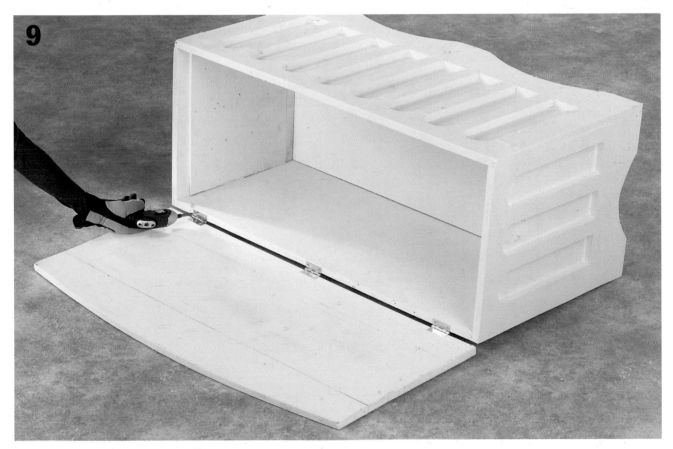

Attach the lid with hinges. Add any additional hardware you may want, such as lid support hardware or chest handles.

Luxury Sun Lounger

Reclining in comfort on a summer afternoon—that's all the motivation most people will need to build this wood sun lounger. It features four recline positions so you can select a comfortable back angle whether you plan to read a book, take an afternoon nap, or bag some serious rays. Fashioned from mahogany for high-end nautical appeal, the lounger features two pullout trays for beverages or books. Mahogany is naturally rot resistant, but it will last longer (and resist staining better) if it is coated with an exterior sealer.

Considering the refined appearance of this woodworking project, you might think you need a shop full of tools, advanced skills, and a pile of custom milled lumber to build it. But the parts that make this lounger are made from stock ¾"-thick and 1½"-thick lumber so you can choose to build it from just about any exterior-grade lumber, such as cedar.

Most of the parts for this lounger are rip-cut to width—a task that's easiest to accomplish with a table saw, but can also be done with a circular saw and straightedge. All of the exposed, sharp edges are eased with a router and roundover bit. If you don't have a router, you can use a power sander, a block plane, or even hand-sand them.

Materials ▸

2 ¾ × 1½" × 8 ft. mahogany	10 ¼" brass flat washers
9 ¾ × 3½" × 8 ft.	4 ¼" brass locknuts
2 ¾ × 5½" × 10 ft.	½"-dia. × 27" rod
2 1½ × 3½" × 8 ft.	2 8"-dia. wheels
1 ¾ -dia. × 24" hardwood dowel	6 ½" galvanized washers
Brass screws (1¼", 2½")	1 ½ -dia. × 19½" CPVC tubing
36 No. 10 brass finish washers	2 ½" push caps
4 ¼ -dia. × 2" brass machine screws	

Made of rich mahogany and dressed up with solid brass hardware, this sun lounger has a nautically inspired appearance that is right at home poolside.

Luxury Sun Lounger

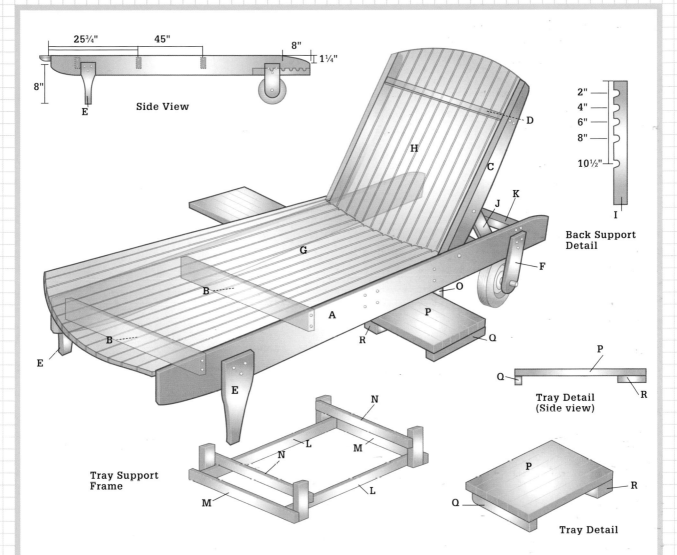

25¾" 45" 8" 1¼"

8"

8"

Side View

E

Back Support Detail

2"
4"
6"
8"
10½"

I

H

C

D

J K

G

F

B

O

A

P

B

R

Q

E

E

N

L

M

N

Tray Support Frame

M

L

Tray Detail (Side view)

P

Q

R

P

Q

R

Tray Detail

Cutting List

Key	Part	Dimension	Pcs.	Material
A	Base rails	¾ × 5½ × 77"	2	Mahogany
B	Base stretchers	1½ × 3 × 24"	4	Mahogany
C	Back rails	¾ × 3 × 30"	2	Mahogany
D	Back stretchers	1½ × 3 × 22"	2	Mahogany
E	Front legs	¾ × 4 × 12"	2	Mahogany
F	Back legs	¾ × 4 × 10¼"	2	Mahogany
G	Base slats	¾ × 1¾ × 51"	13	Mahogany
H	Back slats	¾ × 1¾ × 31½"	12	Mahogany
I	Back support rails	¾ × 1⅝ × 15"	2	Mahogany
J	Back support arms	¾ × 2 × 15"	2	Mahogany
K	Back support rod	¾ dia. × 23¾"	1	Oak dowel

Optional Pull-out Trays

Key	Part	Dimension	Pcs.	Material
L	Tray frame sides	¾ × 1½ × 24"	2	Mahogany
M	Tray frame ends	¾ × 1½ × 13½"	2	Mahogany
N	Tray frame crosspieces	¾ × 1½ × 13½"	2	Mahogany
O	Tray frame supports	¾ × 1-½ × 5½"	4	Mahogany
P	Tray slats	¾ × 1¾ × 12"	12	Mahogany
Q	Tray fronts	¾ × 1½ × 10¾"	2	Mahogany
R	Tray backs	¾ × 3½ × 10¾"	2	Mahogany

Luxury Sun Lounger

BUILD THE BASE FRAME

Begin construction of the sun lounger by making the base frame. Achieving strong joints and perfectly square corners at this stage helps to ensure that your project fits together as designed. Cut the base rails and back rails to length and width. Use a piece of cardboard to make a template of the curved profile (8" long and 1¼" deep) that's cut into the ends of the rails (see drawing, page 69). Trace the curved profile onto the bottom front corner and the top back corner of each base rail and onto the top (back) end only of the seat back rails (**photo 1**). Use a jigsaw to cut along the curved lines (**photo 2**) and then smooth the cuts with a power sander. Round over the top edges of the base rails with a router and ¼"-radius roundover bit (**photo 3**) or ease them with sandpaper.

Cut the front legs to length and width. Use the same curved-profile template that was used for the base and back rails to trace two mirror-image curves on the bottom corners of each front leg (**photo 4**). Use a jigsaw or band saw to cut along the curved lines.

Preparing Your Stock ▶

The sun lounger seen here is designed so it can be built easily with common dimensional lumber found at any home center. Depending on your location, that would include cedar, redwood, or cypress along with treated and untreated SPF (spruce/pine/fir). In some cases, you can find select, sanded hardwoods in standard dimensions at your building center. A well-stocked lumberyard will have much greater selection of dimensioned lumber suitable for exterior projects, such as white oak, mahogany, teak, and ipê. But if you intend to build any project with hardwood, you greatly expand your species options and save significantly on your materials costs by milling your own stock. The most inexpensive way to buy hardwood is in random widths and lengths. Most often, lumber sold this way has been planed or sawn to a uniform thickness that's a bit thicker than standard dimensions. For example, 4/4 ("four quarter") stock is a very common size that is readily planed down to standard ¾" thickness with a surface planer.

In addition to thickness, rough stock must also be squared. This is typically done with a stationary jointer. You run the best edge through the jointer until it is flat and then make a parallel rip cut along the other edge. The squared stock can be run through a planer to create smooth, flat surfaces that will achieve the desired thickness.

Narrow stock can be flattened on the face with a jointer, but for wider stock you need a power planer. Dressing, squaring, and dimensioning random-width lumber is time-consuming but saves a lot of money on materials costs versus pre-milled stock.

Cut the back legs to length and width. Draw a 2"-radius half-circle on the bottom of each leg. Cut along the half-circle line with a jigsaw. Cut the base stretchers to length and width. To mark the curves on the stretchers, bend a flexible 24" long piece of scrap wood (a 1" wide strip of ¼"-thick lauan plywood is a good choice) or metal to create the arc along the top edges of the base stretchers (**photo 5**). Trace the arc on three of the base stretchers. Cut along the arc lines on each base stretcher with your jigsaw or band saw.

Attach the base rails to the base stretchers with 2½" screws and finish washers. Attach the legs to the base rails with exterior wood glue, 1¼" exterior-rated screws, and decorative, rounded finish washers (we used brass hardware but stainless steel is also a good choice). Drill three ⅛"-dia. pilot holes through the legs before driving each screw (**photo 6**).

BUILD THE BACK FRAME

Cut the back rails to length and width. Trace the curved profile on the top back corner of each back rail. Cut along the curve on each back rail. Round over the top edges of the back rails. Cut the back stretchers to length and width. Bend a flexible 24"-long piece of scrap wood or metal to create the arc along the inside

Draw the end profile onto the rails. Using a cardboard template, trace the smooth curve onto the ends of each part as shown in the drawing, on page 69. Draw the curved profile on a piece of heavy cardboard. Cut along the profile line to make the template. This template allows you to trace the curved profile onto the parts.

Cut the curves. Use a jigsaw or band saw to cut the curved profiles on the ends of the base rails and on one end of each back rail. Use a sander to remove any blade marks and smooth the edges.

Round-over the edges of the base rails with a router and ¼" piloted roundover bit. Use a sharp bit and avoid stopping in one place to prevent burning the wood.

Trace the curve profile on the bottom corners of the front legs. Flip the template to create symmetrical curves.

edge of the back stretchers. Trace the arc on both of the back stretchers. Cut along the arc line of both back stretchers. Attach the back rails to the back stretchers with 2½" exterior-rated screws (**photo 7**).

ATTACH THE BASE & BACK SLATS

Rip-cut one ¾ × 3½" board to make two equal width slats. Cut the base and back slats to length and width from this stock. Round-over the long edges of each slat with a router and ¼"-radius piloted roundover bit. Evenly space the base slats across the base stretchers

with the foot ends of the slats extending 3" beyond the foot ends of the base rails. Drill countersunk pilot holes in each slat, centering each hole across the slat and base stretcher. Attach the base slats to the base stretchers with countersunk 1¼" exterior-rated screws (**photo 8**).

Repeat the same process to attach the back slats to the back stretchers. The top edges of the back slats extend 3" beyond the top edges of the back rails. Use a string and pencil as a trammel to draw a 24" radius across the ends of the base and back slats (**photo 9**).

Lay out the stretcher arcs. Tap a finish nail 1" down from the top edge of a base stretcher. Use this nail as a flex point for bending the strip of wood to make the arc on the base stretchers. Cut out and sand along the curve and use this stretcher as a template for tracing arcs on the other two stretchers.

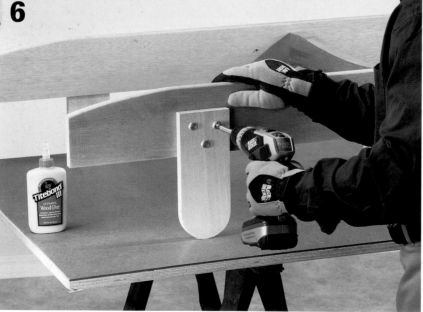

Fasten the back legs to the base rails with brass screws and finish washers.

Cut off the slats ends along the radius line. Sand the cut edges smooth and then round-over the ends of the slats.

ATTACH THE BACK, BASE & ADJUSTABLE BACK SUPPORT

Cut the back support rail to length and width. Mark the center of each notch (the notches are calibrated to create multiple backrest position settings). Drill a ¾"-dia. hole that is centered on each notch layout line and located ½" from the top edge. Make two cuts through the top of the back support rail to open up the top of each notch (**photo 10**). The back cut is made perpendicular to the top edge so that the support bar does not slide out of the notch when you lean on the back. The front cut is beveled slightly forward so that the support bar slides out when the back is raised. Attach the support rails to the base rails with 1¼" screws.

Cut the back support arms to length and width. Draw 1"-radius half-circles at each end of the support arms. Cut along the radius lines. Drill a ¾"-dia. hole

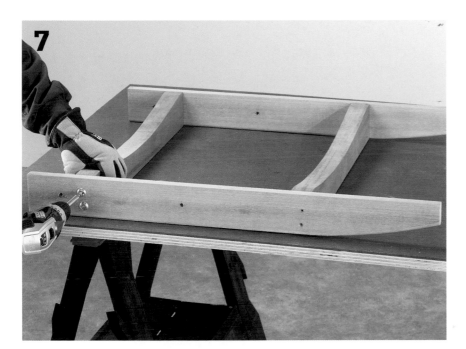

Attach back rails to back stretchers. Use 2½" screws (brass is seen here) and finish washers. The top edges of the back stretchers are flush with the top edges of the back rails.

Attach the base and back slats. Drill ⅛"-dia. countersunk pilot holes centered across each slat and stretcher, and fasten with 1¼" screws (do not use decorative washers here).

on one end of the arm and a ¼"-dia. hole at the other end. Drill ¼"-dia. holes through the back rails where the support arms will be attached. Attach the support arms to the back rails with ¼ × 2" machine screws and locknuts. Place a flat washer between the support arm and back rail and place a finish washer under the screw head.

Cut the back support bar to length and slide it through the ¾"-dia. holes in the support arms. Place the back assembly on the flat support rails, leaving a ½"-wide space between the base slats and back slats. Drill the ¼"-dia. pivot hole through the base rails and back rails. Attach the base rails to the back rails with ¼ × 2" machine screws and locknuts (**photo 11**).

BUILD THE PULL OUT TRAYS

The optional pullout trays are a useful feature that you'll enjoy. To make and install them, start by cutting all tray parts to length and width. Round-over the top edges of the tray slats. Attach the tray slats to the tray front and back with countersunk 1¼" screws. Assemble the tray frame sides, ends, and supports with 1¼" screws. Place the trays on the tray frame sides and then attach the tray crosspieces to the tray supports with 1¼" screws. Position the tray frame and tray assembly against the inside face of the base rails with the tops of the frame supports 3⅛" above the bottom edge of the base rails. Attach the frame by

Draw the slat cutoff profile. To mark the profile on the attached slats, measure 24" from the edge of the middle slat and then use a string and pencil as a trammel to draw the 24"-radius line across the slat ends.

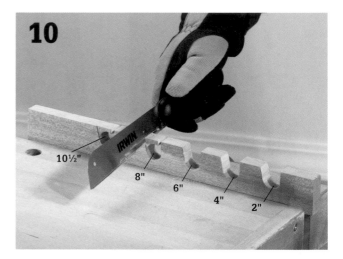

Create the back support notches. After drilling a ¾"-dia. hole at each notch location, make a pair of cuts down from the edge and remove the waste wood to complete each notch.

Mount the back assembly. Attach the back and base with two ¼" machine screws. Insert a washer as a spacer between the base rail and the back to keep them from binding when the back pivots and is raised or lowered.

Install the pullout trays. Place the trays on the tray frame sides and attach the tray frame crosspieces to the supports, keeping the crosspieces ⅛" above the tray slats.

driving 1¼" screws through the base rails and into the edge of the frame supports (**photo 12**).

ATTACH THE WHEELS

The sun lounger wheels allow you to easily move the lounger around to follow the sun or just get it out of the way. It is rather heavy, and pulling and dragging it around constantly will shorten its lifespan. Drill the ⅝"-dia. holes for the axle through the back legs. Slide the ½" aluminum rod axle through the holes, fitting flat washers and a piece of ½"-dia. CPVC over the axle and between the wheels (**photo 13**). Secure the wheels on the axle with ½" push caps (**photo 14**).

Install the axle. Slip the aluminum rod into a CPCV plastic tube sleeve and insert into the guide holes in the wheels.

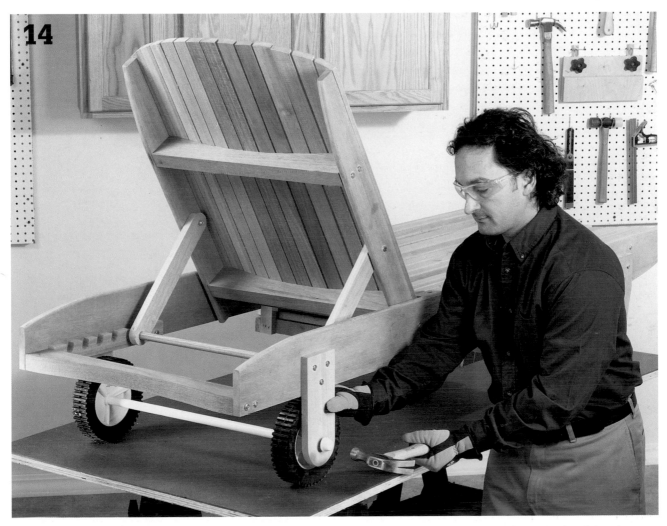

Install the wheels. Make sure the spacers (½" inside-diameter washers) are in place on each side of the wheel and then fasten flanged push caps onto the ends of the rod to secure the wheels to the axle.

Dining & Entertaining Projects

Perhaps the most popular backyard activities are cooking and eating. In fact, throwing backyard barbecues and preparing summertime meals for the family are the primary reasons we acquire most of our yard furnishings. Picnic tables and patio tables are the heart of your outdoor entertaining accommodations, and you'll find several interpretations here. The cedar patio table offers sturdiness, a spacious top, and rich wood tones. The trestle-type table with a pair of matching benches is flexible, comfortable, and low-maintenance, thanks to the composite decking used. The outdoor tea table and chairs sets an Eastern tone that is at once contemporary and classic. You may also want to look over the Children's Picnic Table and the Timberframe Sandbox. For ambitious outdoor cooks, investigate the rolling patio prep cart with built-in refrigerator compartment, or the Pitmaster's Locker—a vertical cabinet with a locking door for fuel and grilling accessory storage. Finally, capture the romance of the great outdoors from an intimate perspective with the bistro-size picnic table for two.

In this chapter:

- Trestle Table & Benches
- Cedar Patio Table
- Teahouse Table Set
- Children's Picnic Table
- Picnic Table for Two
- Patio Prep Cart
- Pitmaster's Locker
- Timberframe Sandbox

Trestle Table & Benches

This modified picnic table and bench set combines the tried-and-true dimensions and durability of a classic picnic table with the style and structure of a traditional trestle dining table. It is built with common exterior lumber. The version seen here uses pressure-treated pine to do the structural work of the base frames, but it has a modern twist. For the tabletop and seat tops it employs low-maintenance composite deck boards. The composite deck boards provide a surface that's easy-to-clean and requires little long-term maintenance. Composite boards are quite a bit heavier than wood, so you might not want to use them if you foresee a need to move your table frequently.

Trestle tables share one principal defining feature: a pair of end leg frames that support a horizontal beam (the trestle). Today, the most common trestle leg tables are the manufactured metal leg folding tables found in almost all schools, hotel banquet rooms, and other commercial settings. But trestle leg construction isn't new; it has been used in table designs for centuries. Early versions were built with large, solid slab-wood legs that were braced with a center stretcher. The stretcher and trestle legs were typically joined by a through-mortise-and-tenon joint that was secured with a pin or key that fit through the tenon.

This outdoor table design reflects the style of those early wood trestle tables. The legs are made from multiple boards instead of a single slab, and the stretcher locks to the leg boards in notches instead of with a through-mortise-and-tenon joint.

Materials ▸

1	1 × 2" × 8 ft. pine	composite deck
9	2 × 4" × 8 ft. pine	boards
1	2 × 8" × 10 ft. pine	Deck screws (2", 2½")
1	2 × 10" × 8 ft. pine	
6	¾" × 12 ft.	

A classic picnic table gets a modern makeover by replacing the wood tabletop and seat boards with low-maintenance composite decking.

Trestle Table & Benches

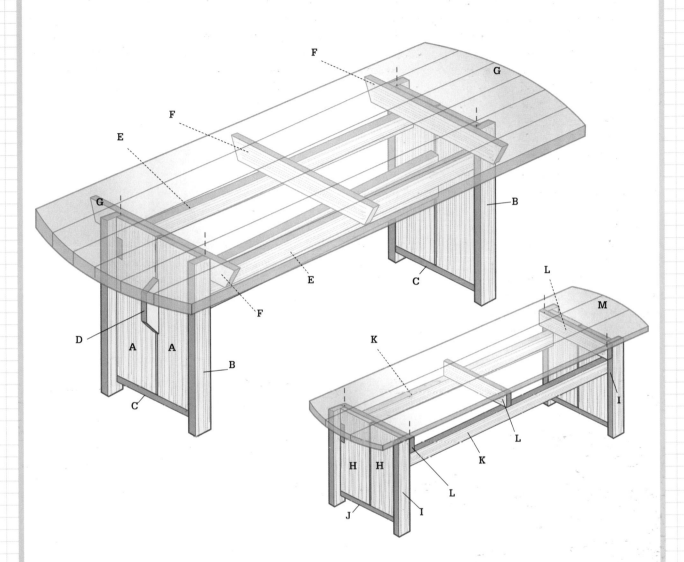

Cutting List

Table

Key	Part	Dimension	Pcs.	Material
A	Inside legs	$1\frac{1}{2} \times 8\frac{3}{4} \times 27"$	4	PT Pine
B	Outside legs	$1\frac{1}{2} \times 2\frac{1}{2} \times 28\frac{3}{4}"$	4	PT Pine
C	Bottom leg rail	$\frac{3}{4} \times 1\frac{1}{2} \times 18"$	2	PT Pine
D	Middle stretcher	$1\frac{1}{2} \times 8\frac{3}{4} \times 52"$	1	PT Pine
E	Side stretchers	$1\frac{1}{2} \times 3 \times 48"$	2	PT Pine
F	Cross supports	$1\frac{1}{2} \times 3 \times 30"$	3	PT Pine
G	Tabletop planks	$1\frac{1}{4} \times 5\frac{1}{2} \times 72"$	6	Decking

Benches (2)

Key	Part	Dimension	Pcs.	Material
H	Inside bench legs	$1\frac{1}{2} \times 6 \times 14\frac{1}{4}"$	8	PT Pine
I	Outside bench legs	$1\frac{1}{2} \times 2\frac{1}{2} \times 16"$	8	PT Pine
J	Bottom bench leg rail	$\frac{3}{4} \times 1\frac{1}{2} \times 12\frac{1}{2}"$	4	PT Pine
K	Side stretchers	$1\frac{1}{2} \times 3 \times 55"$	4	PT Pine
L	Cross stretchers	$1\frac{1}{2} \times 3 \times 15\frac{1}{2}"$	6	PT Pine
M	Seat planks	$1\frac{1}{4} \times 5\frac{1}{2} \times 72"$	6	Decking

Working with Composites ▸

Decking and other building materials made with composite are becoming increasingly popular and are available in a much greater range of sizes, shapes, and colors than they were even a couple of years ago. In fact, composite 2 x 4s that can perform light structural duty are even beginning to hit the market. For any outdoor building project, composites present a number of unique design options. If you are attracted by the low-maintenance qualities of composites and would like to try using them in one of your building projects, as in this trestle table project, you should know a few things about it and how its workability compares to wood.

The basic ingredients in composites are wood dust and plastic resin. This combination gives it some of the look and feel of wood, but little of the structural strength. The plastic makes the material essentially impervious to water damage, hence its popularity as decking. However, because it does contain wood fiber composite, it is susceptible to mold and mildew if you don't clean it regularly.

You can use just about any conventional carpentry tool on composite. However, avoid very fine blades as they can clog up. If you're using a 7¼" circular saw, look for a 40-tooth framing blade. For a 10" power miter saw, use a 60-tooth carbide-tipped blade; for a 12" saw use an 80-tooth blade. For jigsaws, use a 12-TPI (tooth-per-inch) blade.

Composite material does not respond well to sanding. Even coarse sandpapers tend to clog up almost immediately, and the edges of material like decking scratch easily when sanded. For these reasons it's worth taking the time to make your initial cuts as smooth as possible. For the cleanest possible cuts, use a router and straight bit with either a cutting template or a pattern-following sleeve.

Composites can be difficult to get smooth when they're cut. Sanding (left) yields only gummed up papers and a messy edge. Saws (middle) work fine, but avoid blades that are either too fine or too rough. A router and straight bit (right) will yield a perfectly smooth cut but requires multiple passes.

Trestle Table & Benches

CUT THE TABLE PARTS

Cut four 27"-long pieces of 2 × 10 and then trim off the edges to make the four 7¼"-wide inside legs. Use a table saw or circular saw to rip-cut these pieces to width. Clamp the four inner legs together face to face with the ends and edges flush. Draw lines to designate the top and bottom of the notches that hold the middle and side stretchers. Use a router and straight bit to cut out the waste material inside the notch outlines. Clamp a straightedge on each side of the notch layout lines at a distance that is equal to the distance between the edge of the bit and the edge of the router base (**photo 1 and photo 2**). These guides will function as stops for the router base. Cut the notches for the middle stretcher

½" deep by 6¾" long and the notches for the side stretchers 1½" deep by 3" long. The tops of both notches should be 3" down from the top of the leg. Cut the notches by making multiple passes with the router, lowering the bit after each pass (**photo 3**). Do not attempt to remove more than ¼" of material (in thickness) in a single pass.

Cut four 28¾" long pieces of 2 × 4 and then trim approximately ½" off the long edges ½" per edge to make the four 2½" wide outer legs. Cut the two bottom leg rails to length. Cut one 52" long piece of 2 × 10 and then trim approximately ¼" off the long edges to make the 8¾" wide middle stretcher. Use a miter saw or jigsaw to cut each corner to a 30° miter. Make the cuts 1" in from the ends (**photo 4**).

Measure the router bit setback. So you know where to place the straightedge cutting guides to cut the notches with your router, measure the distance from the edge of the straight bit to the outside edge of the base plate.

Gang-cut the stretcher notches into the legs. Clamp a straightedge guide on each side of the notch layout lines so the distance from the blocks to the notch layout line equals the router bit setback distance.

Cut two 48" long pieces of 2 × 4 and then trim approximately ¼" off the long edges to make the 3"-wide side stretchers. Cut three 30"-long pieces of 2 × 4 and then trim approximately ¼" off the long edges to make the 3"-wide cross supports. Cut 30° miters in the ends of the crosspieces.

Sand all of the wood parts to prepare for finishing. Apply an exterior finish to all of the frame parts. In this case a solid-color deck and siding stain was used. Solid color stains are available in a wide range of colors. It looks almost like paint after it is applied, but it doesn't peel as it ages so it is easier to reapply and maintain than paint. Finally, cut the tabletop planks to length. Cut 12-foot deck boards in half to make the 6-foot tabletop and seat top planks

ASSEMBLE THE TABLE

Begin the assembly of the table by attaching one of the inside legs to the middle stretcher using two 2½"

Finish clearing the notches. Don't try to remove all of the waste material from the notches in one pass. Start with a ¼" bit depth and then lower the bit ¼"after each pass.

1" -deep by 1½" -wide notches for lap joint with legs

Trim the middle stretcher. Use a miter saw to trim off each corner at a 30° angle. Make the cuts 1" in from the ends.

screws. Attach one of the cross supports to the inner leg with two 2½" screws (**photo 5**). Attach the second inside leg to the cross support with two 2½" screws and toe-screw it into the middle stretcher with one screw (**photo 6**). Repeat the inside leg and cross support assembly sequence to build the other leg assembly. Fit the side stretchers into the notches on the sides of the inside legs and secure them with two 2½" screws at each joint.

Attach the outside legs to the inside legs with three 2½" screws each (**photo 7**). Attach the bottom leg rail to the bottom of the inside legs with four 2" screws. Clamp the middle cross support in position on the middle stretcher and side stretchers. Drill a ⅜"-dia. × 1½"-deep counterbored hole in the top of the cross support and over the center of the stretchers. Then, drill a 3⁄16" pilot hole the rest of the way through the cross support. Attach the cross support to the stretchers by using an extended driver bit or a hand screwdriver to drive a 2½" screw through each pilot hole and into the side stretcher (**photo 8**).

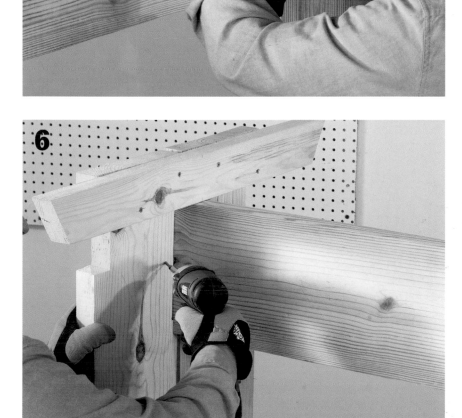

Join the supports and legs. Attach one of the cross supports to the inner leg that has already been attached to the middle stretcher.

Secure the middle stretcher to the leg assemblies. Attach the second inner leg to the cross support and toe-screw this leg into the middle stretcher.

Add outside legs to the leg assemblies. Attach an outside leg to the outer edge of each inside leg. The tops of the inside and outside legs must be flush.

Attach the middle cross support. Drill a deep counterbored hole halfway through the middle cross support and drill a pilot hole through the rest of the cross support. Secure with screws.

Attach the composite tabletop planks to the cross supports with 2" composite decking screws (these are specially designed to minimize "mushrooming" of the composite material around the screw head). Drive two screws in each board, centered over the cross supports.

To make arcs for trimming lines on the ends of the tabletops, measure and mark a point 45" in from each end of the table and centered from side to side. These marks will act as the pivot points for drawing the radius curves on the tabletop ends. Tie a string to a pencil or marker and then measure 45" of string out from the writing utensil. Hold the string on each pivot point and sweep the pencil or marker across the tabletop, keeping it perpendicular

at all times. This will create a radius line (**photo 9**). Cut carefully along the trim lines with a jigsaw and 12-tooth-per-inch blade (**photo 10**). Also draw 3"-radius lines at each corner and then cut along the radius lines. Use a router and ¼" roundover bit to ease the radius edges on the ends of the top boards.

BUILD THE BENCHES

The bench part dimensions are different than the table part dimensions, but the construction process is basically the same. The only notable difference is that the benches do not have a middle stretcher. Cut the bench parts and build the benches using the same steps and techniques that were used to build the table (**photo 11**).

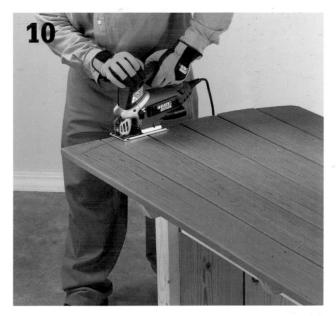

Mark the end curves on the tabletop. Use a 45"-long string or wood strip as a compass (more accurately, as a trammel) and a pencil to mark the 45" radius cutting lines on the ends of the tabletop boards.

Cut the curves. Use a jigsaw and 12-TPI blade to cut the arc at the ends of the tabletop. Be careful to make clean cuts, as composite material is virtually impossible to sand.

Build the benches. Make the trestle benches using the same procedure you used for building the trestle table. The benches do not have a middle stretcher.

Cedar Patio Table

In these days of plastic-resin or aluminum-and-bubble-glass patio furniture, it is refreshing to encounter a nice beefy patio table made of solid wood. With a massive base of 4 × 4 cedar, this square patio table definitely has a surplus of sturdiness. Also boasting warm wood tones, this all-cedar patio table is roomy enough to seat six and strong enough to support a large patio umbrella. The construction process for this table is very straightforward. The legs and cross braces are cut from solid 4 × 4 cedar posts and then they are lag-screwed together. The lag screw heads are countersunk below the wood surface. If you can find them at your local building center, buy heartwood cedar posts. Heartwood, cut from the center of the tree, is valued for its density, straightness, and resistance to decay. Also, take care when selecting the 1 × 4 cedar boards used to make the tabletop. Look for boards that are free of large knots and fairly consistent in tone. Most dimensioned cedar sold at building centers is rough on one face. Either plane the rough faces smooth or face them inward when you install them in this project. Because it's used for an eating surface, apply a natural, clear linseed-oil finish.

Materials ▸

3 4 × 4" × 8 ft. cedar	20 ⅜ × 6" lag screws
3 2 × 2" × 8 ft. cedar	with washers
2 1 × 4" × 8 ft. cedar	Finishing materials
4 1 × 6" × 8 ft. cedar	
Moisture-resistant	
glue	
Deck screws (2", 3")	

This patio table blends sturdy construction with rugged style to offer many years of steady service.

Patio Table

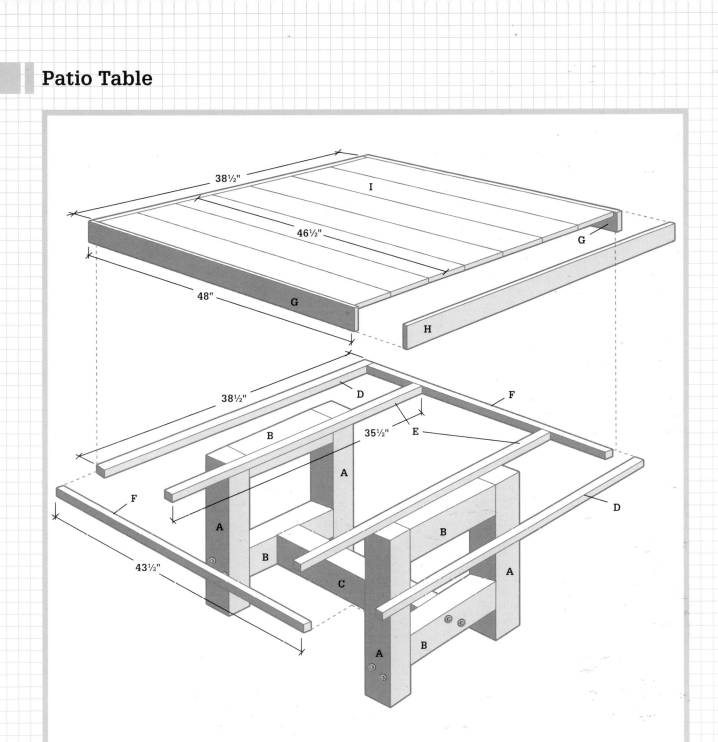

Cutting List

Key	Part	Dimension	Pcs.	Material
A	Leg	3½ × 3½ × 27¼"	4	Cedar
B	Stretcher	3½ × 3½ × 20"	4	Cedar
C	Spreader	3½ × 3½ × 28"	1	Cedar
D	End cleat	1½ × 1½ × 38½"	2	Cedar
E	Cross cleat	1½ × 1½ × 35½"	2	Cedar
F	Side cleat	1½ × 1½ × 43½"	2	Cedar
G	Side rail	¾ × 3½ × 48"	2	Cedar
H	End rail	¾ × 3½ × 38½"	2	Cedar
I	Top slat	¾ × 5¼ × 46½"	7	Cedar

Cedar Patio Table

MAKE THE LEG ASSEMBLIES

Cut the legs, stretchers, and spreader to length. Measure and mark 4" up from the bottom edge of each leg to mark the positions of the bottom edges of the lower stretchers. Test-fit the legs and stretchers to make sure they are square. The top stretchers should be flush with the top leg ends. Carefully position the pieces and clamp them together with pipe clamps. The metal jaws on the pipe clamps can damage the wood, so use protective clamping pads.

Drill ⅞"-dia. × ⅜"-deep counterbores positioned diagonally across the bottom end of each leg and opposite the lower stretchers (**photo 1**). Drill ¼" pilot holes through the counterbores and into the stretchers. Unclamp the pieces and drill ⅜" guide holes for lag screws through the legs, using the pilot holes as center marks. Apply moisture-resistant glue to the ends of the stretchers. Attach the legs to the stretchers by driving lag screws with washers through the legs and into the stretchers. Use the same procedure to attach the spreader to the stretchers.

ATTACH CLEATS & RAILS

Cut the side rails and end rails to length. Drill two evenly spaced, ⅛" pilot holes through the ends of the side rails. Counterbore the holes ¼" deep to accept plugs using a counterbore bit. Apply glue and fasten the side rails to the end rails with 2" deck screws.

Cut the end cleats, cross cleats, and side cleats to length. Fasten the end cleats to the end rails ¾" below the top edges of the rails with glue and 2" deck screws (**photo 2**). Repeat this procedure with the side cleats and side rails.

CUT & ATTACH THE TOP SLATS

Cut the top slats to length. Lay the slats into the tabletop frame so they rest on the cleats. Carefully spread the slats apart so they are evenly spaced. Use masking tape to hold the slats in place once you achieve the correct spacing (**photo 3**). Stand the tabletop frame on one end and fasten the top slats in place by driving two 2" deck screws through the end cleats and into each slat (**photo 4**). Hold or clamp

Counterbore two sets of holes on each leg to recess the lag screws when you attach the legs to the stretchers.

Attach the end cleats to the inside faces of the end rails. Maintain a ¾" distance from the top edge of the rails to the top edge of the cleats.

Install the tabletop slats. Use pencils or dowels as spacers to set even gaps between top slats. Tape the slats in position with masking tape.

Fasten cross cleats to the tabletop for strength and to provide an anchor for the leg assembly.

Attach the tabletop to the table base with 2" deck screws. Do not overdrive the screws.

each slat firmly while fastening to prevent the screws from pushing the slats away from the frame.

CONNECT THE LEGS AND TOP

Turn the tabletop over and center the legs on the underside. Make sure the legs are the same distance apart at the top as they are at the bottom. Lay the cross cleats along the insides of the table legs. Fasten the cross cleats to the tabletop with 2" deck screws (**photo 5**). Fasten the cross cleats to the legs with 3" deck screws.

APPLY FINISHING TOUCHES

Fill screw hole counterbores with cedar plugs or buttons for a more finished appearance. Smooth the edges of the table and legs with a sander or router (**photo 6**). If you want to fit the table with a patio umbrella, use a 1½"-dia. hole saw to cut a hole into the center of the tabletop. Use a drill and spade bit to cut the 1½" dia. hole through the spreader. Finish the table as desired. Use clear linseed oil for a natural, nontoxic, and protective finish.

Sand the surfaces smooth before you stain or treat the patio table. Use the sander to break sharp edges with a slight roundover.

Teahouse Table Set

Inspired by low teahouse tables, this table-and-stool set looks great on a small urban patio or in a Japanese-style garden. The table height offers a unique perspective on the rest of the surroundings and creates a more intimate setting for a casual dinner or evening tea. And if the idea of crouching down to sit in these stools doesn't appeal to you, then you might still consider building it as a child's table.

This set is relatively easy to build, but it still features several appealing and unique design details. The legs of the table and stools feature reverse tapers, reinforcing the Eastern design influence. The seats are cupped slightly for greater comfort. And, the round tabletop has a chamfered edge.

You can build this table using any exterior grade lumber, and the parts are sized so that you can find all of the materials at most home centers or lumberyards. This version was built out of cedar and stained with a dark brown, solid semitransparent deck stain, giving it the look of dark weathered wood.

A few power tools are needed to build this set. First, you need a saw, such as a miter saw or circular saw, to cut the parts to length. You also need a saw to cut the tapers—a band saw is best for this, but you could also use a jigsaw with a long blade or make two mating cuts with a circular saw. The circular top is easiest to cut with a jigsaw or with a router equipped with a circle-cutting jig. The chamfered edge on the tabletop is an optional detail that requires a router and chamfer bit.

Materials ▶

Table		Stools (4)	
3	1 × 8" × 8 ft. cedar	4	1 × 4" × 8 ft. cedar
2	2 × 4" × 8 ft. cedar	5	2 × 4" × 8 ft. cedar
1	4 × 4" × 8 ft. cedar	Deck screws (2", 2½")	

Add a touch of Eastern elegance to your patio or transform your gazebo into a teahouse with this simple-to-make table-and-stool set.

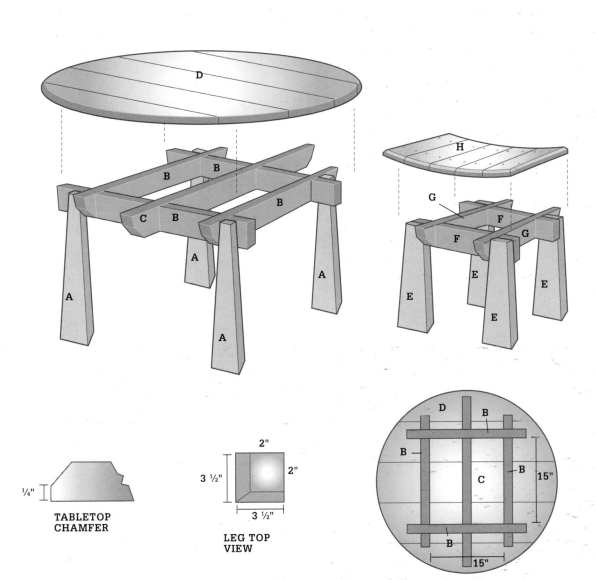

TABLETOP CHAMFER

¼"

2"
2"
3 ½"
3 ½"

LEG TOP VIEW

TABLETOP SUPPORT DETAIL

D   B
B
B   C   B   15"
B
15"

Cutting List

Table

Key	Part	Dimension	Pcs.	Material
A	Legs	3½ × 3½ × 22"	4	Cedar
B	Side supports	1½ × 3½ × 26"	4	Cedar
C	Middle support	1½ × 3½ × 30"	1	Cedar
D	Tabletop planks	¾ × 7¼ × 37"	5	Cedar

Stools (4)

Key	Part	Dimension	Pcs.	Material
E	Legs	1½ × 3½ × 12"	16	Cedar
F	Seat supports	1½ × 3½ × 18"	8	Cedar
G	Seat rails	1½ × 3½ × 12"	8	Cedar
H	Seat planks	¾ × 3½ × 14"	20	Cedar

Teahouse Table Set

BUILD THE TABLE BASE

Begin building the base of the tea table by cutting the leg pieces to length. A 10" or 12" power miter saw can cut through the 4 × 4 in a single pass, but a circular saw requires two joining cuts from opposite sides. Set the saw's cutting depth so it is slightly deeper than one-half the thickness. Cutting with the blade at full depth increases the possibility of uneven cuts.

The table legs are created with reverse tapers—they're wider at the bottom than the top. If you are an experienced woodworker and have a table saw, use a tapering jig to make the parts. A band saw is the next best bet for making taper cuts. Mark the taper lines on two adjacent sides of each leg (**photo 1**). Cut the tapers with a band saw. Cut the first taper (**photo 2**) and then reattach the taper to the leg with tape, flip the leg, and cut the second taper (**photo 3**). Repeat the taper cuts on all four legs and sand the blade marks smooth.

Cut the side supports and middle support to length. Trim off the bottom corners of each support with 30° miter cuts. The miters should end 1½" in from the ends of the bottom edges (**photo 4**). The table supports fit together with half-lap joints. There

One edge of a straightedge should be on the corner of the leg blank on one end. The other end of the blank should be marked 2" in from the edge. Connect the points to create the taper cutting line.

Make the first taper cut. Using a band saw, place one hand on the tabletop to act as a guide and use your other hand to push and steer the leg through the cut.

are several ways to cut the half-laps notches. In this case, the notches are all spaced 15" apart so it makes sense to cut them all at the same time—a technique referred to as "gang cutting." To gang-cut the supports, mark the center on the bottom face of two of the side supports and the middle support. Also mark the center on the top faces of the two remaining side supports. Clamp the supports together with the center marks facing up and aligned. Next, mark the outsides of the notches on the support that is closest to you and then use a try square or combination square to extend that line across all of the supports (**photo 5**). Set your circular saw blade to a depth of 1¾". Make cuts along the notch edge layout lines. Align the blade inside the notch waste area, with the edge of the blade following the layout line.

After cutting the sides of the notches, clean out the rest of the waste material from the notch by making several overlapping cuts with the circular saw (**photo 6**). Smooth any remaining blade marks on the bottom of the notch with a sharp wood chisel. The two bottom side supports also require a middle half-lap notch to hold the middle support. Clamp the two bottom side supports together and repeat the notch cutting process for the middle notch.

Test-fit the parts to make sure everything fits together and then assemble the table base. First, apply exterior-rated glue to the inside faces of the

Make the second taper cut. Temporarily reattach the cutoff taper waste piece with masking tape to support the leg on the table. With the leg oriented so the first taper rests on the table, cut the second taper on the adjoining face.

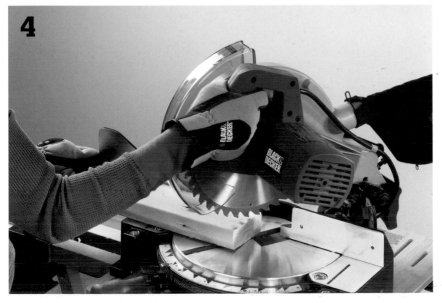

Cut off the bottom corners of the supports. Make marks 1½" in from the ends on the bottom edge of the supports. Align the power miter saw blade with these marks and make 30° miter cuts.

notches. Then, place the top side and middle stretchers in position on the bottom side stretchers. Drive a 2½" screw through the bottom of each half-lap joint. Then, attach the framework to a flat face of each leg.

MAKE THE TABLETOP

Make the teahouse tabletop as a square and then cut it to round after it is assembled. Cut the tabletop planks to length. Then, mark the center of each plank and attach them in succession to the supports using 2" deck screws (**photo 7**). Center each plank across the middle support, leaving a ⅛" gap between the boards. Drill a countersunk, ⅛"-dia. pilot hole for each screw.

To lay out the circular shape for the tabletop, make a compass using a scrap piece of ¼"-thick wood or plywood that is roughly 1½" wide x 20" long. Drill two ⅛"-dia. holes in the scrap, 18⅜" apart. Tap a nail through one of the holes and into the center of the table. *TIP: To find the center, draw straight lines across the tabletop from opposite corners. The point where the lines intersect is the center—provided you were careful and made the top square. Place a pencil tip through the other hole in the scrap wood compass and draw the perimeter of the tabletop* (**photo 8**).

Cut just outside the round tabletop outline with a jigsaw (**photo 9**). Then, use a belt sander to smooth

Lay out the notches. Clamp the stretchers together with the centers aligned. Use a square to extend the notch cut lines across all of the stretchers.

Cut the notch shoulders. Cut the sides of the notch first. Then clean out the middle by making several overlapping cuts.

and shape the wood precisely up to the cutting line. Use a router and 45° chamfer bit to profile the top edge of the table (**photo 10**). Finally, attach the table legs to the tabletop supports with 2½" screws. Drill countersunk pilot holes and drive the screws from the inside faces of the supports.

BUILD THE STOOLS

Make the matching stools. The information on page 91 lists materials and supplies for four stools. Start by cutting the legs to length. Unlike the table legs, the bench legs are only tapered on one side. Make a mark 1½" in from the outside edge of one of the wide faces of the leg. Draw a line from that mark across the wide face down to a point that is 2" up from the opposite bottom corner of the leg (**photo 11**). Cut the tapers with a band saw or jigsaw. Cut the seat supports and seat rails to length. Trim off the bottom corners of the supports with 30° miter cuts. The miters should end 1½" in from the ends of the bottom edge.

Mark and cut the 1½" wide by 1¾" deep notches using the same gang-cutting techniques used to cut the table support notches. Cut the notches in the seat supports as one group and the seat rails as another group. The bottom of the seat arc profile

Assemble the base. The framework of the supports is fastened to the legs with 2" screws.

Lay out the circular cutting line. Draw the perimeter of the tabletop using an 18⅜" long compass. You can also use a piece of string as a compass.

that is cut in the seat supports is located 1" down from the top edge and is centered across the support side. Tap a finish nail in the bottom point and bend a flexible piece of scrap stock to form the arc profile template. Trace the arc profile on the support (**photo 12**). Cut along the arc line on the first support and then use that support as a template to trace the arc on the other supports.

ASSEMBLE THE LEGS

Attach the supports and rails with glue and screws in the same way that you assembled the table

supports. First, cut the seat planks to length. Clamp the seat boards to a flat work surface in groups of five. The boards should be edge to edge with the ends flush. Cut a chamfer profile on both ends of all five boards. Unclamp the boards and rout a chamfer onto the outside edge of each outer board using a piloted chamfer bit (**photo 13**). Space each set of five seat boards evenly across a seat assembly and attach them to the seat supports with 2" screws. Drill a countersunk pilot hole for each screw. Attach the legs to the supports and rails with 2½" screws.

Cut the round tabletop shape. Use a jigsaw to make a rough cut just outside of the cutting line (inset). Then, use a belt sander to remove wood precisely up to the cutting line.

Profile the tabletop edge. Cut a ½" chamfer profile in the top edge of the table with a router and 45° chamfering bit.

11

Lay out the bench legs. Draw a taper line across one of the wide faces of each leg. Cut along the taper line with a band saw or jigsaw.

12

Plot the seat support profile. Use a finish nail as a bending point and flex a piece of scrap stock to create an arc template. Clamp the template and trace the profile on the supports.

13

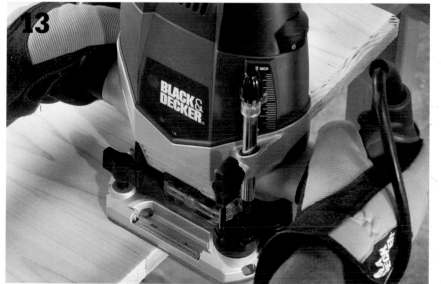

Cut chamfers in the seat boards. With the workpieces for one complete stool clamped together edge-to-edge, rout the chamfer profile across the end grain on both ends. The chamfer matches the tabletop edge profile and eliminates sharp edges on the seat.

Children's Picnic Table

Picnic tables come in many styles, shapes, and sizes, with one of the sizes being "pint." This downscaled kids' picnic table is a wonderful addition to any backyard where children play. Its light weight allows you to move the table around the yard for impromptu tea parties on the deck or dinner under the trees. Yet its wide footprint makes it extremely stable so your rambunctious little ones won't tip it over.

Constructing this kid-sized picnic table is easy. The trickiest part is probably getting the angles cut correctly at the tops and bottoms of the legs. They should be cut at a relatively shallow 50° angle. If they are cut too steeply the table will be taller and less stable; too shallow and it will be shorter and very difficult to seat oneself in.

With a kids' project such as this it is important that you eliminate any sharp edges and do a thorough job sanding the surfaces smooth and splinter free. The edges of the boards can be "broken" by sanding them lightly so they are not sharp. Or, you can install a roundover bit in your router or laminate trimmer and shape the edges all to the same profile.

The table seen here is built with cedar and coated with a clear, UV-protective sealant. You could also make it from modern pressure-treated pine (arsenic free) and paint it or finish it with a semitransparent deck stain. If you do use treated lumber, be sure to choose hot-dipped lag bolts that are triple-coated to limit corrosion. Or, better yet, use all stainless steel fasteners.

Materials ▸

2 2 × 4" × 6 ft. cedar	16 ⅜ x 3" carriage
3 2 × 6" × 8 ft. cedar	bolts with nuts
3 2 × 8" × 8 ft. cedar	32 washers
Deck screws (2½")	

This kid-scale table with benches makes picnicking in the backyard even more fun for children. And with its broad legs and low top it is very stable.

Children's Picnic Table

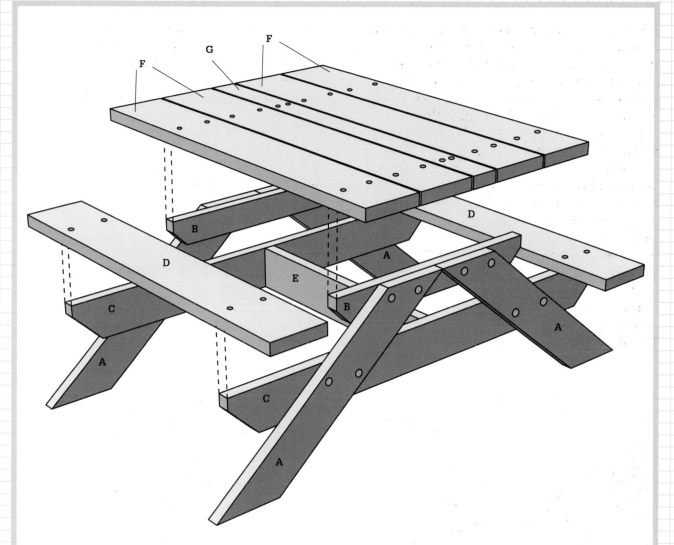

Cutting List

Key	Part	Dimension	Pcs.	Material
A	Leg	1½ × 5½ × 32"	4	Cedar
B	Table support	1½ × 3½ × 29¾"	2	Cedar
C	Seat support	1½ × 5½ × 60"	2	Cedar
D	Seat	1½ × 7½ × 48"	2	Cedar

Key	Part	Dimension	Pcs.	Material
E	Brace	1½ × 5½ × 30"	1	Cedar
F	Table top	1½ × 7½ × 48"	4	Cedar
G	Table top	1½ × 3½ × 48"	1	Cedar

Children's Picnic Table

CUT THE ANGLED LEGS & SUPPORTS

To make the angled legs, use a saw protractor to mark a 50° angle on one end of a 2 × 6 (**photo 1**). Cut the angle using a circular saw. Measure 32" from the tip of the angle, then mark and cut another 50° angle parallel to the first. Do this for all four legs, cutting two legs from one piece of lumber.

Cut the table supports to length. Measure 1½" in from each end of both supports and make a mark. Make a 45° angle starting at the mark and going in the direction of the board end. This relieves the sharp end of the board to prevent injuries and also looks more pleasing. Cut the seat supports to length. Measure 2½" from the ends of both supports, make a mark, and cut a 45° angle to relieve the sharp ends.

ASSEMBLE THE A-FRAMES

Place one of the legs against the tabletop support so the inside edge of the leg is at the centerpoint of the support. Align the top of the leg with the top of the support. Clamp the pieces together. Drill two ⅜" holes through the leg and support. Stagger the holes. To keep the bolts from causing scrapes, recess both the bolt head and nut. Drill 1"-dia. counterbored holes about ¼" deep into the legs and the tabletop supports. Insert a ⅜ × 3" carriage bolt and washer into each hole. Tighten a washer and nut on the end of the bolt using a ratchet wrench. Repeat these steps to fasten the second leg in place. *Note: If your washers are larger than 1", drill a larger counterbore.*

Measure along the inside edge of each leg and make a mark 12½" up from the bottom. Center the seat support over the leg assembly, on the same side of the legs as the tabletop support, with the 45° cuts facing down and the bottom flush with the 12½" marks. Clamp the two pieces together and then drill ⅜" holes with 1"-dia. counterbored holes. Fasten the seat support to the legs using carriage bolts, nuts, and washers (**photo 2**). Repeat this step to assemble the second A-frame.

ATTACH THE TABLETOP & SEATS

Cut the seat boards to length. Stand one of the A-frames upright. Place a seat on the seat support so the seat overhangs the outside of the support by 7½". Align the back edge of the seat with the end of the support. Drill two ³⁄₃₂" pilot holes through the seat into the support and then insert 2½" deck screws. Attach the seat to the second A-frame the same way. Fasten the seat on the other side of the table using the same method.

Cut the brace. Center the brace between the seat supports, making sure they're flush at the bottom. Drill two ³⁄₃₂" pilot holes through the supports on each side, then fasten the brace to the supports using 2½" deck screws. Cut the tabletop boards to length. Place the 2 × 4 tabletop across the center of the tabletop supports, overhanging the supports by 7½". Drill two ³⁄₃₂" pilot holes on both ends of the top board where it crosses the supports. Attach it to the supports with 2½" deck screws.

Place a 2 × 8 tabletop board across the supports, keeping a ¼" gap from the 2 × 4. Drill pilot holes in the end of the board, then insert 2½" deck screws (**photo 3**). Install the remaining top boards the same way, spacing them evenly with a ¼" gap. Allow the outside boards to overhang the end of the tabletop supports.

FINISHING TOUCHES

Sand any rough surfaces and splinters, and round over edges on the seat and tabletop using 150-grit sandpaper. Apply a stain, sealer (foodsafe boiled linseed oil is a good choice), or paint following the manufacturer's instructions.

Use a saw protractor to mark a 50° angle on the end of the table leg, and then cut the angle using a circular saw.

Fasten the tabletop and seat supports to the legs with carriage bolts. Do not use washers with carriage bolt heads. The washers and nuts are recessed in counterbored holes to prevent injury.

Install the tabletop boards by drilling pilot holes and driving 2½" deck screws. Insert ¼" spacers between boards.

Picnic Table for Two

A picnic table doesn't have to be a clumsy, uncomfortable family feeding trough. Instead, create a unique picnic table that's just the right size for two people to enjoy. Portable and lightweight, it can be set in a corner of your garden, beneath a shade tree, or on your deck or patio to enhance outdoor dining experiences.

The generously proportioned tabletop can be set with full table settings for a fancy, multicourse meal in the garden. Or, you can take advantage of the intimacy the table and benches foster by sharing a cool beverage with a special person as you watch the sun set.

Made with plain dimensional cedar, this picnic table for two is both sturdy and long-lasting. As shown, deck screws and glue complete the fastening work for this project. The deck screws are driven through countersunk pilot holes. For a more refined look, counterbore the pilot holes and fill them with cedar plugs. Sanding all cedar surfaces smooth will contribute to the refined appearance. For a more rustic look, position the rough faces of the cedar face outward on the structural members. The seat boards and tabletop should be smooth.

Materials ▸

1 2 × 8" × 6 ft. cedar	Moisture-resistant glue
1 2 × 6" × 8 ft. cedar	Deck screws (1⅝",
4 2 × 4" × 8 ft. cedar	2½")
3 1 × 6" × 8 ft. cedar	Finishing materials
4 1 × 2" × 8 ft. cedar	

Turn a quiet corner of your yard into an intimate setting for dining alfresco with this compact picnic table for two.

Picnic Table for Two

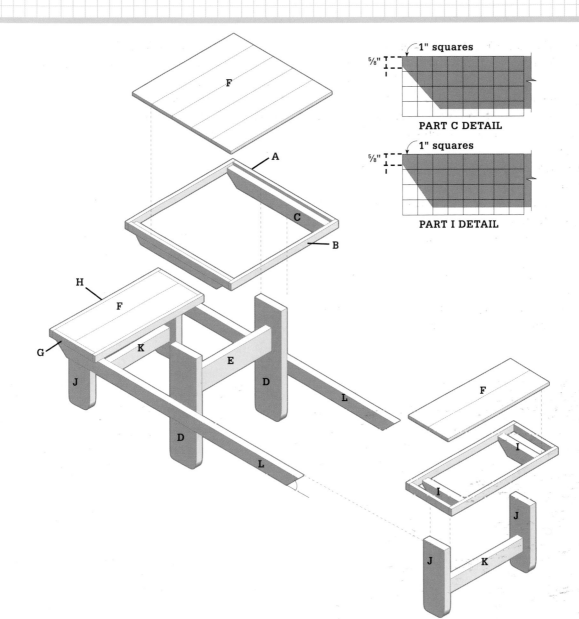

1" squares

⁵⁄₈"

PART C DETAIL

1" squares

⁵⁄₈"

PART I DETAIL

Cutting List

Key	Part	Dimension	Pcs.	Material
A	Tabletop frame	⁷⁄₈ × 1½ × 27¾"	2	Cedar
B	Tabletop frame	⁷⁄₈ × 1½ × 30"	2	Cedar
C	Table stringer	1½ × 3½ × 27¾"	2	Cedar
D	Table leg	1½ × 7¼ × 27¼"	2	Cedar
E	Table stretcher	1½ × 5½ × 22¼"	1	Cedar
F	Slat	⁷⁄₈ × 5½ × 28¼"	9	Cedar

Key	Part	Dimension	Pcs.	Material
G	Bench frame	⁷⁄₈ × 1½ × 11¼"	4	Cedar
H	Bench frame	⁷⁄₈ × 1½ × 30"	4	Cedar
I	Bench stringer	1½ × 3½ × 11¼"	4	Cedar
J	Bench leg	1½ × 5½ × 15¼"	4	Cedar
K	Bench stretcher	1½ × 3½ × 22¼"	2	Cedar
L	Cross rail	1½ × 3½ × 68"	2	Cedar

Picnic Table for Two

BUILD THE TABLETOP

Cut the tabletop frame pieces, the table stringers, and the table slats to length. Sand the parts. Draw cutting lines that start 2½" from one end of each stringer and connect with a point at the same end, ⅝" in from the opposite edge of the board (see Diagram, page 103). Cut along the lines with a circular saw to make the cutoffs (**photo 1**).

Fasten the shorter tabletop frame pieces to the sides of the stringers. The tops of the frame pieces should extend ⅞" above the tops of the stringers and the ends should be flush. First, drill ⅛" pilot holes in the frame pieces. Counterbore the holes ¼" deep using a counterbore bit. Attach the pieces with glue and drive 1⅝" deck screws through the frame pieces and into the stringers.

Position the longer tabletop frame pieces so they overlay the ends of the shorter frame pieces. Fasten them with glue and 1⅝" deck screws to complete the frames. Set the slats inside the frame so the ends of the slats rest on the stringers. Space the slats evenly. Drill two pilot holes through the tabletop frame into the ends of each slat. Counterbore the holes. Drive 1⅝" deck screws through the frame and into the end of each slat, starting with the two end slats (**photo 2**).

ATTACH THE TABLE-LEG ASSEMBLY

Cut the table legs and table stretcher to length. Use a compass to draw a 1½"-radius roundover curve on the corners of one end of each leg. Cut the curves with a jigsaw. Hold an end of the stretcher against the inside face of one of the table legs, 16" up from the bottom of the leg and centered side to side. Trace the outline of the stretcher onto the leg. Repeat the procedure on the other leg.

Drill two evenly spaced pilot holes through the stretcher outlines on the legs. Counterbore the holes on the outside faces of the legs. Attach the stretcher with glue and drive 2½" deck screws through the legs and into the ends of the stretcher. Turn the tabletop upside down. Apply glue to the table stringers where they will contact the legs. Position the legs in place within the tabletop frame. Attach them by driving 2½" deck screws through the legs and into the table stringers (**photo 3**).

BUILD THE BENCH TOPS

Cut the bench slats, bench frame pieces, and bench stringers. Cut the ends of the bench stringers in the same way you cut the table stringers, starting ⅝" from the top edge and 2" from the ends on the

Make triangular cutoffs at the ends of the table stringers using a circular saw.

Install the tabletop slats by driving screws through the tabletop frame and into the ends of the slats..

Attach the legs. Position the table legs inside the tabletop frame, and attach them to the table stringers.

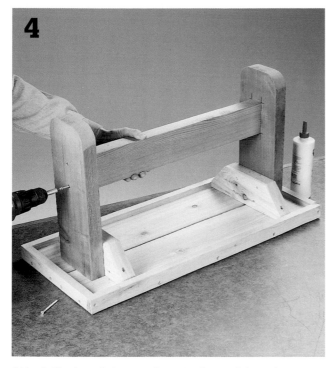

4

Attach the bench legs to the outer faces of the stringers and then attach a stretcher between each leg pair.

5

Center the table within the cross rails, and then clamp it in place. Secure the cross rails to the table legs with decks screws driven into counterbored pilot holes.

bottom edges. Assemble the frame pieces into two rectangular frames by driving 1⅝" deck screws through the longer frame pieces and into the ends of the shorter pieces.

Turn the bench frames upside down. Center the bench slats inside them so the outer edges of the slats are flush against the frame. Attach the slats by driving 1⅝" deck screws through the frames and into the ends of the slats. Fasten the stringers inside the frame so the tops of the stringers are flat against the undersides of the slats, 3" from the inside of each frame end. Attach with glue and drive 1⅝" deck screws through the angled ends of the stringers and into the undersides of the slats. Locate the screws far enough away from the ends of the stringers so they don't stick out through the tops of the slats. The stringers are not attached directly to the bench frames.

BUILD THE BENCH LEGS
Cut the bench legs and bench stretchers to length. With a compass, draw a roundover curve with a 1½" radius on the corners of one end of each leg. Cut the roundovers with a jigsaw. Center the tops of the bench legs against the outside faces of the bench stringers. Drill pilot holes in the stringers. Counterbore the holes.

Attach the legs to the stringers with glue, and then drive 2½" deck screws through the stringers and into the legs.

Drill pilot holes in the bench legs and counterbore the holes in a similar fashion to the approach described on page 104. Glue the bench stretchers and attach them between the legs with 2½" deck screws (**photo 4**).

JOIN THE TABLE & BENCHES
Cut the cross rails to length, miter-cutting the ends at a 45° angle. Position the benches so the ends of the cross rails are flush with the outside ends of the bench frames. Drill counterbored pilot holes in the cross rails. Apply glue and attach the cross rails to the bench legs with 2½" deck screws. Stand the benches, and then center the table legs between the cross rails. Apply glue to the joints between the cross rails and legs. Clamp the table legs to the cross rails, making sure the parts are perpendicular (**photo 5**). Secure the parts by driving several 2½" deck screws through the cross rails and into the outside face of each leg.

APPLY FINISHING TOUCHES
Sand or round over all of the sharp edges and then sand all surfaces of the table using up to 150-grit sandpaper. Apply a nontoxic wood sealant.

Patio Prep Cart

This elegant rolling cook's cart will take your outdoor cooking to a higher level without breaking your bank account. Whether the point is to impress or simply to make your outdoor entertaining a bit more pleasant, setting up an outdoor kitchen that revolves around this clever cart and an ordinary grill is easy. And, because this cart (and most grills) are on wheels, they're easy to move as needed and to roll away into storage.

This cart features 8 square feet of countertop space, a storage cabinet with shelves, and a dedicated place for a refrigerator. The sides are made from 1 × 4 cedar or a similar exterior-grade lumber. Use corrosion-resistant screws to assemble this cart. The screws that attach the siding are driven from the outside, leaving the heads exposed to act as a design feature.

This outdoor kitchen cart employs eight 12 × 12" tiles for the countertop, minimizing the joints in the countertop surface. To simplify construction the tiles are set with construction adhesive (instead of thinset mortar) and the joints between the tiles are filled with exterior caulk (instead of tile grout).

Materials ▸

18 1 × 4" × 8 ft. cedar	Exterior-rated screws
4 2 × 4" × 8 ft. cedar	(1¼", 2½")
1 ¾ × 4" × 8 ft. cedar	Lag screws (16 @ ¼" ×
plywood	1½")
1 ½ × 3" × 5 ft.	2 3" utility hinges
cementboard	4 Casters
1 ¾ × 2" × 4 ft. exterior	1 Door handle
plywood	1 Catch
8 12 × 12" floor tiles	

Both attractive and functional, this rolling cook's cart will make your deck or patio almost as convenient as your kitchen for entertaining friends and family.

Patio Prep Cart

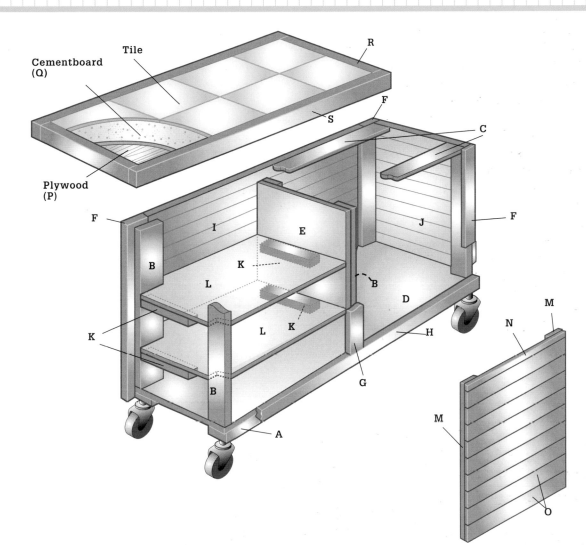

Cutting List

Key	Part	Dimension	Pcs.	Material
A	Bottom supports	$1\frac{1}{2} \times 3\frac{1}{2} \times 46"$	2	Cedar
B	Posts	$1\frac{1}{2} \times 3\frac{1}{2} \times 35"$	6	Cedar
C	Top rails	$\frac{7}{8} \times 3\frac{1}{2} \times 46"$	2	Cedar
D	Bottom panel	$\frac{3}{4} \times 22 \times 46"$	1	Cedar plywood
E	Center panel	$\frac{3}{4} \times 22 \times 35"$	1	Cedar plywood
F	Corner stiles	$\frac{7}{8} \times 2\frac{1}{2} \times 37\frac{1}{4}"$	4	Cedar
G	Front center stile	$\frac{7}{8} \times 2\frac{1}{2} \times 35\frac{3}{8}"$	1	Cedar
H	Front bottom rail	$\frac{3}{4} \times 1\frac{3}{4} \times 42\frac{3}{4}"$	1	Cedar
I	Back siding	$\frac{7}{8} \times 3\frac{1}{2} \times 42\frac{1}{4}"$	10	Cedar
J	Side siding	$\frac{7}{8} \times 3\frac{1}{2} \times 22"$	20	Cedar

Key	Part	Dimension	Pcs.	Material
K	Shelf supports	$\frac{7}{8} \times 1 \times 17"$	4	Cedar
L	Shelves	$\frac{3}{4} \times 19\frac{1}{2} \times 21\frac{3}{4}"$	2	Cedar plywood
M	Door stiles	$\frac{7}{8} \times 3\frac{1}{2} \times 34\frac{1}{2}"$	2	Cedar
N	Top door siding	$\frac{7}{8} \times 1 \times 18\frac{1}{2}"$	1	Cedar
O	Door siding	$\frac{7}{8} \times 3\frac{1}{2} \times 18\frac{1}{2}"$	9	Cedar
P	Worksurface subbase	$\frac{3}{4} \times 24 \times 48"$	1	Ext. plywood
Q	Tile backer	$\frac{1}{2} \times 24 \times 48"$	1	Cementboard
R	Side edging	$\frac{7}{8} \times 1\frac{1}{2} \times 24"$	2	Cedar
S	Front/back edging	$\frac{7}{8} \times 1\frac{1}{2} \times 49\frac{1}{2}"$	2	Cedar

Patio Prep Cart

BUILD THE FRAME

This outdoor kitchen cart is essentially a skeleton of 2 × 4 cedar wrapped in cedar siding and capped off with large tiles. Start by building the skeleton: that is, the frame. Cut the bottom supports, posts, and top rails to length. Cut the bottom panel and center panel to length and width. Attach two of the posts to the center panel with 1¼" screws. Place the center panel and bottom panel on their sides and attach the bottom panel to the posts with 2½" screws (**photo 1**). With the panels on their edges, attach two of the corner posts to the bottom panel. Flip the assembly right-side up and attach one of the top rails to the top of the corner posts and center panel post. Attach the other two corner posts and top rail (**photo 2**). Attach the bottom supports to the bottom panel with 1¼" screws.

INSTALL THE CORNERS, TRIM & SIDING

Cut the corner stiles to length and width. Attach the corner stiles to the corner posts with four 1¼" screws. Drill a countersunk, ⅛"-dia. pilot hole and countersunk hole for each screw (**photo 3**). Cut the front-bottom rail to length and width and attach it to the front-bottom support with four 1¼" screws and decorative

finish washers. Cut the side siding and back siding pieces to length. Drill two ⅛" pilot holes in each end of each siding board. Space the holes 1" in from the ends and ¾" in from the edges. Attach the siding boards to the corner posts with 1¼" screws, spacing the boards ¼" apart (**photo 4**). Drill a 1¼"-dia. hole near the bottom of the back of the refrigerator section for the power cord to fit through.

INSTALL THE SHELVES

The shelves for this outdoor cart are optional. As shown, they're spaced to allow storage of items of varying height, such as plates and cups. But if you want to store taller items, such as bags of charcoal or a turkey fryer, eliminate the shelves from the plan.

Measure and mark the shelf heights on the inside faces of the left side siding and center divider. Here, the shelves are spaced so the lowest shelf opening is 15" high. The middle opening is 10" high and the top opening is 8" high. The shelf supports are sized so the shelves will not interfere with the front corner posts. Attach the shelf supports with 1¼" screws driven through countersunk pilot holes in the supports and into the cabinet walls. Cut the shelves from ¾"-thick

Attach the bottom panel to the posts. Drive 2½" screws through the underside of the bottom panel and into the ends of the center panel posts.

Install corner posts and top rails. Each top rail should be attached to a corner post and a center panel post with 2½" screws. Drive one screw into each post.

Install cornerboards. Attach the corner stiles to the corner posts with 1¼" screws. Align the inside edges of the stiles and posts.

Add siding. Drill two ⅛"-dia. pilot holes through each end of each siding board. Locate the holes 1" from the ends and ¾" from the top and bottom edges. Attach the siding boards with 1¼" screws, spaced with a ¼" gap between boards.

plywood (preferably cedar plywood). Cut 1½" × 3½" notches in the left corners of each shelf board to fit around the posts. Drive a few brads down through the shelves and into the supports to secure them (**photo 5**).

BUILD THE DOOR

Cut the door stiles to length. Cut the door siding to length and the top door siding board to length and width. Drill two ⅛" pilot holes in each end of each full-width door siding board. Space the holes 1" in from the ends and ¾" in from the edges. Drill one ⅛" pilot hole in each end of the top door siding board. Attach the siding boards to the door stiles with 1¼" screws (**photo 6**).

ATTACH THE WHEELS & HARDWARE

Tip the cabinet upside down and place one caster in each corner (here, 2½" casters are being installed). Mark the caster screw holes and drill ³⁄₁₆" pilot holes for each screw. Fasten the casters with ¼" × 1½" hot-dipped lag screws (**photo 7**). To hang the door, attach zinc-plated or brass hinges (a pair of 3" butt hinges will do) to the door and the left corner post and corner stile (**photo 8**). Also add a handle (an aluminum door pull installed vertically is used here) as well as a latch and strikeplate to hold the door closed.

Install the shelves. Attach the shelf supports with screws and then tack the shelves into position with 1¼" brads.

6

Attach the door siding boards to the door stiles. The top door siding board is attached with only one screw in each end.

BUILD & ATTACH THE TOP

The top for this cart features a ¾"-thick plywood subbase that supports a cementboard backer for the tiles (here, eight 12 × 12" porcelain tiles). Cut the plywood subbase to size from exterior plywood and attach it to the top rails with 1¼" deck screws. Cut a piece of tile backer board (here, ½" thick cementboard) to 24 × 48". Attach the backer board to the subbase with construction adhesive and 1" screws (make sure the screwheads are recessed below the cementboard surface). Attach the tiles to the backer board with construction adhesive (**photo 9**).

Cut the top sides, front and back edging pieces to length from cedar 1 × 2. Drill countersunk, ⅛"-dia. pilot holes in the edging pieces and attach them to the subbase edges with construction adhesive and brads (**photo 10**). Fill gaps around tile with caulk. Apply a clear, UV-protectant finish to the wood surface and seal the tiles.

7

Attach the casters. Position each caster and drill pilot holes for each caster screw. Attach the casters with the suggested or supplied fastener (here, ¼" × 1¼" lag screws).

8

Hang the door and install hardware. Fasten the door hinges to the door (or doors if you choose to cover each opening) and then attach the door to the cart frame. Use a ¼" spacer under the door to position it.

Install the tile work surface.
Instead of traditional thinset mortar, exterior construction adhesive is being used because it better withstands temperature and humidity changes.

Attach countertop edging. Made from strips of 1 × 2 cedar, the edging hides the countertop edges and protects the tile. Fill the gaps around the edge tiles and between tiles with caulk.

Pitmaster's Locker

Supplies and accessories for your outdoor grilling and barbecuing have special storage requirements. Some, such as charcoal starter fluid and propane tanks and bottles, are hazardous, flammable chemicals that should be locked safely away outside of the house or garage. Other supplies, such as big bags of charcoal briquettes, turkey fryers, or starter chimneys, are bulky and often dirty or dusty. Additional tools, like grille brushes, thermometers, rib racks, and Texas-size kitchen utensils, are best kept together in a neat area close to your grill. This Pitmaster's locker addresses all of these concerns in a rugged-looking package that fits in well with today's popular grilling equipment.

The frame for this grill locker is made with solid aluminum angle iron, sold at most building centers. Aluminum is rigid, sturdy, and withstands exposure to the elements very well. It is also relatively easy to drill, which you will appreciate. Because the metals market is fairly volatile, costs for aluminum can run on the high side. But if you buy in volume you can usually save a little money. Our eight pieces of 72" aluminum angle cost us $130 from an Internet seller (this is at a time of high metal costs). If you like this design but want to save some money, you can substitute paintable hardwood, such as poplar, for the frame parts. This requires recalculating the shelf and panel dimensions, however.

The lower shelf of this locker has 24" of height capacity. If you plan to store a 20-pound propane tank on this shelf, you can lower the supports for the middle shelf by 6" and still have enough room for the 17½" tall standard tanks. This creates a middle shelf that has 30" of height capacity (or two shorter shelves).

Materials ▸

8	¹⁄₁₆ × 1½ × 72" solid aluminum angle
2	³⁄₈ × 4" × 8 ft. sheet rough cedar siding
1	¾ × 4" × 8 ft. exterior plywood
1	¼ × ¾" × 8 ft. wood shelf edge
2	1 × 2" × 8 ft. cedar

Exterior hasp with padlock
3 2 × 2" butt hinges
¼ × ¾" bolts
¼" lock nuts
¾" hex-head wood screws
Aluminum pop rivets

For the serious grill cook (a Pitmaster in barbecuer's parlance), a lockable, dedicated storage locker is the best place to keep tools, fuel, and other supplies organized and safe.

Pitmaster's Locker

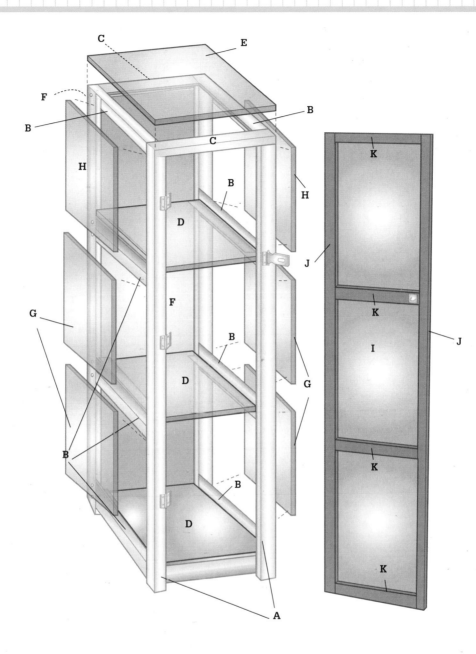

Cutting List

Key	Part	Dimension	Pcs.	Material
A	Frame leg	$\frac{1}{16} \times 1\frac{1}{2} \times 72$"	4	Aluminum angle
B	Shelf support	$\frac{1}{16} \times 1\frac{1}{2} \times 18$"	12	Aluminum angle
C	Frame top	$\frac{1}{16} \times 1\frac{1}{2} \times 18\frac{1}{4}$"	2	Aluminum angle
D	Shelf	$\frac{3}{4} \times 17 \times 16$"	3	Ext. plywood
E	Top*	$\frac{3}{4} \times 17\frac{1}{2} \times 18\frac{1}{2}$"	1	Ext. plywood
F	Back panel	$\frac{3}{8} \times 18 \times 70$"	1	Cedar siding
G	Side panel	$\frac{3}{8} \times 16 \times 23\frac{1}{2}$"	4	Cedar siding
H	Side panel (top)	$\frac{3}{8} \times 16 \times 21$"	2	Cedar siding
I	Door	$\frac{3}{8} \times 14 \times 67$"	1	Ext. plywood
J	Door stiles	$\frac{3}{4} \times 1\frac{1}{2} \times 68$"	2	Cedar
K	Door rails	$\frac{3}{4} \times 1\frac{1}{2} \times 12$"	4	Cedar
L	Top trim(opt.)**	1×1" × cut to fit	4	Corner molding

*Exposed edges finished with $\frac{1}{4} \times \frac{3}{4}$" wood shelf edge

**Not shown

Pitmaster's Locker

MAKE THE METAL FRAME

The framework for this locker is built from solid aluminum angle (1/16" thick × 1½" wide each direction). Although aluminum is very rigid, it is also relatively soft and very workable for cutting and drilling. You can easily cut the metal parts for this project with a hacksaw, though keeping the cuts straight can be tricky. If you have access to a metal cutoff saw, it will save a lot of time—you might consider renting one. Do not install an abrasive blade in a power miter saw. You can also use a reciprocating saw or a jigsaw with a bimetal blade, as seen here (**photo 1**). Whichever saw you use, clean up and deburr the cut edges with a bench grinder.

Lay out shelf locations on the frame legs with a wax crayon or pencil (avoid permanent markers, as they work but the marks cannot be erased). Install shelf supports between pairs of legs at selected heights. Clamp each support to each leg with a locking pliers. Drill one ¼" guide hole in the middle of each joint (**photo 2**). Use a carbide-tipped twist bit. *TIP: Lubricate the drilling point with a drop of cutting oil before drilling.* Add more oil if the metal begins to smoke. Once the guide hole is drilled, insert a ¼ × ¾" bolt and add a locknut on the interior side (**photo 3**). Hand-tighten the nut, but wait until the entire frame is assembled and squared before tightening nuts all the way.

After all of the joints are secured with hand-tightened bolts, check the assembly with a framing square and adjust as needed. Begin fully tightening the locknuts. Grasp each nut with a locking pliers and tighten the bolt head with a socket and ratchet or cordless impact driver (**photo 4**).

ADD THE PLYWOOD PANELS & SHELVES

Cut the shelves to size from ¾" (thick plywood use decent plywood such as AB or BC as opposed to sheathing or CDX). Cut the panels from rough-textured cedar siding panels (these come in 4 × 8-foot sheets, usually around ⅜" thick). Sand and stain both faces and the edges of the panels and shelves with exterior stain before installing them.

Attach the back panel, top panel, and side panels in the correct locations with ¾" pop rivets (**photo 5**). Clamp each panel in place and drill guide holes for the

Cut the aluminum angle for the frame parts (top) and then deburr the cut ends on a bench grinder (lower). Don't overdo it on the grinder.

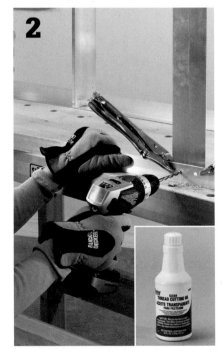

Drill guide holes for bolts. Clamp the part for each joint together with locking pliers and then drill for one ¼" bolt per joint. Apply a drop of cutting oil (inset) to the metal before drilling.

Assemble the frame. Secure each frame joint with a ¼ × ¾" bolt and lock nut. If you're able to locate aluminum fasteners use them, otherwise use stainless steel or hot-dipped fasteners.

Assemble the frame by tightening the locknuts onto the bolts. Hand-tighten all nuts first and then check the frame to make sure it is square. Tighten the nuts with a cordless impact driver or a ratcheting socket set.

Attach the panels using aluminum pop rivets driven through guide holes in the frame and the panels.

Hang the door. Attach the hinges to the metal frame first and then attach the other plates to the back of the door on the edge with no shelf edge molding.

rivets through the frames and the panels. Install the pop rivets from the exterior side of the cabinet. Install the back panel first because it helps to square up the cabinet.

HANG THE DOOR & INSTALL HARDWARE

The locker door is sized to fit in between the metal frame members, and it closes against the slightly recessed shelf edges. It is made from ⅜"-thick siding and framed with 1 × 2 trim. Install three butt hinges to the left leg with bolts and lock nuts. You will probably need to enlarge the screw holes in the hinge plates to accept the ¼"-dia. bolts. After installing all three butt hinges, attach the edge of the door to the free hinge plates (**photo 6**). Test the door. If it works properly, attach the locking hasp. Use exterior-rated wood glue and 1" brass brads to attach ¼" thick × ¾"-wide wood shelf edge to the front edges of the shelves (**photo 7**).

Make the panels and shelves. Cut the shelves and door to size from exterior plywood and attach wood shelf edge molding to select edges as instructed. Cut the side, back, and top panels from cedar plywood (siding). Stain the parts before installing them in the frame.

Timberframe Sandbox

Building this sandbox requires a good deal more effort than if you simply nailed four boards together and dumped a pile of sand in the middle. The timber construction is both charming and solid. A storage box at one end gives kids a convenient place to keep their toys. The opposite end has built-in seats, allowing children to sit above the sand as they play.

The gravel bed and plastic sheathing provide a nice base for the sandbox, allowing water to drain while keeping weeds from sprouting in the sand. The gravel and liner also keep sand from migrating out of the box. The structure is set into the ground for stability and to keep the top of the pavers at ground level so you can easily mow around them. When your children outgrow the sandbox, turn it into a garden bed.

Materials ▸

14 4 × 4" × 8 ft. cedar	Sand
1 1 × 8" × 12 ft. cedar	Wood sealer/ protectant
2 1 × 6" × 8 ft. cedar	Heavy-duty plastic sheeting
2 2 × 2" × 6 ft. cedar	2" galvanized screws
Coarse gravel	6" barn nails
	Pavers
	Hinges

If you have small children, a backyard just isn't complete without a sandbox. This version is nicely sized, sturdy, and designed for ease of cleaning.

Timberframe Sandbox

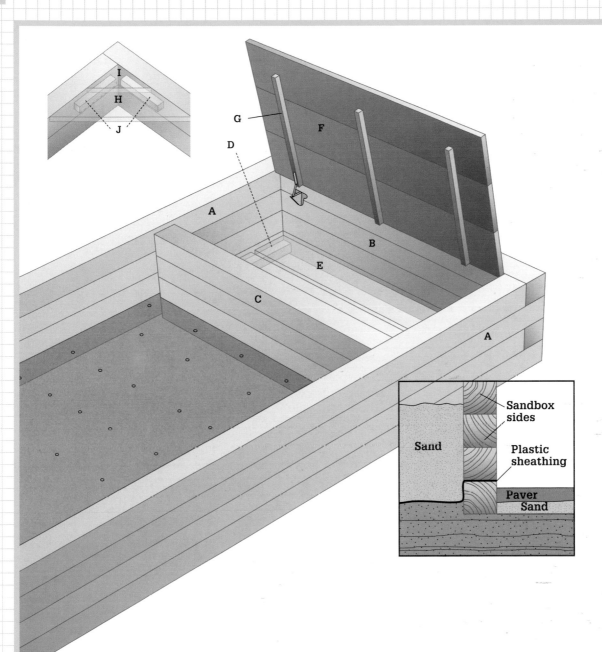

Sandbox sides

Sand

Plastic sheathing

Paver Sand

Cutting List

Key	Part	Dimension	Pcs.	Material
A	Sandbox sides	3½ x 3½ x 92½"	8	Cedar
B	Sandbox ends	3½ x 3½ x 44½"	8	Cedar
C	Storage box wall	3½ x 3½ x 41"	4	Cedar
D	Floor cleats	1½ x 1½ x 18"	2	Cedar
E	Floorboards	¾ x 5½ x 43"	3	Cedar

Key	Part	Dimension	Pcs.	Material
F	Lid boards	¾ x 7½ x 43½"	3	Cedar
G	Lid cleats	1½ x 1½ x 18"	3	Cedar
H	Bench boards	¾ x 5½ x 18"	2	Cedar
I	Corner bench boards	¾ x 5½ x 7"	2	Cedar
J	Bench cleats	1½ x 1½ x 10"	4	Cedar

Timberframe Sandbox

PREPARE THE SITE

Outline a 48 × 96" area using stakes and strings. Use a shovel to remove all of the grass inside the area. Dig a flat trench that's 2" deep × 4" wide around the perimeter of the area, just inside the stakes and string (**photo 1**).

LAY THE FIRST ROW OF TIMBERS

Cut the side, end, and storage box wall timbers using a reciprocating saw. Coat the timbers with a wood sealer and let them dry completely. Place the first tier of sides and ends in the trench so the corners on successive rows will lap over one another. Place a level across a corner, then add or remove soil to level it. Level the other three corners the same way. Drill two $\frac{3}{16}$" pilot holes through the timber sides, then drive 6" barn nails through the pilot holes.

Measuring from the inside of one end, mark for the inside edge of the storage box at 18" on both sides. Align the storage box wall with the marks, making sure the corners are square, and then score the soil on either side of it. Remove the timber and dig a 3" deep trench at the score marks.

Replace the storage box timber in the trench. Its top edge must be ¾" lower than the top edge of the first tier of the sandbox wall. Add or remove dirt until the storage box timber is at the proper height. Drill $\frac{3}{16}$"-dia. pilot holes through the sandbox sides into the ends of the storage box timber, then drive 6" barn nails through the pilot holes.

Pour 2" of coarse gravel into the sandbox section. Compact the gravel with a hand tamper or simply by stomping on it for a while. Cover the gravel bed section with heavy-duty plastic sheathing (**photo 2**). Pierce the plastic with an awl or screwdriver at 12" intervals for drainage.

BUILD THE SANDBOX FRAME

Set the second tier of timbers in place over the first tier and over the plastic sheathing, staggering the joints with the joint pattern in the first tier. Starting at the ends of the timbers, drill $\frac{3}{16}$"-dia. pilot holes every 24", then drive 6" galvanized barn nails through the pilot holes. Repeat for the remaining tiers of timbers, staggering the joints.

Stack the remaining storage box timbers over the first one. Drill $\frac{3}{16}$"-dia. pilot holes through the sandbox

Remove the grass in the sandbox location with a flat-end spade, and then dig a trench for the first row of timbers.

Prepare the base. Lay the first row of timbers, including the wall for the storage box. Fill the sandbox area with a 2" layer of gravel, and cover with plastic sheathing.

Build the rest of the sandbox frame, staggering the corner joints. Drill holes and drive barn nails through the holes.

Attach the bench lid using heavy-duty hinges. Install a child-safe lid support to prevent the lid from falling shut.

Install 2 x 2 cleats ¾" from the top of the sandbox to support the seats in the corners. Attach the corner bench boards using galvanized screws.

Place the pavers into the sand base. Use a rubber mallet to set them in place.

sides into the ends of the storage box timbers, and then drive 6" barn nails into the pilot holes (**photo 3**). Cut the excess plastic from around the outside of the sandbox timbers, using a utility knife.

BUILD THE STORAGE BOX FLOOR & LID

Cut the floor cleats and position one against each side wall along the bottom of the storage box. Attach them using 2" galvanized screws. Cut the floorboards and place them over the cleats with ½" gaps between boards to allow for drainage. Fasten the floorboards to the cleats using 2" screws.

Cut the lid boards and lay them out side-by-side, with the ends flush. Cut the lid cleats and place across the lid, one at each end and one in the middle, making sure the end of each cleat is flush with the back edge of the lid. Drill pilot holes and attach the cleats using 2" galvanized screws. Attach the lid to the sandbox frame using heavy-duty child-safe friction hinges (**photo 4**).

BUILD CORNER BENCHES

Cut the bench cleats. Mark ¾" down from the top edge of the sandbox at two corners. Align the top edges of the bench cleats with the marks and fasten them using 2" deck screws.

Cut the corner bench boards to length with a 45° angle at each end. Place it in the corner and attach it to the cleats using 2" screws (**photo 5**). Cut the bench boards to length with a 45° angle at each end. Butt it against the corner bench board, and then attach it to the cleats. Repeat this step to install the second corner bench.

FILL SANDBOX & INSTALL BORDER

Fill the sandbox with play sand to within 4 to 6" of the top. Mark an area the width of your pavers around the perimeter of the sandbox. Remove the grass and soil in the paver area to the depth of your pavers, plus another 2", using a spade. Spread a 2" layer of sand into the paver trench. Smooth the sand level using a flat board. Place the pavers on top of the sand base, beginning at a corner of the sandbox (**photo 6**). Use a level or a straightedge to make sure the pavers are even and flush with the surrounding soil. If necessary, add or remove sand to level the pavers. Set the pavers in the sand by tapping them with a rubber mallet. Fill the gaps between the pavers with sand. Wet the sand lightly to help it settle. Add new sand as necessary until the gaps are filled.

Yard & Garden Projects

Outdoor carpentry projects are not limited to patio tables and garden benches. The projects in this chapter share a common theme: their main purpose is to improve the appearance of your yard.

Yards and gardens do not take care of themselves. So several projects in this chapter are designed to make yard and garden maintenance easier: a yard cart that looks just like the ones you see on gardening television shows but at a fraction of the price, a scaled-down garden shed, a clever potting bench with work surfaces at two levels (because potted plants are not one-size-fits-all), and more.

There are design and instructions for several planters and containers: a triple-threat trellis planter for potting, climbing, and hanging; a planter based on a design from the Gardens at Versailles. And for pure decorative fun, we've included a wishing well/pump house with recirculating water, a stately garden bridge, and a Japanese-inspired luminary.

In this chapter:

- High-low Potting Bench
- Trellis Planter
- Versailles Planter
- Mailbox Stand
- Plant Boxes
- Mini Garden Shed
- Pump House
- Garden Bridge
- Compost Bin
- Pagoda Lantern
- Yard Cart

High-low Potting Bench

Working the soil is part of the fun of gardening, but crouching down all day can be exhausting. Many gardening tasks are easier if you can work at a standard workbench height instead of on the ground. That's where a potting bench comes in handy. A potting bench provides a comfortable and efficient place to work on gardening jobs that don't have to happen on the ground.

What makes this potting bench different from most other potting benches is that the work surfaces are at appropriate heights for gardening tasks. The work surface is 30" high, making it easier to reach down into pots. The low work surface is just over a foot high, so you won't have to lift heavy objects such as large pots or bags of soil. In addition to the high-low work surfaces, this bench also features a shelf and hook rail to keep small supplies and tools within reach, yet still off the main work area.

A potting bench gets wet and it gets dirty, so rot- and moisture-resistant materials were chosen to build this bench. The frame is made with pressure-treated pine lumber and the work surfaces are composite deck boards. The composite material provides a smooth surface that will not splinter and is easy to clean.

Materials ▸

1 1 × 2" × 8 ft. pine	Exterior-rated screws
2 1 × 4" × 8 ft. pine	(1¼", 2")
4 2 × 4" × 8 ft. pine	Cup hooks
1 1¼ × 5½" × 6 ft. pine	
4 ⅝" × 8 ft. deck boards	

Not all pots are the same height. With two different working heights, this bench is comfortable to use whether you're planting seeds in starter trays or planting a 5-gallon planter with tomatoes.

High-low Potting Bench

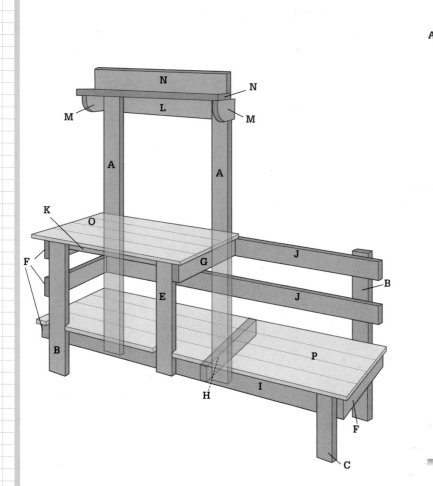

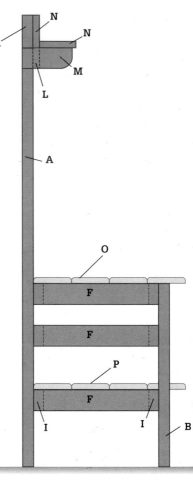

Cutting List

Key	Part	Dimension	Pcs.	Material
A	Long leg	1½ × 3½ × 62¾"	2	Treated pine
B	Mid length leg	1½ × 3½ × 29"	2	Treated pine
C	Short leg	1½ × 3½ × 12"	1	Treated pine
D	Back strut*	1½ × 3½ × 54¼"	1	Treated pine
E	Front strut	1½ × 3½ × 20½"	1	Treated pine
F	Outside cross supports	¾ × 3½ × 22 "	4	Treated pine
G	Middle top cross support	1½ × 3½ × 19¾"	1	Treated pine
H	Middle bottom cross support	1½ × 3½ × 16"	1	Treated pine

Key	Part	Dimension	Pcs.	Material
I	Bottom rails	1½ × 3½ × 60"	2	Treated pine
J	Back rails	¾ × 3½ × 60"	2	Treated pine
K	Front rail	¾ × 1½ × 30"	1	Treated pine
L	Hook rail	¾ × 3½ × 30"	1	Treated pine
M	Shelf supports	¾ × 3½ × 7"	2	Treated pine
N	Shelf/shelf back	1¼ × 5½ × 31½"	2	Treated pine
O	High worktop	1¼ × 5½ × 33½"	4	Deck boards
P	Low worktop	1¼ × 5½ × 62½"	4	Deck boards

*Not Shown

High-low Potting Bench

CUT THE FRAME PARTS

Cut all of the frame and shelf parts to length. Draw a 3½" radius on the front bottom corner of each shelf support. Cut along the radius lines with a jigsaw or bandsaw (**photo 1**). Sand the profiles smooth. Apply a solid color exterior deck and siding stain to all sides of the frame and shelf parts. Staining these parts isn't mandatory, but it's an opportunity to customize your workbench and the stain will extend the life of the parts.

ASSEMBLE THE FRAME

Attach two back rails and one bottom rail to the long leg, back strut, and back right mid-length leg with 2" deck screws. Check that all of the parts intersect at 90-degree angles. Attach the front rail and one bottom rail to the left front mid-length leg, front strut, and short leg. Connect the back assembly and front assembly by attaching them to the cross supports (**photo 2**).

ATTACH THE WORKTOP PLANKS

Cut the deck boards that will be used to create the work surfaces to length. We used composite deck boards because they require little maintenance and are easy to clean. See pages 78 to 85 for more information on working with composites). Place the front deck board for the lower work surface against the backside

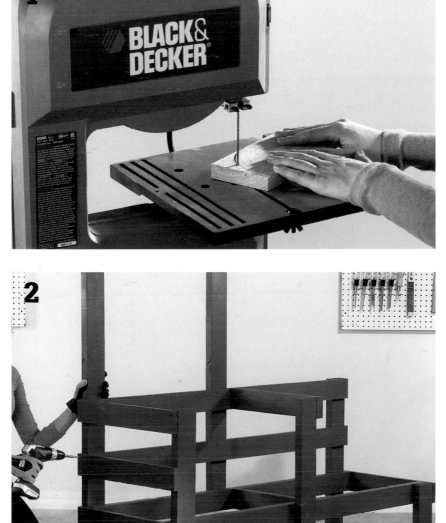

Cut the shelf supports. Use a bandsaw or a jigsaw to make the 3½" radius roundovers on the ends of the shelf supports. Sand smooth.

Assemble the bench frame. Clamp the cross supports to the front and back assemblies. Attach the cross supports with 2" deck screws.

of the front left leg and front strut. Mark the point where the front leg and strut intersect the deck board. Using these marks, draw the 3¾" deep notch outlines and cut out the notches with a jigsaw (**photo 3**).

Place the top and bottom deck boards on the cross supports, leaving a ¼" space between the boards. Drill two pilot holes that are centered over the cross supports in each deck board. Attach the deck boards with 2" deck screws (**photo 4**). If you are using composite deck boards, use specially designed decking screws.

ATTACH THE SHELF & RACK

Attach the shelf back, shelf hook rail, and shelf supports to the long leg and back strut with 2½" deck screws. Attach the shelf to the shelf supports with 2" deck screws. Fasten the hooks to the shelf hook rail (**photo 5**).

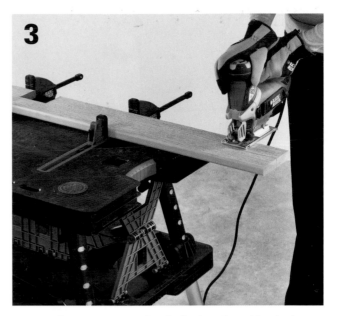

Cut notches. Lay out notches in the front board for the low work surface where the board must fit around the front leg and front strut. Use a jigsaw to cut the notches.

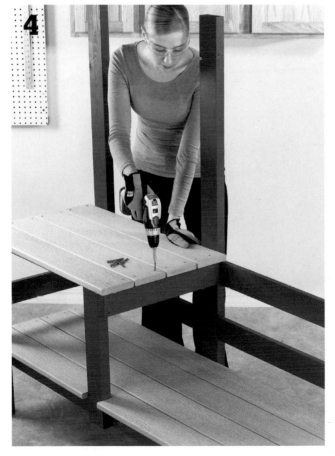

Install the worktop slats. Use composite screws to attach the composite deck boards that create the upper and lower worktops.

Install the shelf and hook rail. Attach the shelf to the shelf supports. Drill pilot holes for each screw to prevent splitting the shelf supports. Once the hook rail is installed twist in the cup hooks.

Trellis Planter

You don't need a large yard—or any yard at all for that matter—to have a garden. Planting in containers makes it possible to cultivate a garden just about anywhere. A container garden can be as simple as a small flowering annual planted in a single 4" pot or as elaborate as a variety of shrubs, flowering plants, and ornamental grasses planted in a large stationary planter.

This planter project combines a couple of different container options to create a larger garden in a relatively small space. The base is an 18 × 30" planter box that is large enough to hold several small plants, a couple of medium-sized plants, or one large plant. It features a trellis back that can be covered by climbing plants.

In addition to the planter and trellis, this project features two plant hangers that extend out from the back posts. Adding a couple of hanging plant baskets further extends the garden display without increasing the space taken up by the planter.

This project is easiest to build with a table saw, miter saw, jigsaw, and drill/driver. If you don't have access to a

table saw, use a circular saw or jigsaw and straightedge to rip the 1 × 6 siding boards. An even easier option is to replace the 2¾"-wide siding boards with 3½"-wide 1 × 4s. This modification makes the planter 4½" taller, so you also have to make the front posts 24½" long instead of 20" long and add 4½" to the front posts trim.

Materials ▸

3	1 × 2" × 8 ft. cedar	Exterior-rated screws
3	1 × 6" × 8 ft. cedar	(2", 3")
1	2 × 4" × 10 ft. cedar	2 ⅜ × 2-½" eyebolts
2	4 × 4" × 8 ft. cedar	4 ⅜" flat washers
1	2 × 2" × 6 ft. cedar	2 ⅜" locknuts
1	¾ × 4" × 4 ft. Ext. plywood	

This efficient planter combines a box for container gardening with a climbing trellis and a pair of profiled arms for hanging potted plants.

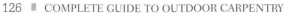

Trellis Planter

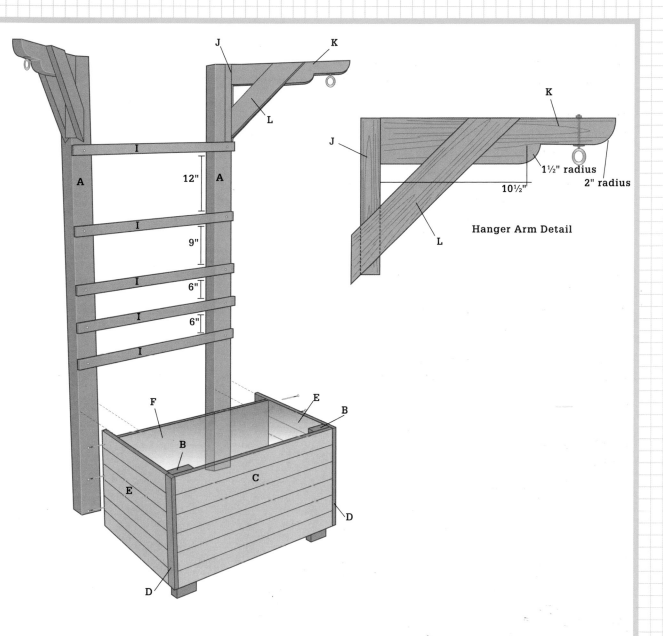

Hanger Arm Detail

1½" radius

2" radius

10½"

Cutting List

Key	Part	Dimension	Pcs.	Material
A	Back posts	3½ × 3½ × 72"	2	Cedar
B	Front posts	1½ × 3½ × 20"	2	Cedar
C	Front siding	¾ × 2¾ × 30"	6	Cedar
D	Front post trim	¾ × 1½ × 18"	2	Cedar
E	Side siding	¾ × 2¾ × 21½"	12	Cedar
F	Back panel	¾ × 18 × 30"	1	Ext. Plywood
G	Bottom supports*	¾ × 1½ × 22¼"	2	Cedar

*Not shown

Key	Part	Dimension	Pcs.	Material
H	Bottom panel*	¾ × 22¼ × 30"	1	Ext. Plywood
I	Climbing rails	¾ × 1½ × 30"	5	Cedar
J	Hanger backs	1½ × 1½ × 12"	2	Cedar
K	Hanger arms	1½ × 3½ × 18"	2	Cedar
L	Hanger braces	1½ × 3½ × 18"	4	Cedar

Trellis Planter

CUT THE BASE PARTS

Cutting the front posts (2 × 4) and back posts (4 × 4) to length is easy. Cutting the hanger parts is a bit trickier, primarily because the plant hangers splay out from the corners of the posts at a 45° angle. The top, outside post corners must be beveled to create flat mounting surface for the hangers. Mark the bevel cut lines on the outside and front faces of the posts (**photo 1**). Tilt the shoe of a jigsaw to 45° and bevel-cut along the layout lines (**photo 2**). Use a handsaw to make a stop cut that meets the bottom of the bevel cut in each back post, forming a shoulder (**photo 3**). Rip-cut some 1 × 6 stock to 2¾" wide (**photo 4**) using a table saw or a circular saw and a straightedge cutting guide. Cut six 30" long pieces and twelve 21½" long pieces to make the siding strips.

Also use a circular saw or table saw to cut the bottom and back panels to length and width. Cut 1½" long × 3½" wide notches out of the front corners of the bottom panel. Cut the front post trim, bottom supports, and back climbing rails to length from 1 × 2 boards.

ASSEMBLE THE BASE PLANTER

Attach the front siding strips to the front posts with 2" exterior screws. Align the ends of the siding pieces flush with the sides of the front legs. Leave a ¼" space between the siding boards. Drive one screw

Mark the post bevel cuts. The lines at the top of each back post should be drawn 1" out from the corner and should run down the post for 12" long.

Cut the bevels. Tilt the foot of a jigsaw at a 45° angle so it will ride smoothly on the post face and follow the bevel cutting line. Make a bevel cut along the layout line.

through each end of each siding board and into the front legs. Drill a countersunk pilot hole for each screw. Attach the front post trim pieces to the front posts with three or four 2" brad nails or finish nails. Align the front edge of the trim pieces flush with the front face of the front siding. Attach the back panel to the back posts with six 2" screws. Drive three screws into each post.

Attach the back lattice rails to the back posts. Drive one screw through each end of each climbing rail (**photo 5**). Refer to the construction drawing on page 127 for lattice spacing. Place the front and back assemblies on their sides and install siding on the side that's facing up. The siding boards should be positioned against the front post trim board and flush with the back edge of the back post, spaced ¼" apart.

Attach the siding with 2" screws (**photo 6**). Flip the project over and repeat the process to attach siding to the other side.

Attach the bottom supports to the front and back legs. The bottom of the front end of the bottom support should be flush with the bottom of the siding. The bottom of the back end of the bottom support should be positioned 2" up from the bottom of the back post. Drive one screw through the front end of the support and into the front leg and two screws into the back legs. Attach the bottom to the bottom supports with four 2" screws—two into each support.

BUILD THE PLANT HANGERS

Cut the hanger backs, hanger arms, and hanger braces to length. Draw the hanger arm profile onto the side of

3

Make the shoulder cut. Use a handsaw to cut into the corner of the post to meet the bevel cut, creating a shoulder for the beveled corner.

4

Rip 1 × 6 stock for siding. Using a table saw or a circular saw and cutting guide, rip enough material for the sides and the front to 2¾".

each hanger arm, and use a compass to draw the radius profiles. Profile details are shown on the construction drawings (page 127). Use a jigsaw to cut along the profile layout lines on the hanger arms. Both ends of the hanger brace are mitered at 45 °, but the back or bottom end is a compound miter cut, meaning that it has both a miter and a bevel component. Cut the top end 45° miters on all four braces. Then, make compound cuts at the bottom ends of the hanger braces (**photo 7**). Make the cuts so the beveled end faces the post when it is attached.

Drill a ⅜"-dia. hole through the top of each hanger arm. Locate the hole 3" in from the end of the hanger arm. Fasten one eyebolt, two flat washers, and a locknut

through each hanger arm. Attach the hanger back to the back end of the hanger arm with two 3" screws. Position a 2 × 2 hanger back and a 2 × 4 hanger arm against the beveled corner of each back post. Drive two 3" screws through the hanger back and into the back posts. Attach the hanger braces to the hanger back and hanger arm with 2" screws (**photo 8**). Make sure the hanger arms remain perpendicular to the posts when you attach the braces.

FILL PLANTER
The planter itself is lined with heavy (at least 4-mil thick) black plastic sheeting. Cut the sheeting pieces

Add the latticework. Attach the horizontal climbing rails to the back posts with 2" screws. Use one screw at each lattice connection to the posts.

Install siding. Attach the siding to the front and back posts with 2" screws. After completing one side, flip the project and complete the other side. Then, install siding strips on the front.

that cover the sides, front, and bottom several inches oversized so they overlap in the corners. Cut the back sheeting the same size as the back panel. Attach the plastic to the inside faces of the planter with staples (**photo 9**). Start with the bottom sheet, overlap the sides on the bottom, and then overlap the front over the sides and bottom. Finally overlap the back over the sides, leaving a small gap between the bottom of the back sheet and the bottom sheet to allow water to drain out. Fill the planter with potting soil and add your plants. *TIP: Adding a few inches of gravel to the bottom of the planting compartment allows for better drainage.*

Cut the hanger brace angles. After cutting a flat 45° miter in the top end of the hanger brace, make a compound bevel/miter cut in the bottom end so it will fit flat against the bevel cut in the post.

Install the hanger braces. Clamp the hanger" braces to the hanger arms and hanger backs. Attach the hanger braces with 2" screws driven into the hanger back and into the hanger arm. Drive two screws at each connection.

Line the container. Attach 4-mil black plastic liner with ⅜" stainless steel staples. Overlap the plastic in the corners and leave a small gap along the back bottom edge for drainage.

Versailles Planter

Possibly the most famous gardens in the world, the gardens at King Louis XIV's Versailles palace are the birthplace of this famous rolling planter style. Reportedly created by landscape architect Andre Le Notre, the Versailles Planter was originally designed to accommodate the many orange trees that were moved in and out of the orange groves on the grounds. The planter seen here differs in several ways from the classic Versailles model, but anyone who has a historical sense of gardening will recognize the archetypal form immediately.

The classic Versailles planter is constructed from oak slats and is bound together with cast iron straps. Cast iron ball or acorn finials atop the corner posts are also present on virtually every version of the planter. Most of the planters that existed (and still exist) on the Versailles grounds today are considerably larger than the one seen here, with sides as wide as 5 feet, as tall as 7 feet. These larger models typically have hinged corners so the sides can be removed easily to plant the tree or shrub, as well as to provide care and maintenance. The X-shaped infill on the design seen here is present in some of the Versailles models, but many others consist of unadorned vertical slats.

At 24 × 24", this historical planter can be home to small- to medium-sized ornamental or specimen trees. The trees can be planted directly into the planter or in containers that are set inside the planter. If you wish to move the plants to follow sunlight or for seasonal protection, install the casters as they are shown. Otherwise, the casters can be left out.

Not a gardener? Try building a slatted top for the planter to create a rolling storage bin that, conveniently, is roughly the same height as a patio table. Or even make a few to serve multiple purposes around your yard while maintaining a consistent design theme.

Based on a classic design originated by the landscape architect for Louis XIV's Gardens at Versailles, this rolling planter can hold small fruit trees (its original purpose) or be put to use in any number of creative ways in your garden or yard.

Materials ▶

1	4 × 4" × 10 ft. cedar	4	2 × 2" × 8 ft. treated pine
1	4 × 4" × 4 ft. cedar		
1	2 × 4" × 8 ft. cedar	1	1 × 6" × 8 ft. cedar
1	2 × 6" × 8 ft. cedar		
1	¾ × 4" × 8 ft. Ext plywood	4	3" casters
			Deck screws

Versailles Planter

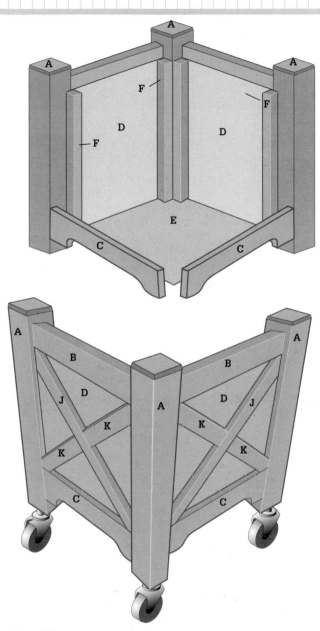

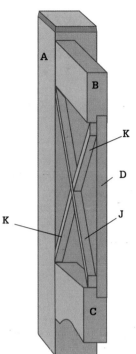

Cutting List

Key	Part	Dimension	Pcs.	Material
A	Corner post	$3\frac{1}{2} \times 3\frac{1}{2} \times 30"$	4	Cedar (4x4)
B	Top rail	$1\frac{1}{2} \times 3\frac{1}{2} \times 17"$	4	Cedar (2x4)
C	Bottom rail	$1\frac{1}{2} \times 5\frac{1}{2} \times 17"$	4	Cedar (2x6)
D	Side panel	$\frac{3}{4} \times 17 \times 18\frac{1}{2}"$	4	Ext. Plywood
E	Bottom panel	$\frac{3}{4} \times 17 \times 17"$	1	Ext. Plywood
F	Corner nailer	$1\frac{1}{2} \times 1\frac{1}{2} \times 23"$	8	PT pine (2x2)
G	Bottom brace*	$1\frac{1}{2} \times 1\frac{1}{2} \times 17\frac{1}{8}"$	2	PT pine (2x2)

Key	Part	Dimension	Pcs.	Material
H	Bottom brace*	$1\frac{1}{2} \times 1\frac{1}{2} \times 14\frac{1}{4}"$	4	PT pine (2x2)
I	Blocking*	$1\frac{1}{2} \times 1\frac{1}{2} \times 7"$	3	PT pine (2x2)
J	X Leg — full	$\frac{3}{4} \times 2 \times 24"$	4	Cedar
K	X Leg — half	$\frac{3}{4} \times 2 \times 11"$	8	Cedar

*Not shown (see step 4, page 135)

Versailles Planter

MAKE THE BOX

Building the box for the Versailles Planter constitutes most of the work for this project. Start by cutting four 30"-long 4 × 4 cedar posts. Install a ¼" piloted chamfering bit in your router and chamfer all four sides of each post top to create 45° bevels (**photo1**). You may find that this is easier if you gang all four posts together edge-to-edge and then spin them each 90° after each cut.

Cut the 2 × 2 pressure-treated corner nailers to length and attach them to the inside faces of the posts so the nailers meet at the inside corners. The bottoms of the nailers should be 4" above the post bottoms
and the tops should be 3" down from the post tops. Use exterior adhesive and 3" deck screws to attach the nailers.

Prepare a 2 × 4 for the top rails and a 2 × 6 for the bottom rails by cutting a rabbet into each work piece (**photo 2**). Located on the bottom inside edge of the 2 × 4 and the top inside edge of the 2 × 6, the rabbets should be ¾" wide x ¾" deep. You can cut it with a table saw or a router. After cutting the rabbet, cut the rails to length. Lay out the profile on the bottom rails and cut with a jigsaw. Sand smooth.

Cut the side panels from ¾" exterior plywood. Create four side assemblies by attaching the panels in the rabbets on pairs of mating top and bottom rails. Use adhesive and 1¼" deck screws driven through the plywood and into the rails.

Attach the side assemblies to the 2 × 2 nailers on the inside faces of the posts. The top rails should all align 1" down from the post tops. Use adhesive and 3" deck screws driven through the nailers and into the rails. Also drive a few 1¼" deck screws through the panels and into the nailers, making sure to countersink the screwheads slightly so they can be concealed with wood putty (**photo 3**).

Flip the box so it is top-down on your work surface and then install the 2 × 2 bottom braces and blocking. It will work best if you first create the brace grid by end-screwing through the four outer braces and into the inner braces and blocking. Then, attach the four outer braces to the bottom rails with adhesive and 3" deck screws driven every 4" or so (**photo 4**). Then, cut the bottom panel to size. Drill a 1" drain hole every 6" (resulting in nine drain holes). Cut 1½" notches at the corners of the bottom panel using a jigsaw. Set the box with the top up and attach the bottom panel to the braces with adhesive and 1¼" deck screws.

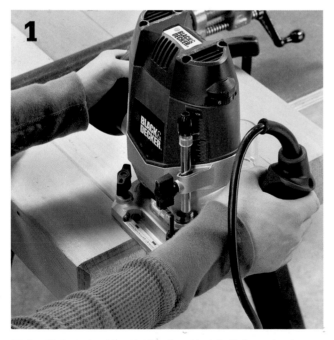

Make the posts. After cutting them to length from 4 x 4 cedar, make a ¼" chamfer cut around all the tops. Gang the posts together for profiling if you like.

Cut panel rabbets. Make the ¾ x ¾" rabbet cuts in the rail stock using a table saw or router. The rabbets will accept the plywood side panels.

ADD DECORATIVE TOUCHES

Rip-cut an 8-ft.-long cedar 1 × 6 into two 2"-wide strips using a tablesaw or circular saw and straightedge guide. Cut the legs of the X's to length. Cut off the corners of the full-length legs on a miter saw to create arrow shapes. Install the legs between opposite corners of the side panel on the outside faces using adhesive and a few 1" brass brads. Cut the half-length X legs with a square end and a pointed end and attach them to the side panels, completing the X shapes (**photo 5**).

Turn the box back upside down and install 3" exterior-rated casters at the corners of the bottom panel. Flip it onto the casters and attach cedar post cap finials (acorn-shape or round) to the tops of the posts if you wish. Or, leave the tops unadorned. Apply two or three coats of exterior trim paint to the outside of the planter and to the inside at least 6" down from the top. If you will be placing dirt directly into the planter, line it with sheet plastic first. A better idea is to plant your tree or shrub in a square pot and set the pot into the planter. *TIP: If you wish to use the planter form as a patio table, attach some cedar 1× 4 slats to a pair of 17"-long 2 × 4 stretchers and set the top (called a duckboard) onto the planter.*

Attach the side assemblies. First, drive 3" deck screws through the corner nailers and into the rails. Then, drive 1¼" deck screws through the side panels and into the nailers. Reinforce the joints with adhesive.

Attach the bottom braces. Assemble the braces into a square grid using adhesive and screws and then attach the whole assembly to the base rails by screwing through the four outer braces that meet the rails.

Make the X shape. The distinctive X shape on the outer surfaces of the side panels is made with 2" wide strips of cedar that are fastened with adhesive and 1" brass brads.

Mailbox Stand

This weekend project combines building skills and a love for flowering perennial plants. In addition to the building materials, visit a salvage yard to find an interesting rectangular planter to suspend below the mailbox. We used a brass planter with an antique patina.

Or, build your own planter from material of your choosing. This mailbox stand is made from a 4 × 4 cedar post that supports a pair of cross arm rails on which you set the mailbox. It is designed for a typical rural mailbox that's sized from 6 to 7" wide and 19 to 20" long. The planter is mounted by hanging it from ropes attached to Shaker pegs in the cross arm rails. Of course, you may prefer to leave the planter off entirely.

It is recommended that you set your mailbox stand post into concrete. It doesn't need to extend all the way down past the frost line unless you're really worried about your mailbox height changing by a fraction of an inch as the ground freezes and thaws. A depth of around 20" is more than adequate for relatively stable soil. A post cap at the top of the post keeps moisture out of the post's end grain and gives your project a neat, finished appearance.

Materials ▸

1	4 × 4" × 8 ft. cedar post	16 #6 × 1½" brass wood screws
2	2 × 4" × 8 ft. cedar	Exterior wood glue
1	1 × 6" × 8 ft. cedar	Mailbox
1	2 × 8" × 8 ft. cedar	Rectangular planter box
1	1 × 2" × 8 ft. cedar	
1	decorative post cap	Nylon rope (or cord or chain)
6	¼ × 5½" stainless steel bolts with nuts and washers	Potting soil
		12 wood caps
		8 Shaker pegs
6	#8 × 2" brass wood screws	

This appealing mailbox stand creates a welcome entry marker for your driveway, especially if you hang the optional planter from it and fill it with bedding plants.

Mailbox Stand

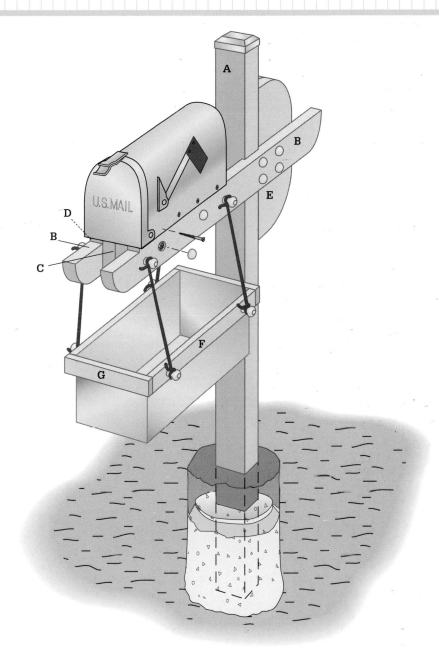

Cutting List

Key	Part	Dimension	Pcs.	Material
A	Post	$3\frac{1}{2} \times 3\frac{1}{2} \times 96"$	1	Cedar
B	Side rails	$1\frac{1}{2} \times 3\frac{1}{2} \times 47"$	2	Cedar
C	Spacers	$1\frac{1}{2} \times 3\frac{1}{2} \times 10\frac{3}{4}"$	2	Cedar
D	Box shelf	$\frac{7}{8} \times 5\frac{1}{2} \times 17\frac{1}{2}"$	1	Cedar
E	Brace	$1\frac{1}{2} \times 7\frac{1}{4} \times 16\frac{1}{2}"$	2	Cedar
F	Long frames	$\frac{7}{8} \times 1\frac{1}{2} \times 27"$	2	Cedar
G	Short frames	$\frac{7}{8} \times 1\frac{1}{2} \times 6\frac{1}{4}"$	2	Cedar

Mailbox Stand

MAKE THE PARTS

Cut the side rails as indicated on the cutting list. On one end of each side rail, make a mark at 14" and another mark at 17½". Set the depth on a circular saw to ¼"; starting at the first mark and working to the second, make a series of cuts ¼" apart. Using a mallet and chisel, remove the waste material between the cuts (**photo 1**). Sand the face of the mortise as necessary. On each end of each side rail, use a jigsaw to cut a 3½"-radius arc.

Cut two braces as indicated on the cutting list. Use a jigsaw to cut an arc 5½" in radius in each end of each brace (**photo 2**).

ASSEMBLE THE POST & RAILS

Cut the spacers. Lay out one side rail, and set the post into the mortise. Position the spacers and the braces and add the second side rail. Square and clamp the assembly. Use a 1" spade bit to drill six counterbored holes that are ½" deep and centered at each bolt location. Turn the assembly over and drill holes on the other side.

Use a ⁵⁄₁₆" spade bit to through-drill the six bolt holes. Fasten the assembly with bolts, washers, and nuts (**photo 3**). Set the nuts finger tight, plus a half-turn. Use exterior wood glue and a wooden cap to plug each bolt hole (**photo 4**). Tap each cap into place, using a rubber mallet wrapped with a soft cloth.

Cut a mortise into each side rail by making a series of ¼"-deep kerf cuts and then removing the waste wood with a mallet and chisel.

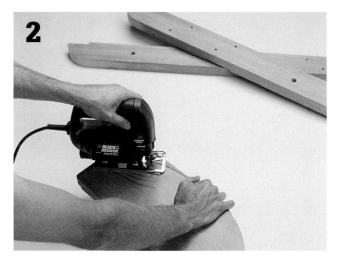

Cut and shape two braces. Draw an arc with a 5½" radius on the braces and cut with a jigsaw.

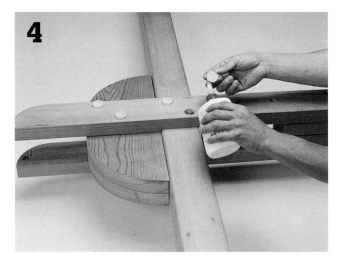

Fasten the post, rails, and braces with lag bolts. Drill counterbores for the bolt heads and the nuts.

Glue a wood cap into both counterbores for each bolt.

Drill four receiving holes for the four Shaker pegs that will support the planter. Use exterior wood glue to fasten the pegs into the side rails (**photo 5**). The heads of the pegs should extend 1" from the side rails. Trim off the excess peg shank so the ends are flush with the inside faces of the rails. Attach the decorative cap onto the top of the post.

ATTACH THE SHELF & MAILBOX

Cut the box shelf as indicated on the cutting list. Position the shelf on top of the side rails, 2½" from the front. Drill pilot holes and attach the mailbox shelf to the side rails using six #8 wood screws (**photo 6**). Fasten the mailbox to the mailbox shelf with eight #6 wood screws driven through the side flanges (**photo 7**). Adjust the box position to allow the door to open freely.

MAKE THE PLANTER HANGING FRAME

Cut two long frame pieces and two short frame pieces. Drill pilot holes for four Shaker pegs. Position the short frame pieces between the long frame pieces. Drill pilot holes and fasten the frame with two #6 wood screws at each corner (**photo 8**). Glue the pegs into their guide holes and trim the ends. Allow the assembly to dry overnight.

Fill the planter box with potting soil and plants. Water thoroughly. Insert the planter box into the support frame and suspend it from the cabinet pulls with nylon rope, cord, or chain.

Insert a Shaker peg into each guide hole so the cap extends 1" out from the rail. Glue in place and trim the end flush.

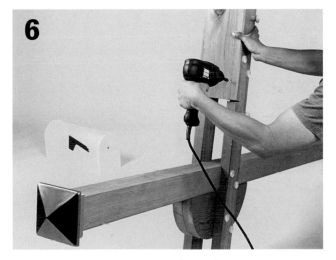

Attach the shelf for the mailbox to the side rails.

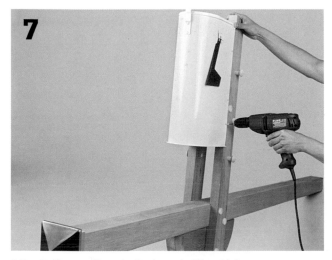

Attach the mailbox to the box shelf by driving screws through the side flanges of the mailbox.

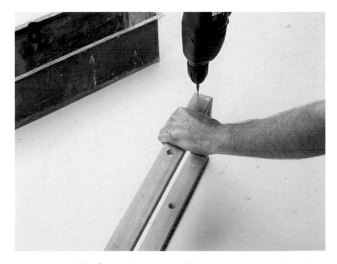

Fasten the planter hanging frame with a pair of #6 wood screws driven in pilot holes at each corner.

Plant Boxes

Planters and plant boxes come in a vast array of sizes and styles, and there is a good reason for that. Everyone's needs are different. Rather than build just one style of planter that may or may not work for you, try this versatile planter design. The boxes can easily be modified to fit your space and planting demands.

This project provides measurements for planters in three sizes and shapes: short and broad for flowers or container plants; medium for spices and herbs or small trees and shrubs; and tall and narrow for vegetables or flowering vines that will cascade over the cedar surfaces. The three boxes are proportional to one another—build all three and arrange them in a variety of patterns, including the tiered effect shown below. Or, adjust the dimensions to make boxes in any size you wish. On larger boxes, consider adding casters so the boxes can easily be relocated or shifted to follow the sun once they are filled.

Whatever the size of the plant box or boxes you are building, the same basic steps for construction

are employed. The only difference between the three boxes is the size of some components. If you need larger, smaller, broader, or taller plant boxes than those shown, it's easy to create your own cutting list based on the diagram and dimensions shown on the next page. If you are building several planters, do some planning and sketching to make efficient use of wood and to save time by gang-cutting parts that are the same size and shape.

Materials ▸

3 1 × 2" × 8 ft. cedar	Deck screws (1¼",
6 1 × 4" × 8 ft. cedar	1½" and 3")
1 ⅝ × 4" × 8 ft. fir siding	6d galvanized finish nails
1 ¾ × 2" × 4 ft. CDX plywood	Finishing materials

Simple cedar boxes can be grouped or arranged individually to meet your container gardening needs.

Plant Boxes

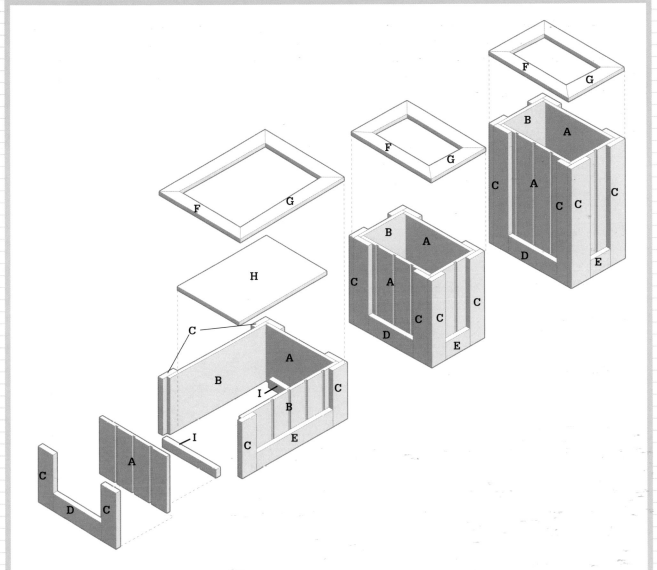

Cutting List

Key	Part	Pcs.	Front Bin Dimension	Middle Bin Dimension	Back Bin Dimension	Material
A	End panel	2	5/8 × 15 × 11⅛"	5/8 × 15 × 17⅛"	5/8 × 15 × 23⅛"	Siding
B	Side panel	2	5/8 × 22¼ × 11⅛"	5/8 × 10¼ × 17⅛"	5/8 × 10¼ × 23⅛"	Siding
C	Corner trim	8	7/8 × 3½ × 11⅛"	7/8 × 3½ × 17⅛"	7/8 × 3½ × 23⅛"	Cedar
D	Bottom trim	2	7/8 × 3½ × 9¼"	7/8 × 3½ × 9¼"	7/8 × 3½ × 9¼"	Cedar
E	Bottom trim	2	7/8 × 3½ × 17"	7/8 × 3½ × 5"	7/8 × 3½ × 5"	Cedar
F	Top cap	2	7/8 × 1½ × 18"	7/8 × 1½ × 18"	7/8 × 1½ × 18"	Cedar
G	Top cap	2	7/8 × 1½ × 24"	7/8 × 1½ × 12"	7/8 × 1½ × 12"	Cedar
H	Bottom panel	1	¾ × 14½ × 19½"	¾ × 14½ × 8½"	¾ × 14½ × 8½"	Plywood
I	Cleat	2	7/8 × 1½ × 12"	7/8 × 1½ × 12"	7/8 × 1½ × 12"	Cedar

Plant Boxes

MAKE & ASSEMBLE THE BOX

The end and side panels are rectangular pieces of sheet siding that are tacked together with deck screws to form a box. The corner joints are then reinforced with trim when it is installed. Cut the end panels and side panels to size using a circular saw and straightedge cutting guide (**photo 1**).

Lay an end panel face down on a flat work surface and butt the side panel, face-side out, up to the end of the end panel. Mark positions for pilot holes in the side panel. Drill ⅛" pilot holes through the end panels and into the edges of the side. Counterbore the holes slightly so the heads are beneath the surface of the end panel. Fasten the side panel to the end panel with 1½" deck screws. Position the second side panel at the other end of the end panel and repeat the procedure.

Lay the remaining end panel face down on the work surface. Position the side panel assembly over the end panel, placing the end panel between the side panels and keeping the edges of the side panels flush with the edges of the end panel. Fasten the side panels to the end panel.

ATTACH THE TRIM

The cedar trim serves not only as a decorative element, but also as a structural reinforcement to the side panels. Most cedar has a rough texture on one side. For a rustic look, install your trim pieces with the rough side facing out. For a more finished appearance, install the pieces with the smooth side facing out.

Cut the corner trim to length. Overlap the edges of the corner trim pieces at the corners to create a square butt joint. Fasten the corner trim pieces directly to the panels by driving 1¼" deck screws through the inside faces of the panels and into the corner trim pieces (**photo 2**). Do not countersink pilot holes for screws and take care not to overdrive the screws—the points will stick out through the face of the trim pieces. For additional support, drive countersunk screws through the overlapping corner trim pieces and into the edges of the adjacent trim piece.

Cut the bottom trim pieces to length. Fasten the pieces to the end and side panels between the corner trim pieces. Drive 1¼" deck screws through the side and end panels and into the bottom trim pieces.

INSTALL THE CAP FRAMES

The top caps fit around the top of the plant box to create a thin ledge that keeps water from seeping into the end grain of the panels and trim pieces. Cut 45° miters at both ends of one cap piece using a power miter saw or a miter box and backsaw. Tack the mitered cap piece to the top edge of the planter, keeping the outside edges flush with the outer edges

Line the Boxes ▶

Although the boxes are constructed with exterior-rated materials, they will last longer if you line them with landscape fabric before adding soil. This also helps keep the boxes from discoloring and keeps the soil in the box where it belongs. Simply cut a piece of fabric large enough to wrap the box (as if you were gift-wrapping it), and then fold it so it fits inside the box. Staple it at the top, and trim off the excess. For better soil drainage, drill a few 1"-dia. holes in the bottom of the box and add a layer of small stones at the bottom of the box.

Cut the end panels and side panels to size from cedar siding using a circular saw and a straightedge cutting guide.

of the corner trim pieces. For a proper fit, use this cap piece as a guide for marking and cutting the miters on the rest of the cap pieces. Miter both ends of each piece and tack it to the box so it makes a square corner with the previously installed piece. If the corners do not work out exactly right, loosen the pieces and adjust the arrangement until everything is square. Permanently fasten all the cap pieces to the box with 6d galvanized finish nails.

INSTALL THE BOX BOTTOM

The bottom of the planter box is supported by cleats that are fastened inside the box, flush with the bottoms of the side and end panels. Cut the cleats to length. Screw them to the end panels with 1½" deck screws (**photo 3**). On the taller bins you may want to mount the cleats higher on the panels so the box won't need as much soil when filled. If you choose to do this, add cleats on the side panels for extra support. Cut the bottom panel to size from ¾"-thick exterior-rated plywood, such as CDX plywood. Set the bottom panel onto the cleats. You do not need to fasten it in place.

APPLY FINISHING TOUCHES

If you've oriented your lumber so the smooth face is out, sand all edges and surfaces to remove rough spots and splinters. Apply two or three coats of exterior wood stain or clear protectant to all wood surfaces. When the finish has dried, fill the boxes with potting soil. If you are using shorter boxes, you can simply place your potted plants inside the planter box.

Fasten the corner trim to the panels by driving 1¼" deck screws through the panels into the trim. Don't overdrive the screws.

Attach a pair of 1 x 2 cleats to the inside faces of the box ends to support the bottom panel.

This scaled-down garden shed is just small enough to be transportable. Locate it near gardens or remote areas of your yard where on-demand tool storage is useful.

Mini Garden Shed

Whether you are working in a garden or on a construction site, getting the job done is always more efficient when your tools are close at hand. Offering just the right amount of on-demand storage, this mini garden shed can handle all of your gardening hand tools but with a footprint that keeps costs and labor low.

The mini shed base is built on two 2 × 8 front and back rails that raise the shed off the ground. The rails can also act as runners, making it possible to drag the shed like a sled after it is built. The exterior is clad with vertical-board-style cementboard siding. This type of siding not only stands up well to the weather, it is very stable and resists rotting and warping. It also comes preprimed and ready for painting. Cement siding is not intended to be in constant contact with moisture, so the manufacturer recommends installing it at least 6" above the finished ground grading. You can paint the trim and siding any color you like. You might choose to coordinate the colors to match your house or you might prefer a unique color scheme so that it stands out as a garden feature.

The roof is made with corrugated fiberglass roof panels. These panels are easy to install and are available in a variety of colors, including clear, that will let more light into the shed. An alternative to the panels is to attach plywood sheathing and then attach any roofing material you like over the sheathing. These plans show how to build the basic shed, but you can customize the interior with hanging hooks and shelves to suit your needs.

Materials ▸

24 2 × 4" × 8 ft. SPF	Roof panel closure
2 2 × 8" × 8 ft.	strips
treated pine	Clear acrylic
2 ¾" × 4 × 8 ft. Ext.	(20 x 28")
plywood	Exterior-rated screws
17 1 × 4" × 8 ft. SPF	(1½", 2½")
1 1 × 6" × 8 ft. SPF	1½" siding nails
2 24"-wide × 8 ft.	2" finish nails
roof panels	1" neoprene gasket
1 Large utility or	screws
gate handle	

Working with Fiber Cement Siding ▸

Fiber cement siding is sold in ¼"-thick, 4 x 8-ft. sheets at many home centers. There are specially designed shearing tools that contractors use to cut this material, but you can also cut it by scoring it with a utility knife and snapping it—just like cement tile backer board or drywall board. *Note: You can also cut cementboard with a circular saw, but you must take special precautions.* Cementboard contains silica. Silica dust is a respiratory hazard. If you choose to cut it with a power saw, then minimize your dust exposure by using a manufacturer-designated saw blade designed to create less fine dust and by wearing a NIOSH/MSHA-approved respirator with a rating of N95 or better.

Cutting List

Key	Part	Dimension	Pcs.	Material
	Lumber			
A	Front/back base rails	1½ × 7¼ × 55"	2	Treated pine
B	Base cross pieces	1½ × 3½ × 27"	4	Treated pine
C	Base platform	¾ × 30 × 55"	1	Ext. plywood
D	Front/back plates	1½ × 3½ × 48"	4	SPF
E	Front studs	1½ × 3½ × 81"	4	SPF
F	Door header	1½ × 3½ × 30"	1	SPF
G	Back studs	1½ × 3½ × 75"	4	SPF
H	Side bottom plate	1½ × 3½ × 30"	2	SPF
I	Side top plate	1½ × 3½ × 27"	2	SPF
J	Side front stud	1½ × 3½ × 81"	2	SPF

Key	Part	Dimension	Pcs.	Material
	Lumber			
K	Side middle stud	1½ × 3½ × 71"	2	SPF
L	Side back stud*	1½ × 3½ × 75¼"	2	SPF
M	Side cross piece	1½ × 3½ × 27"	2	SPF
N	Door rail (narrow)	¾ × 3½ × 29¾"	1	SPF
O	Door rail (wide)	¾ × 5½ × 23"	2	SPF
P	Door stiles	¾ × 3½ × 71"	2	SPF
Q	Rafters	1½ × 3½ × 44"	4	SPF
R	Outside rafter blocking*	1½ × 3½ × 15¼"	4	SPF
S	Inside rafter blocking*	1½ × 3½ × 18¾"	2	SPF

*Not shown

Key	Part	Dimension	Pcs.	Material
	Siding & Trim			
T	Front left panel	¼ × 20 × 85"	1	Siding
U	Front top panel	¼ × 7½ × 30"	1	Siding
V	Front right panel	¼ × 5 × 85"	1	Siding
W	Side panels	¼ × 30½ × 74½"	2	Siding
X	Back panel	¼ × 48 × 79"	1	Siding
Y	Door panel	¾ × 29¾ × 74"	1	Ext. plywood
Z	Front corner trim	¾ × 3½ × 85"	2	SPF
AA	Front top trim	¾ × 3½ × 50½"	1	SPF
BB	Side casing	¾ × 1½ × 81½"	2	SPF
CC	Top casing	¾ × 1½ × 30"	1	SPF
DD	Bottom casing	¾ × 2½ × 30"	1	SPF
EE	Trim rail (narrow)	¾ × 1½ × 16½"	3	SPF

Key	Part	Dimension	Pcs.	Material
	Siding & Trim			
FF	Trim rail (wide)	¾ × 3½ × 16½"	1	SPF
GG	Side trim	¾ × 2½ × 27"	2	SPF
HH	Side trim	¾ × 2½ × 27¾"	2	SPF
II	Side corner trim	¾ × 1¾ × 85¼"	2	SPF
JJ	Side corner trim	¾ × 1¾ × 79½"	2	SPF
KK	Side trim	¾ × 3½ × 27"	2	SPF
LL	Side trim	¾ × 1½ × 69"	2	SPF
MM	Back corner trim	¾ × 3½ × 79"	2	SPF
NN	Back trim	¾ × 3½ × 50½"	2	SPF
OO	Back trim	¾ × 1½ × 72"	2	SPF
PP	Side windows	¼ × 10 × 28"	2	Acrylic

Key	Part	Dimension	Pcs.	Material
	Roof			
QQ	Purlins	1½ × 1½ × 61½"	5	
RR	Corrugated closure strips	61½" L	5	
SS	Corrugated roof panels	24 × 44"	3	

Mini Garden Shed

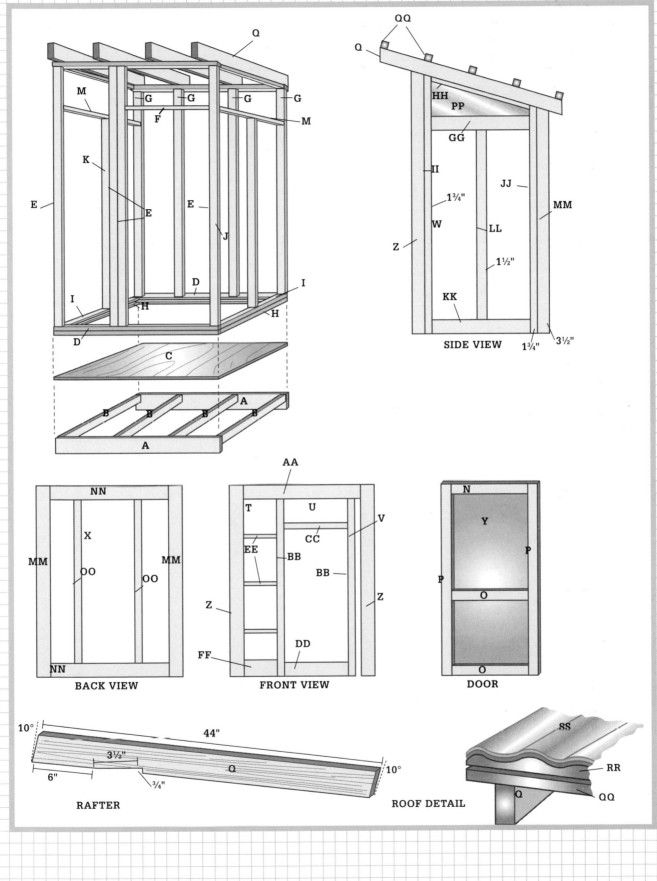

Q

QQ

Q

HH
PP
GG
II
JJ
MM
W
LL
Z
1¾"
1½"
KK
SIDE VIEW
1¾"   3½"

M
G   G   G   G
F
M
K
E
E
E
J
D
I   I
H   H
D
C

A
B   B   B   B
A

NN
X
MM   MM
OO   OO
NN
BACK VIEW

AA
T   U
CC
EE
BB
BB
Z   Z
FF   DD
FRONT VIEW

N
Y
P
P
O
O
DOOR

10°   44"   10°
3½"
6"   Q
¾"
RAFTER

SS
RR
Q   QQ
ROOF DETAIL

Mini Garden Shed

BUILD THE BASE

Even though moving it is possible, this shed is rather heavy and will require several people or a vehicle to drag it if you build it in your workshop or garage. When possible, determine where you want the shed located and build it in place. Level a 3 × 5 foot area of ground. The shed base is made of treated lumber, so you can place it directly on the ground. If you desire a harder, more solid foundation, dig down 6" and fill the area with tamped compactable gravel.

Cut the front and back base rails and base crosspieces to length. Place the base parts upside-down on a flat surface and attach the crosspieces to the rails with 2½" deck screws. Working with the parts upside-down makes it easy to align the top edges flush. Cut the base platform to size. Flip the base frame over and attach the base platform (functionally, the floor) with 1½" screws. Set and level the base in position where the shed will be built.

FRAME THE SHED

Cut the front wall framing members to size, including the top and bottom plates, the front studs, and the door header. Lay out the front wall on a flat section of ground, such as a driveway or garage floor. Join the wall framing components with 10d common nails (**photo 1**). Then, cut the back-wall top and bottom plates and studs to length. Lay out the back wall on flat ground and assemble the back wall frame.

Cut both sidewall top and bottom plates to length, and then cut the studs and crosspiece. Miter-cut the ends of the top plate to 10°. Miter-cut the top of the front and back studs at 10° as well. Lay out and assemble the side walls on the ground. Place one of the side walls on the base platform. Align the outside edge of the wall so it is flush with the outside edge of the base platform. Get a helper to hold the wall plumb while you position the back wall. If you're working alone, attach a brace to the side of the wall and the platform to hold the wall plumb (**photo 2**).

Place the back wall on the platform and attach it to the side wall with 2½" deck screws. Align the outside edge of the back wall and the edge of the platform (**photo 3**). Place the front wall on the platform and attach it to the side wall with 2½"

Build the wall frames. For the front wall, attach the plates to the outside studs first and then attach the inside studs, using the door header as a spacer to position the inside studs.

Raise the walls. Use a scrap of wood as a brace to keep the wall plumb. Attach the brace to the sidewall frame and to the base platform once you have established that the first wall is plumb.

Fasten the wall frames. Attach the shed walls to one another and to the base platform with 2½" screws. Use a square and level to check that the walls are plumb and square.

Make the rafters. Cut the workpieces to length, then lay out and cut a bird's mouth notch in the bottom of the two inside rafters. These notches will keep the tops of the inside rafters in line with the outside rafters. The ends should be plumb-cut at 10°.

Install rafter blocking. Some of the rafter blocking must be attached to the rafters by toe-screwing (driving screws at an angle). If you own a pocket screw jig you can use it to drill angled clearance holes for the deck screw heads.

Install the roof. Attach the corrugated roof panels with 1" neoprene gasket screws (sometimes called pole barn screws) driven through the panels at closure strip locations. Drill slightly oversized pilot holes for each screw and do not overdrive screws—it will compress the closure strips or even cause the panels to crack.

screws. Place the second side wall on the platform and attach it to the front and back walls with 2½" screws.

Cut the rafters to length, then miter-cut each end to 10° for making a plumb cut (this way the rafter ends will be perpendicular to the ground). A notch, referred to as a "bird's mouth," must be cut into the bottom edge of the inside rafters so the tops of these rafters align with the outside rafter tops while resting solidly on the wall top plates. Mark the bird's mouth on the inside rafters (see Diagram, page 147) and cut them out with a jigsaw (**photo 4**). Cut the rafter blocking to length—these parts fit between the rafters at the front and back of the shed to close off the area above the cap plates. Attach the rafters to the rafter blocking and to the top plates. Use blocking as spacers to position the rafters and then drive 2½" screws up through the top plates and into the rafters. Then, drive 2½" screws through the rafters and into the blocking (**photo 5**). Toe-screw any rafter blocking that you can't access to fasten through a rafter. Finally, cut the door rails and stiles to length. Attach the rails to the stiles with 2½" screws.

INSTALL THE ROOF

This shed features 24"-wide corrugated roofing panels. The panels are installed over wood or foam closure strips that are attached to the tops of 2 × 2 purlins running perpendicular to the rafters. Position the purlins so the end ones are flush with the ends of the rafters, and the inner ones are evenly spaced. The overhang should be equal on the purlin ends.

Cut five 61½"-long closure strips. If the closure strips are wood, drill countersunk pilot holes through the closure strips and attach them to the purlins with 1½" screws. Some closure strips are made of foam with a self-adhesive backing. Simply peel off the paper backing and press them in place. If you are installing foam strips that do not have adhesive backing, tack them down with a few pieces of double-sided carpet tape so they don't shift around.

Cut three 44"-long pieces of corrugated roofing panel. Use a jigsaw with a fine tooth blade or a circular saw with a fine-tooth plywood blade to cut fiberglass or plastic panels. Clamp the panels together between scrap boards to minimize vibration while

Cut the wall panels. Use a utility knife to score the fiber cement panel along a straightedge. Place a board under the scored line and then press down on the panel to break the panel as you would with drywall.

Attach siding panels. Attach the fiber cement siding with 1½" siding nails driven through guide holes. Space the nails 8" to 12" apart. Drive the nails a minimum ⅜" away from the panel edges and 2" from the corners..

Cut the acrylic window material to size. One way to accomplish this is to sandwich the acrylic between two sheets of scrap plywood and cut all three layers at once with a circular saw (straight cuts) or jigsaw.

they're being cut (but don't clamp down so hard you damage the panels). Position the panels over the closure strips, overlapping roughly 4" of each panel and leaving a 1" overhang in the front and back.

Drill pilot holes 12" apart in panels and located over the overlapping panel seams. The pilot hole diameter should be slightly larger than the diameter of the screw shanks. Fasten the panels to the closure strips and rafters with hex-head screws that are pre-fitted with neoprene gaskets (**photo 6**).

ATTACH THE SIDING

Cut the siding panels to size by scoring them with a a utility knife blade designated for scoring concrete and them snapping them along the scored line (**photo 7**). Or, use a rented cementboard saw (see page 145). Drill guide holes in the siding and then attach the siding to the framing with 1½" siding nails spaced at 8 to 12" intervals (**photo 8**). (You can rent a cementboard coil nailer instead.) Cut the plywood door panel to size. Paint the siding and door before

you install the windows and attach the wall and door trim. Apply two coats of exterior latex paint.

INSTALL THE WINDOWS

The windows are fabricated from ¼"-thick sheets of clear plastic or acrylic. To cut the individual windows to size, first mark the cut lines on the sheet. To cut acrylic with a power saw, secure the sheet so that it can't vibrate during cutting. The best way to secure it is to sandwich it between a couple of pieces of scrap plywood and cut through all three sheets (**photo 9**). Drill ¼"-dia. pilot holes around the perimeter of the window pieces. Position the holes ½" from the edges and 6" apart. Attach the windows to the side wall framing on the exterior side using 1½" screws (**photo 10**).

ATTACH THE TRIM

Cut the wall and door trim pieces to length. Miter-cut the top end of the side front and back trim pieces to 10°. Attach the trim to the shed with 2" galvanized finish nails (**photo 11**). The horizontal side trim overlaps the window and the side siding panel. Be careful not to drive any nails through the plastic window panels. Attach the door trim to the door with 1½" exterior screws.

HANG THE DOOR

Fasten a utility handle or gate handle to the door. Fasten three door hinges to the door and then fasten the hinges to a stud on the edge of the door opening (**photo 12**). Use a scrap piece of siding as a spacer under the door to determine the proper door height in the opening. Add hooks and hangers inside the shed as needed to accommodate the items you'll be storing. If you have security concerns, install a hasp and padlock on the mini shed door.

Attach the window panels. Drill a ¼"-dia. pilot hole for each screw that fastens the window panels. These oversized holes give the plastic panel room to expand and contract. The edges of the windows (and the fasteners) will be covered by trim.

Attach the trim boards with 2" galvanized finish nails. In the areas around windows, predrill for the nails so you don't crack the acrylic.

Hang the door using three exterior-rated door hinges. Slip a scrap of ¼" thick siding underneath the door to raise it off the base plate while you install it.

Pump House

With this decorative yard feature, anyone can enjoy the rural charm of an old-fashioned well and pump house. Although it doesn't actually pump water from an underground source, this well is equipped with a pump and recirculating water supply so it adds the sight and sound of real running water to enhance your garden scene.

The wood pump mechanism features a handle that moves. Inside the well is a bucket of water and a small recirculating water pump. The pump draws water from the bucket and moves it through a tube that dumps the water out through the wood spout and back into the bucket. As long as there is water in the bucket and power to the pump the water never stops flowing. In hot climates the water in the bucket should be replenished daily.

Building this little well and pump house is not difficult. The base of the well is made by beveling the edges of eight boards to create a short octagonal column that bears some resemblance to a classic wishing well. These cuts are easy to make using a table saw. The roof of this well is clad with cedar shingles, but you can use any roofing material you like. Or, simply paint the roof to look as if it is shingled.

Materials ▸

2	1 × 4" × 8 ft. cedar	1¼" exterior-rated
2	1 × 6" × 8 ft. cedar	screws
2	1 × 8" × 8 ft. cedar	2" deck screws
3	2 × 4" × 8 ft. cedar	Small water feature
1	¾ × 2" × 4 ft.	pump (30 to 75
	plywood	gallons per hour)
1	¾"-dia. × 12" dowel	Plastic bucket
1 bundle cedar		Tubing
	shingles	
1¼" galvanized brad		
	nails	

This cute wishing well will liven up any garden or yard, especially if you outfit it with a water pump and recirculate water through the spout.

Pump House

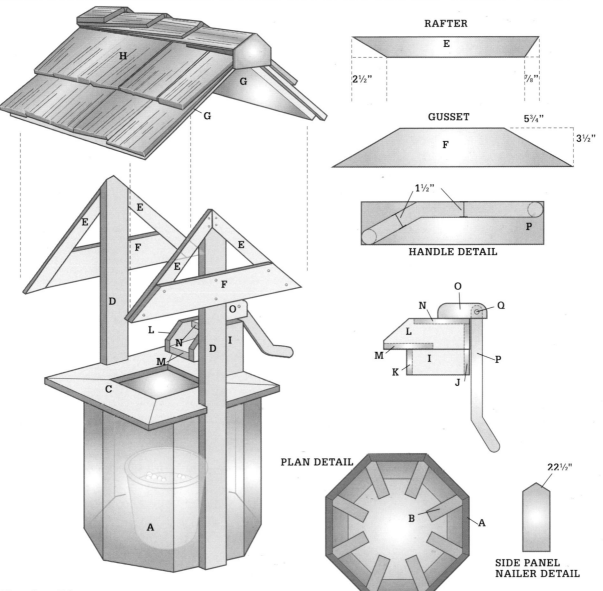

RAFTER

E

2½" ⅞"

GUSSET

F

5¾"

3½"

1½"

P

HANDLE DETAIL

O

N Q

L

M I P

K J

PLAN DETAIL

22½"

B A

SIDE PANEL
NAILER DETAIL

Cutting List

Key	Part	Dimension	Pcs.	Material
A	Side panels	¾ × 7¼ × 18"	8	Cedar
B	Side panel nailers	1½ × 3½ × 18"	8	Cedar
C	Top caps	¾ × 5½ × 22"	4	Cedar
D	Posts	1½ × 3½ × 38"	2	Cedar
E	Rafters	¾ × 1½ × 12"	4	Cedar
F	Roof gussets	¾ × 3½ × 24"	2	Cedar
G	Roof panels	¾ × 15 × 24"	2	Ext. plywood
H	Shingles	various width × 18"		Cedar
I	Pump sides	¾ × 5½ × 21¼"	2	Cedar

Key	Part	Dimension	Pcs.	Material
J	Pump back	¾ × 3½ × 24"	1	Cedar
K	Pump front	¾ × 2¾ × 3½"	1	Cedar
L	Spout sides	¾ × 3½ × 8½"	2	Cedar
M	Spout bottom	¾ × 3½ × 6½"	1	Cedar
N	Spout top	¾ × 3½ × 5"	1	Cedar
O	Handle hinges	¾ × 2¼ × 4"	2	Cedar
P	Handle	¾ × 3½ × 15"	1	Cedar
Q	Handle pin	¾" dia. × 2½"	1	Hardwood dowel

Pump House

BUILD THE OCTAGONAL WELL

Cut the side panels and side panel nailers to length. Use a table saw to bevel-cut the edges of the side panels inward so they meet flush. Set the blade bevel angle to 22½ ° (half of a 45° angle) and bevel-cut both long edges of each side panel (**photo 1**). Bevel-cut the side panel nailers. These bevels are cut to form a peak along one edge (**photo 2**). Attach each side panel edge to one side panel nailer using exterior-rated glue and galvanized nails. If you have a pneumatic brad nail gun, then you can use 1½" brad nails. Otherwise, use 3d × 1½" finish nails. The beveled edge of the panel side should line up with the peak of the nailer. Attach all of the panels and nailers to form the octagonal well base (**photo 3**).

Cut the top caps to length with opposing 45° miters on each end. Lay out a 1½"-deep x 3½"-wide notch in the center of the outside edge of two of the top caps. Lay out a 1½"-deep × 5"-wide notch in the center of the outside edge of one of the remaining two caps. Cut out the notch with a jigsaw. Attach the top caps to the well base with glue and nails (**photo 4**).

BUILD THE WOOD PUMP HOUSING

Cut the pump, spout, and tray parts to size. Use a jigsaw to cut the pump sides into an L shape. Cut the top corner off the spout side pieces at a 45° angle, leaving 1½" of the front edge face below the angle cut. Cut 1"-radius curves in the top corners of the handle

1

Bevel stock for the side panels. Set a table saw blade bevel angle to 22½°. Bevel-cut both long edges of a 1 x 8 to create the material from which to cut the side panels.

2

Bevel the nailers. Run the side panel nailers through the table saw on-edge twice, creating two bevels that form a peak on each edge.

hinge pieces. The handle is cut from a piece of 1 × 4. Lay out the handle shape on the 1 × 4 and cut it out with a jigsaw. Drill ¾"-dia. holes for the handle pin through the handle hinge and handle pieces. Slip the handle pin through the handle hinge and handle holes. Bore one ¹⁄₃₂" pilot hole through the top of each handle hinge and into the pin. Secure the pin in the hinges with 1½" finish nails. The handle should swing freely both on the pin and between the hinge pieces. Attach the handle hinge pieces to the spout top with glue and 1¼" screws (**photo 5**).

Attach the spout sides to the spout top with glue and nails. Attach the pump sides to the pump front and back with glue and nails. Slide the spout and handle assembly over the pump assembly and connect them with glue and nails. Slide the spout bottom between the spout sides and on top of the pump front piece. Attach the spout bottom to the spout sides with glue and nails (**photo 6**). Position the completed pump assembly in the 5"-wide notch on the backside of the well. Drive 1¼" screws through the inside faces of the side panels and into the pump sides.

ATTACH THE ROOF

Cut the posts, rafters, and gussets for the roof structure to length. Lay out the miter angles on the ends of these parts. The miters are steeper than 45°, so use a jigsaw or circular saw and a straightedge to cut along the miter lines. Place a post inside each notch and against the side panels. Drive three 2" screws to attach the post. Attach the gussets to the posts and the rafters to the gussets with glue and 1¼" screws (**photo 7**).

Assemble the well base. Apply glue to the beveled faces of the nailers, clamp the panels to the nailers, and then drive three nails through the side panel and into the nailers, creating the octagonal base assembly.

Cap the well. Attach each top cap to the well base so that the back edge of the notch is flush with the outside face of the side panel, and the mitered ends of the top caps form corners.

Cut the roof panels to size and attach them to the rafters with 1¼" screws. In this case, cedar shingles are attached to the roof panels. Secure the shingles with 1" nails (**photo 8**). Because there will be water flowing and dripping inside the well, it's a good idea to apply some type of water-repelling exterior finish to all surfaces. In this case we applied two coats of a clear exterior deck sealer to all of the surfaces except the spout that would have water flowing over it. Coat the inside faces of the spout sides and the top face of the spout bottom with several coats of marine varnish.

INSTALL THE PUMP

Place a plastic bucket on the ground where the well is to be installed. Set a small recirculating pond pump in the bucket, with roughly 24 to 36" of water tubing attached to the pump (**photo 9**). Fill the bucket half full of water and test the pump operation. With the assistance of a helper, place the well structure over the bucket (**photo 10**). Then, thread the water tubing up through the bottom of the wood pump and up to the back of the spout. Secure the water tubing to the spout bottom with a couple of cable staples—the same type used to anchor electrical cables to wood framing.

Make the pump handle assembly. Attach the handle hinge pieces to the spout top with glue and 1¼" screws.

Assemble the spout. The front bottom edge of the spout bottom is flush with the bottom edge of the spout sides. The middle rests on the pump front. Attach it between the spout sides with glue and nails.

Assemble the roof structure. Glue and clamp the gussets to the posts and the rafters to the gussets. Attach the parts with 1¼" screws.

Shingle the roof. Drive two nails into each cedar shingle and stagger the shingle widths so that the vertical seams do not align in adjacent rows.

Hook up the pump. The well must be located near an electrical outlet. Place the pond pump in a plastic bucket that is half filled with water. Run the water tubing line through the wooden pump so that it comes out on top of the spout bottom piece.

Lower the pump house. With assistance, lower the pump house structure over the functioning pump and then hook the pump tubing up to the spout.

Garden Bridge

A bridge can be more than simply a way to get from point A to point B without getting your feet wet. This striking cedar footbridge will be a design centerpiece in any backyard or garden.

Even if the nearest trickle of water is miles from your home, this garden bridge will give the impression that your property is graced with a tranquil brook, and you'll spend many pleasurable hours absorbing the peaceful images it inspires. If you happen to have a small ravine or waterway through your yard, this sturdy bridge will take you across it neatly and in high style. Or, you can fortify the illusion of flowing water by laying a "stream" of landscaping stones beneath this garden bridge. Often, shallow drainage ditches are dug and lined with stones to help control water runoff and prevent soil erosion. Such a ditch is a perfect candidate for locating a decorative garden bridge.

Materials ▸

4 4 × 4" × 8 ft. cedar	8 1 × 2" × 8 ft. cedar
2 2 × 10" × 8 ft. cedar	2 ½ × 2" × 8 ft. cedar lattice
11 2 × 4" × 8 ft. cedar	⅜ × 4" lag screws
2 1 × 8" × 8 ft. cedar	Deck screws (2", 3")
2 1 × 3" × 8 ft. cedar	Finishing materials

This handsome bridge will add romance and charm to your yard whether it's positioned over a real stream, a small swirl of stones, or even a gently sloped ravine.

Garden Bridge

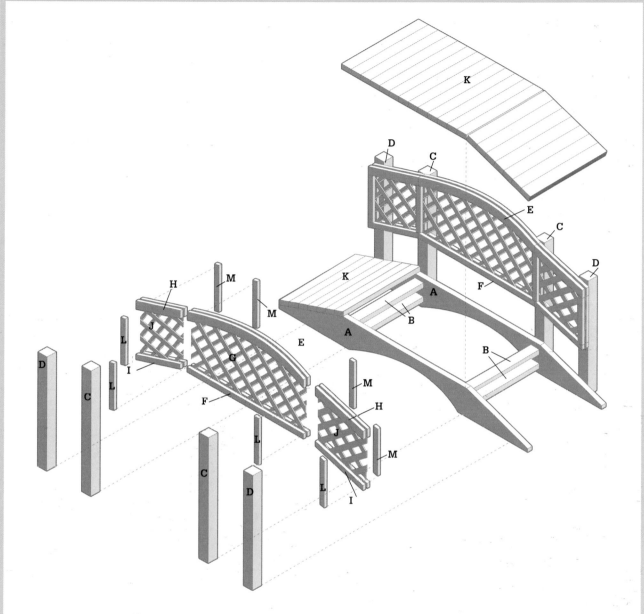

Cutting List

Key	Part	Dimension	Pcs.	Material
A	Stringer	1½ × 9¼ × 96"	2	Cedar
B	Stretcher	1½ × 3½ × 27"	4	Cedar
C	Middle post	3½ × 3½ × 42"	4	Cedar
D	End post	3½ × 3½ × 38"	4	Cedar
E	Center handrail	⅞ × 7¼ × 44½"	4	Cedar
F	Center rail	⅞ × 1½ × 44½"	4	Cedar
G	Center panel	½ × 23½ × 44½"	2	Cedar lattice

Key	Part	Dimension	Pcs.	Material
H	End handrail	⅞ × 2¼ × 19½"	8	Cedar
I	End rail	⅞ × 1½ × 24"	8	Cedar
J	End panel	½ × 19 × 24"	4	Cedar lattice
K	Tread	1½ × 3½ × 30"	27	Cedar
L	Filler strip	⅞ × 1½ × 19"	8	Cedar
M	Trim strip	⅞ × 1½ × 21"	8	Cedar

Garden Bridge

MAKE THE STRINGERS

The stringers are the main structural members of this bridge. Both stringers have arcs cut into their bottom edges, and the ends are cut at a slant to create the gradual tread incline of the garden bridge. Draw several guidelines on the stringers before cutting. First, draw a centerline across the width of each stringer; then mark two more lines across the width of each stringer 24" to the left and right of the centerline; finally, mark the ends of each stringer 1" up from one long edge and draw diagonal lines from these points to the top of each line to the left and right of the center.

Use a circular saw to cut the ends of the stringers along the diagonal lines. Tack a nail on the centerline, 5¼" up from the bottom long edge. Also tack nails along the bottom edge, 20½" to the left and right of the centerline. Lay out the arc at the bottom of each stringer with a marking guide made from a thin, flexible strip of scrap wood or plastic. Hook the middle of the marking guide over the center nail and slide the ends under the outside nails to form a smooth curve. Trace along the guide with a pencil to make the cutting line for the arc (you can mark both

stringers this way, or mark and cut one, then use it as a template for marking the other). Remove the nails and marking guide, and cut the arcs on the bottom edge of each stringer with a jigsaw (**photo 1**).

ASSEMBLE THE BASE

Once the two stringers are cut to shape, they are connected with four straight boards, called "stretchers", to form the base of the bridge. Cut the stretchers, middle posts, and end posts to size. Mark the stretcher locations on the insides of the stringers 1½" from the top and bottom of the stringers. The outside edges of the stretchers should be 24" from the centers of the stringers, leaving the inside edges flush, with the bottoms of the arcs.

Stand the stringers upright and position the stretchers between them. Support the bottom stretchers with 1½"-thick spacer blocks for correct spacing. Fasten the stretchers between the stringers with countersunk 3" deck screws driven through the stringers and into the ends of the stretchers. Turn the stringer assembly upside down, and attach the top stretchers (**photo 2**). The footbridge will get quite

Make the arched cutouts in the bottoms of the 2 x 10 stringers using a jigsaw.

Attach pairs of stretchers between the stringers with 3" deck screws.

Cut the 4 x 4 posts to their finished height, then use lag screws to attach them to the outsides of the stringers.

Attach the treads to the stringers with deck screws.

heavy at this stage: you may want to build the rest of the project on site.

Clamp the middle posts to the outsides of the stringers so the outside edges are 24" from the centers of the stringers. Make sure the middle posts are perpendicular to the stringers. Drill ¼"-dia. guide holes through the stringers and into the middle posts. Attach the middle posts with ⅜"-dia. × 4"-long lag screws driven through the stringers and into the posts (**photo 3**). Clamp the end posts to the stringers, starting 7" from the stringer ends. Drill guide holes and secure the end posts to the stringers with lag screws.

ATTACH THE TREADS
Cut the treads to length. Position the treads on the stringers using a spacer to make sure they are separated by consistent gaps of about ¼". Test-fit all the treads before you begin installing them. Then, secure the treads with 3"-long countersunk deck screws (**photo 4**). Try to keep the screwheads aligned for a more pleasing visual effect.

ATTACH THE CENTER HANDRAIL PANELS
The center panels are made by sandwiching lattice sections between 1 × 2 cedar frames. Each center

panel has an arched top handrail. This arc can be laid out with a flexible marking guide, using the same procedure used for the stringers. Cut the center handrails, center rails, and center panels to size. Using a flexible marking guide, trace an arc that begins 2½" up from one long edge of one center handrail. The top of this arc should touch the top edge of the workpiece. Lower the flexible marking guide 2¼" down on the center handrails. Trace this lower arc, starting at the corners, to mark the finished center handrail shape (**photo 5**). Cut along the bottom arc with a jigsaw. Trace the finished center handrail shapes onto the other workpieces, and cut along the bottom arc lines.

Cut the center panels to size from ½"-thick cedar lattice. Sandwich each center panel between a pair of center handrails so the top and side edges are flush. Clamp the parts, and gang-cut through the panel and center handrails along the top arc line with a jigsaw (**photo 6**). Unfasten the boards, and sand the curves smooth.

Refasten the center panels between the centered rails, ½" down from the tops of the arcs. Drive 2" deck screws through the inside center handrail and into the center panel and outside center handrail. Drive one screw every 4 to 6". Be sure to use pilot holes and make an effort to drive screws through areas where the lattice strips cross, so the screws won't be visible from above.

Fasten the center rails to the bottom of the center panels flush with the bottom edges. Center the panels between the middle posts, and fasten them to the posts so the tops of the handrails are flush with the inside corner of the middle posts at each end. The ends of the handrails are positioned at the center of the posts. Drive 3" deck screws through the center handrails and center rails to secure the panel to the center posts.

Cut the filler strips to size. The filler strips fit between the center handrails and center rails, bracing the panel and providing solid support for the loose ends of the lattice. Position the filler strips in the gaps between the center panels and the middle posts, and fasten them to the middle posts with 2" deck screws (**photo 7**).

ATTACH THE END HANDRAIL PANELS

Like the center panels, the end panels are made by sandwiching cedar lattice sections between board frames and fastening them to posts. The ends of the end panels and the joints between the end and center

panels are covered by trim strips, which are attached with deck screws.

Cut the end handrails, end rails, and end panels to size. Position an end handrail and an end rail on your work surface, then place an end panel over the pieces. Adjust the end handrail and end rail so the top of the panel is ½" down from the top edge of the end handrail. Sandwich the end panels between another set of end handrails and end rails, and attach the parts with 2" deck screws. Repeat the above steps for each end panel.

Clamp or hold the panels against the end posts and middle posts, and adjust the end panels so they are aligned with the center panel and the top inside corner of the end posts. Draw alignment marks near the end of the panels along the outside of the end posts (**photo 8**), and cut the end panels to size. Unclamp the panels, and draw cutting lines connecting the alignment marks. Cut along the lines with a jigsaw.

Sand the end panels, and attach them to the posts with countersunk 3" deck screws, driven through the end handrails and end rails. Slide filler strips between the end panels and the posts. Fasten the filler strips

Lay out the handrails. Use a flexible piece of plastic or wood as a marking guide when drawing the cutting lines for the center handrails.

Cut the panels and center handrails to shape using a jigsaw.

Fasten 1 x 2 filler strips to the posts to close the gaps at the sides of the lattice panels.

Clamp the rough end panels to the posts at the ends of the bridge, and draw alignment markers so you can trim them to fit exactly.

Attach a trim strip over each joint between the end panels and center panels, using deck screws.

with 2" deck screws. Cut the trim strips to size. Attach the trim strips over each joint between the end and center panels and at the outside end of each end panel with countersunk 3" deck screws (**photo 9**).

APPLY FINISHING TOUCHES

Sand all the surfaces to smooth out any rough spots. Apply an exterior wood stain to protect the wood, if desired. You may want to consider leaving the cedar untreated, since that will cause the wood to turn gray—this aging effect may help the bridge blend better with other yard elements. Get some help, and position the bridge in your yard. For a dramatic effect, dig a narrow, meandering trench between two distinct points in your yard, line the trench with landscape fabric, and then fill the trench with landscaping stones to simulate a creek.

Handling Lattice Panels ▸

Lattice panels must be handled carefully, or they may fall apart. This is especially true when you are cutting the lattice panels. Before making any cuts, clamp two boards around the panel, close to the cutting line, to stabilize the lattice and protect it from the vibration of the saw. Always use a long, fine blade on your saw when cutting lattice.

Compost Bin

Composting yard debris is an increasingly popular practice that makes good environmental sense. Composting is the process of converting organic waste into rich fertilizer for the soil, usually in a compost bin. A well-designed compost bin has a few key features. It's big enough to contain the organic material as it decomposes. It allows cross-flow of air to speed the process. And the bin area is easy to reach whether you're adding waste, turning the compost, or removing the composted material. This compost bin has all these features, plus one additional benefit not shared by most compost bins: it's very attractive.

Grass clippings, leaves, weeds, and vegetable waste are some of the most commonly composted materials. Just about any formerly living organic material can be composted, but DO NOT add any of the following items to your compost bin:

- animal material or waste
- dairy products
- papers with colored inks

For more information on composting, contact your local library or agricultural extension office.

Materials ▸

4 4 × 4" × 4 ft. cedar posts	Hook-and-eye latch mechanism
5 2 × 2" × 8 ft. cedar	3 × 3" brass butt hinges (one pair)
8 1 × 6" × 8 ft. cedar fence boards	
1½", 3" galvanized deck screws	

Convert organic waste into garden fertilizer inside the confines of this easy-to-make cedar compost bin.

Compost Bin

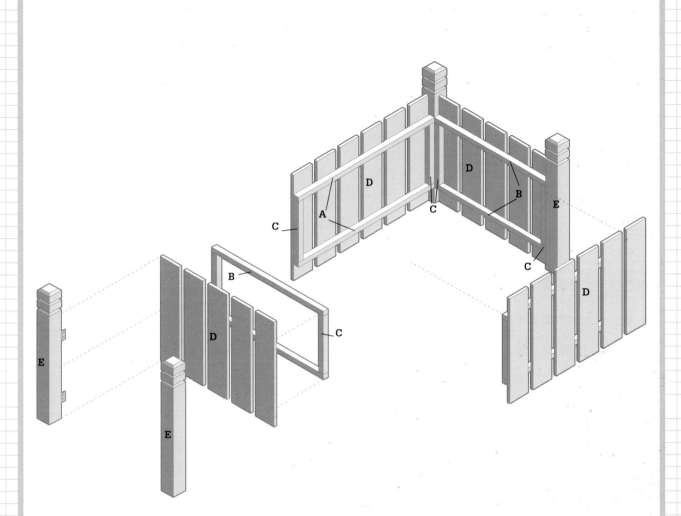

Cutting List

Key	Part	Dimension	Pcs.	Material
A	Side rail	1½ × 1½ × 40½"	4	Cedar
B	End rail	1½ × 1½ × 33½"	4	Cedar
C	Cleat	1½ × 1½ × 15"	8	Cedar
D	Slat	¾ × 5½ × 27"	22	Cedar
E	Post	3½ × 3½ × 30"	4	Cedar

Compost Bin

BUILD THE PANELS

The four fence-type panels that make up the sides of this compost bin are cedar slats that attach to panel frames. The panel frames for the front and back of the bin are longer than the frames for the sides. Cut the side rails, end rails, and cleats to length. Group pairs of matching rails with a pair of cleats. Assemble each group into a frame—the cleats should be between the rails, flush with the ends. Drill ⅛"-dia. pilot holes into the rails. Counterbore the holes ¼" deep using a counterbore bit. Fasten all four panel frames together by driving 3" deck screws through the rails and into each end of each cleat (**photo 1**).

Cut all of the slats to length. Lay the frames on a flat surface and place a slat at each end of each frame. Keep the edges of these outer slats flush with the outside edges of the frame and let the bottoms of the slats overhang the bottom frame rail by 4". Drill pilot holes in the slats. Counterbore the holes slightly. Fasten the outer slats to the frames with 1½" deck screws (**photo 2**).

When you have fastened the outer slats to all of the frames, add slats between each pair of outer slats to fill out the panels. Insert a 1½" spacing block between the slats to set the correct gap. This will allow air to flow into the bin. Be sure to keep the ends of the slats aligned.

Check with a tape measure to make sure the bottoms of all the slats are 4" below the bottom of the panel frame (**photo 3**).

ATTACH THE PANELS & POSTS

The four slatted panels are joined with corner posts to make the bin. Three of the panels are attached permanently to the posts, while one of the end panels is installed with hinges and a latch so it can swing open like a gate. You can use plain 4 × 4 cedar posts for the corner posts. For a more decorative look, buy prefabricated fence posts or deck rail posts with carving or contours at the top.

Cut the posts to length. If you're using plain posts, you may want to do some decorative contouring at one end or attach post caps. Stand a post upright on a flat work surface. Set one of the longer slatted panels next to the post, resting on the bottoms of the slats. Hold or clamp the panel to the post, with the back of the panel frame flush with the inside face of the post. Fasten the panel to the post by driving 3" deck screws through the frame cleats and into the posts. Space screws at roughly 8" intervals.

Stand another post on end, and fasten the other end of the panel frame to it, making sure the posts

Fasten the cleats between the rails to construct the panel frames.

Attach a slat at each end of the panel frame so the outer edges of the slats are flush with the outer edges of the frame.

are aligned. Fasten one of the shorter panels to the adjoining face of one of the posts. The back faces of the frames should meet at the inside corner of the post (**photo 4**). Fasten another post at the free end of the shorter panel. Fasten the other longer panel to the posts so it is opposite the first longer panel, forming a U-shaped structure.

ATTACH THE GATE

The unattached shorter panel is attached at the open end of the bin with hinges to create a swinging gate for loading and unloading material. Exterior wood stain or a clear wood sealer with UV protectant will keep the cedar from turning gray. If you are planning to apply a finish, it's easier to apply it before you hang the gate. Make sure all hardware is rated for exterior use.

Set the last panel between the posts at the open end of the bin. Move the sides of the bin slightly, if needed, so there is about ¼" of clearance between each end of the panel and the posts. Remove this panel gate and attach a pair of 3" butt hinges to a cleat, making sure the barrels of the hinges extend past the face of the outer slats. Set the panel into the opening, and mark the location of the hinge plates onto the post. Open the hinge so it is flat, and attach it to the post (**photo 5**). Attach a hook-and-eye latch to the unhinged end of the panel to hold the gate closed.

Continue to attach slats. The inner slats should be 1½" apart, with the ends 4" below the bottom of the frame.

Stand the posts and panels upright, and fasten the panels to the posts by driving screws through the cleats.

Attach exterior-rated hinges to the end panel frame and then fasten them to the post. Add a latch on the other side of the hinged panel.

Pagoda Lantern

Enhance your landscape with this decorative pagoda lantern. It will act as an interesting focal point within your garden by day and its glow makes it even more inviting at night. It's made from commonly available dimensional lumber—four pieces of 1 × 6 and one piece of 2 × 2. You can stain the wood to complement the surrounding landscape or you might choose to stain it or paint it to look like the Asian structures that inspired its design.

The stacked tiers of the pagoda are frames that are attached to four corner legs. Connecting four crosspieces with half-lap joints makes each frame. The top frame features similar construction to the sides and is capped with a square piece and a wood ball to create the peak. Any 2"-dia. wood ball (or even a copper ball) will work as the cap ball, but it should ideally be made from exterior-rated wood. You can also use a manufactured post cap for the cap plate and ball.

Candles illuminate this lantern. The candles are placed on a tile base and can be placed within a glass vase or hurricane lantern shade to prevent burning the wood structure.

Materials ▸

1 1½ × 1½" × 8 ft. white oak	1 6" to 10"-dia. glass hurricane shade
4 ¾" × 5½" × 8 ft. white oak	2" exterior-rated screws
1 2" dia. ball white oak or other	1½" galvanized finish nails
1 12 × 12" ceramic tile	

Big enough to make a statement but compact enough to fit just about anywhere, this oak lantern can house large outdoor candles or even a low-voltage landscape light.

Pagoda Lantern

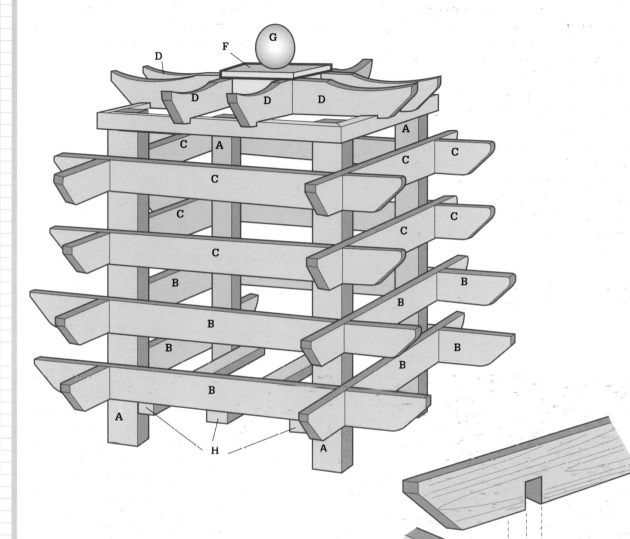

HALF-LAP DETAIL

Cutting List

Key	Part	Dimension	Pcs.	Material
A	Legs	$1\frac{1}{2} \times 1\frac{1}{2} \times 21"$	4	White Oak
B	Bottom crosspieces	$\frac{3}{4} \times 2\frac{1}{4} \times 27"$	8	White Oak
C	Middle crosspieces	$\frac{3}{4} \times 2\frac{1}{4} \times 24"$	8	White Oak
D	Crown crosspieces	$\frac{3}{4} \times 2\frac{1}{4} \times 21"$	4	White Oak
E	Top rails	$\frac{3}{4} \times 1 \times 15"$	4	White Oak
F	Crown plate	$\frac{3}{4} \times 5\frac{1}{2} \times 5\frac{1}{2}"$	1	White Oak
G	Crown ball	2" dia. ball	1	Wood or copper
H	Bottom slats	$\frac{3}{4} \times 1\frac{1}{2} \times 15"$	3	White Oak

Pagoda Lantern

MAKE THE CROSSPIECES & TOP RAIL

If you do some careful planning and marking, the crosspieces can be cut from three 8-foot-long, 1 × 6 boards. First, cut the boards to length. Cut one 1 × 6 into four 24" pieces. Then cut two 27" boards and two 21" boards from each of the other two 1 × 6s. Cut the 1 × 6 pieces in half lengthwise, leaving you with the twenty 2¼" wide crosspieces (**photo 1**).

Use a miter saw to trim the bottom corners (1¾ × 1¾") off each end of the crosspieces (**photo 2**). You can also use a table saw and miter gauge to make these cuts. The crosspieces fit together with half-lap joints in much the manner of toy building logs.

The half-lap notches are 1⅛" deep and equal to the thickness of the crosspieces (¾ to ⅞"). To lay out the notches, mark the center of the middle and bottom crosspieces and then make a mark 7½" on each side of the centerline to designate the inside edge of the notches. Mark the center of the top crosspieces and then make a mark 1¾" on each side of the centerline to designate the inside edge of the notches. Cut the notches in several crosspieces at the same time to save time and ensure consistent notch widths.

You must flip half of the crosspieces for each size upside-down so that you end up with an equal number of pieces with notch cuts on the top and on the

Rip-cut the stock. On a table saw (if you have access to one), rip-cut each piece of 1 × 6 stock for the crosspieces into two equal strips that are approximately 2¼" wide.

Trim the crosspiece corners. Set the miter saw to make a 45° cut and make each cut 1¾" from each end.

bottom edge. You can use a table saw, router, or circular saw to cut the half-lap notches. Use a miter gauge to guide the pieces on a table saw, making several passes to cut the full width. Use a straight-edge to guide a circular saw or router (**photo 3**).

Mark the arc profile along the top edge of the four top crosspieces. Cut along the arc line with a jigsaw or band saw.

Cut 15"-long top rail pieces to length from 1× 2 stock. Then, rip the four pieces down to 1" wide. Cut 45° miters in each end of the top rails. Mark the center of each top rail piece and then make a mark 1¾" on each side of the centerline to designate the inside edge of the notches that will hold the top crosspieces. Use the same method

you used to cut the notches in the crosspieces to cut two ¼"-deep notches in the top edge of each top rail piece (**photo 4**). Sand the faces smooth and ease the outside edges of all of the crosspieces.

BUILD THE BASE

Assemble the crosspiece frames. Apply exterior-rated glue to the notches and clamp the crosspiece frames together. Drill countersunk pilot holes through the bottom of each joint and drive a 2" screw into each joint (**photo 5**).

Cut the legs to length and then attach them to the crosspiece frames. Cut four 3"-wide spacer blocks to position the bottom frame on the legs. Apply glue to the inside faces of the crosspiece-frame corners and

Cut half-lap notches. Clamp the crosspieces together with the notch cutout marks aligned. Use several passes with a router and straight bit to remove the waste material from the notches, lowering the bit ¼" for each pass.

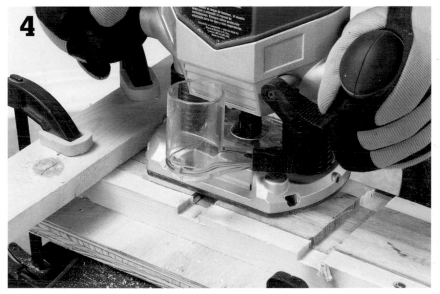

Notch the top rails. Clamp the top rails together and cut two ¼"-deep notches that are the same width as the rail stock. Use a router setup with a straight bit and straightedge guide. *TIP: Position a piece of scrap the same thickness as the workpieces on each side so the router bit will enter the workpieces cleanly with no tear-out.*

clamp them to the legs. Drill one countersunk pilot hole at each corner and secure with a 2" screw.

Cut four 2"-wide spacer blocks to position each of the next three frames over the previous frame. Secure each frame to the legs with glues and 2" screws (**photo 6**). Glue and clamp the top rails to the legs and attach them with 2" screws. Attach the bottom slats to the bottom crosspiece frame with 2" screws.

BUILD THE CROWN

Apply glue to the crown crosspiece notches and clamp them together. Secure them by driving 2" screws through the bottom of the joint. Cut the crown plate to size and drill a ¼"-dia. pilot hole through the center of the crown plate and a ³⁄₁₆"-dia. x 1¼" pilot hole in

the center of the base of the ball. Position the crown ball over the center of the cap plate and attach it with a 2" screw (**photo 7**). Attach the cap plate to the top crosspiece frame with 1½" galvanized finish nails (**photo 8**). Drill a ¹⁄₁₆" pilot hole for each nail.

LIGHT YOUR LANTERN

You can apply an exterior stain to add color to the wood and help protect it from decay or you can let it age naturally. Place a 12" square tile on the bottom slats inside the base. Use one to three candles to illuminate the lantern. Place large candles inside a glass vase or hurricane shade to protect the wood parts from burning and protect the candle flame from the wind.

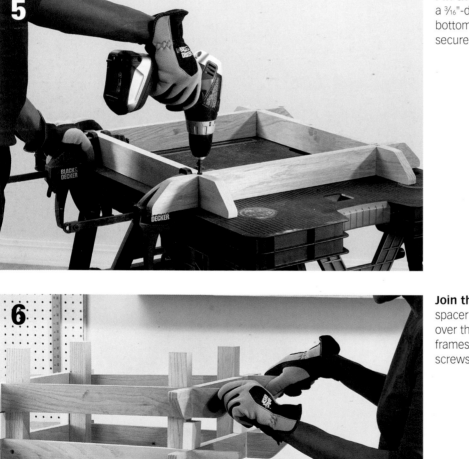

Pin the crosspieces together. Drill a ³⁄₁₆"-dia. x 2"-deep pilot hole in the bottom of each crosspiece joint and secure the joints with 2" screws.

Join the crosspiece frames. Use 2" spacer blocks to position each frame over the previous frame. Attach the frames to the legs with glue and 2" screws.

7

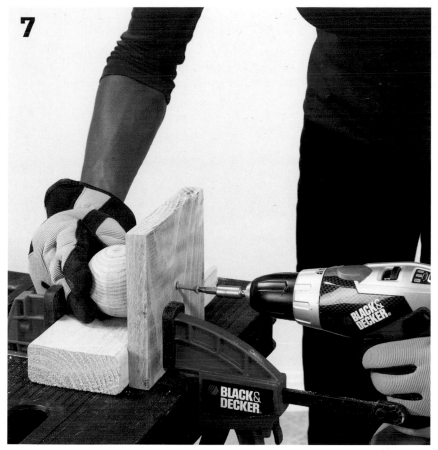

Make the crown. Attach the crown plate to the crown ball with a 2" screw.

8

Make the crowning touch. Attach the cap plate to the top crosspiece frame with galvanized finish nails. Drill a pilot hole for each nail to prevent splitting the wood.

Yard Cart

A good yard cart makes your work easier and saves time. This is just such a yard cart. It doesn't feature any fancy gadgets, bells, or whistles, but it's versatile, durable, and handles nicely so you can move tools and materials around your yard with ease. It is also easy to build.

The hauling bed for this cart is large enough to hold a quarter of a cubic yard of mulch or yard waste, a large mortar mixing tub, a dozen cans of paint, or several potted plants. The front gate lifts out for ease of access when loading contents in the front and makes dumping your cart even easier.

This yard cart is designed to roll on a pair of 26" bicycle wheels. The large diameter wheels won't get hung up on rocks, bumps, or any other rough yard terrain. You can use pneumatic (air filled) tires, but airless, solid tires are less expensive and won't go flat when you need the cart most. In addition, this cart is built with pressure-treated lumber and corrosion-resistant hardware, so it will hold up to years of helping you haul wet or dry materials.

Materials ▸

4 2 × 4" × 8 ft. treated pine	Exterior-rated screws (1¼", 1½")
1 1 × 2" × 8 ft. treated pine	2 ½ × 8" stainless steel bolts
1 ½" × 4 × 8 ft. ext. plywood	2 ½"stainless steel locknuts
1 1"-dia. × 24" conduit	6 ½" stainless steel washers
2 26"-dia. wheels	

These familiar yard carts have plenty of carrying capacity and the large bicycle-style tires help them navigate rough terrain. New carts of this type cost around $300, but you can build one yourself for much less

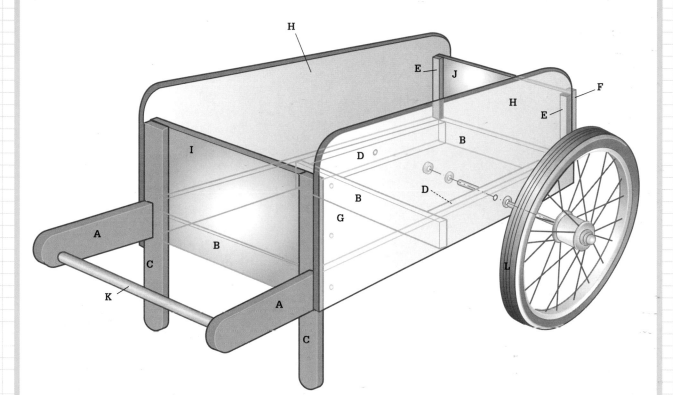

Cutting List

Key	Part	Dimension	Pcs.	Material
A	Base rails	1½ × 3½ × 61½"	2	Treated pine
B	Cross supports	1½ × 3½ × 21"	3	Treated pine
C	Legs	1½ × 3½ × 24"	2	Treated pine
D	Axle blocks	1½ × 3½ × 20"	2	Treated pine
E	Short gate guide	¾ × 1½ × 8"	2	Treated pine
F	Long gate guide	¾ × 1½ × 12"	2	Treated pine

Key	Part	Dimension	Pcs.	Material
G	Bottom	½ × 24 × 45"	1	Ext. Plywood
H	Sides	½ × 16 × 48"	2	Ext. Plywood
I	Back	½ × 8 × 23½"	1	Ext. Plywood
J	Gate	½ × 8 × 23½"	1	Ext. Plywood
K	Handle	1"-dia. × 22½"	1	Conduit
L	Wheels	26"-dia.	2	

Yard Cart

BUILD THE FRAME

Cut the base rails, cross supports, legs, and axle blocks to length. Cut a 1¾" radius in one end of each base rail and leg. Cut a 1½ x 3½" notch in each leg to fit around the base rail (**photo 1**). The bottom of the notch is located 12" up from the bottom of the leg. The handle is secured between the base rails inside round mortises that are 1"-dia. x ¾"-deep. Measure in 2½" from the end and 1" up from the bottom edge of the base rail to find the center of the handle mortises. Bore the handle mortises with a 1" Forstner bit mounted in a drill press (**photo 2**) or use a 1" spade bit in a portable drill.

Cut the 22½" long piece of 1"-dia. dowel or aluminum conduit that will be the handle. Clamp the handle and cross supports between the base rails. Attach the cross supports to the base rails with 2½" screws. Attach the axle blocks to the base rails with

Cut the base rail notch. Draw the notch edge lines on each leg. Use a jigsaw to cut along the notch layout lines.

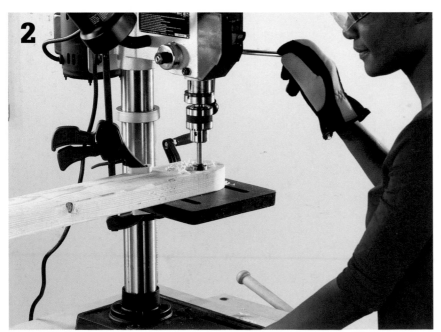

Cut the round handle mortises. Use a Forstner bit to bore the handle mortises. Forstner bits feature flat sharp edges on the bottom that cut a flat bottom hole. They are designed for use with drill presses, not portable drills. If you don't have a drill press use a 1" spade bit and a portable drill.

2½" screws. Attach the legs to the base rails with 2½" screws (**photo 3**).

ATTACH THE PANELS

Cut the bottom, sides, back, and gate to length and width. Round the corners of the gate with a jigsaw or sander. Then, cut the grip hole in the gate (**photo 4**). Cut 3"-radius curves into the top corners of the sides. Attach the bottom panel to the base rails and cross supports with 1¼" deck screws. Attach the back to the legs with 1¼" deck screws. Attach the sides to the base rails and legs with 1¼" screws (**photo 5**). Cut the gate guides to length and attach them with 1" screws (**photo 6**).

ATTACH THE WHEELS

Bore ½"-dia. holes in the base rails for the axle bolts. Pay special attention to keep these holes perpendicular to the base rails. Fasten the wheels with ½"-dia. x 8" stainless steel (or hot dipped galvanized) bolts. Place flat washers at each end of the bolt and between the wheel and the side panel (**photo 7**).

Assemble the base frame parts. Fit the leg notches over the base rails and attach the legs with 2½" screws.

Cut the grip hole in the gate. Drill 1"-dia. holes at each end of the grip hole in the gate. Then use a jigsaw to make cuts connecting the two holes, forming a 6"-long slot.

Attach the cart sides. Fasten the bottom panel, back panel, and side panels to the cart frame with 1¼" deck screws.

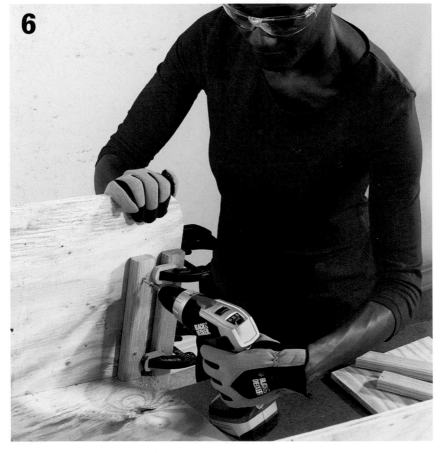

Install the gate guides. Apply exterior glue to the gate guides and clamp them to the side panels. Secure the gate guides with 1" screws.

7

Attach the wheels. Fasten the wheels to the base rails with ½" bolts and locknuts. Position flat washers between the wheel and base rails.

Another Way to Roll ▸

Yard and garden carts come in many sizes and shapes designed for various purposes. Some, like the bicycle-tire cart featured in this chapter, are designed to haul a relatively large volume of yard waste or supplies. But if your primary need is for a manageable cart that can be used to transport tools (especially long-handled garden tools) from your garage or shed to your gardens, one like this may be more to your liking. Made from solid cedar, its 4 cu. ft. won't handle more than one or two bags of potting soil on the cargo side. But the handle racks make transporting shovels and rakes much easier and safer.

Yard Structures

Building permanent or semipermanent structures is the essence of carpentry. In our yards, structures take many forms. The arbor-and-trellis, the pergola, gates, and small specialty shelters are among the most common. In this chapter, we explore such carpentry projects.

The main purpose of many outdoor yard structures is to provide shade. Often, this goal is achieved with an arbor that is used to train vines and other climbing plants. In the warmth of summer, when shade is most needed, the plants reach full flower and cut the harsh sunlight within the arbor. We show you how to build a freestanding arbor that can be moved around the yard and another arbor that has lattice sides to block both wind and sun, even without plants. Several other arbor designs are incorporated into gate and fence structures.

Finally, there is wood fencing. Because fencing projects are very popular among outdoor carpenters, we include comprehensive projects for the two major types: those made with prefabricated wood panels, and those built stick by stick.

In this chapter:

- Freestanding Arbor
- Lattice Arbor
- Trash Can Corral
- Firewood Shelter
- Picket Fence
- Wood Panel Fence
- Basic Gates
- Arched Gate
- Trellis Gate
- Classical Pergola

Freestanding Arbor

This freestanding arbor combines the beauty and durability of natural cedar with an Asian-inspired design. Set it up on your patio or deck or in a quiet corner of your backyard. It adds just the right finishing touch to turn your outdoor living space into a showplace geared for relaxation and quiet contemplation.

The arbor has a long history as a focal point in gardens and other outdoor areas throughout the world. And if privacy and shade are concerns, you can enhance the sheltering quality by adding climbing vines that weave their way in and out of the trellis. Or, simply set a few potted plants around the base to help the arbor blend in with the outdoor environment. Another way to integrate plant life into your arbor is to hang decorative potted plants from the top beams.

This arbor is freestanding, so it can be easily moved to a new site whenever you desire. Or, you can anchor it permanently to a deck or to the ground and equip it with a built-in seat.

Sturdy posts made from 2 × 4 cedar serve as the base of the arbor, forming a framework for a 1 × 2 trellis system that scales the sides and top. The curved cutouts that give the arbor its Asian appeal are made with a jigsaw, then smoothed out with a drill and drum sander for a more finished appearance.

Materials ▸

7 1 × 2" × 8 ft. cedar	8 ⅜"-dia. × 2½" lag
9 2 × 4" × 8 ft. cedar	screws
3 2 × 6" × 8 ft. cedar	4 6" lag screws
Wood glue (exterior)	Deck screws
Wood sealer or stain	(2½", 3")
#10 × 2½" wood	Finishing materials
screws	

Create a shady retreat on a sunny patio or deck with this striking cedar arbor.

Freestanding Arbor

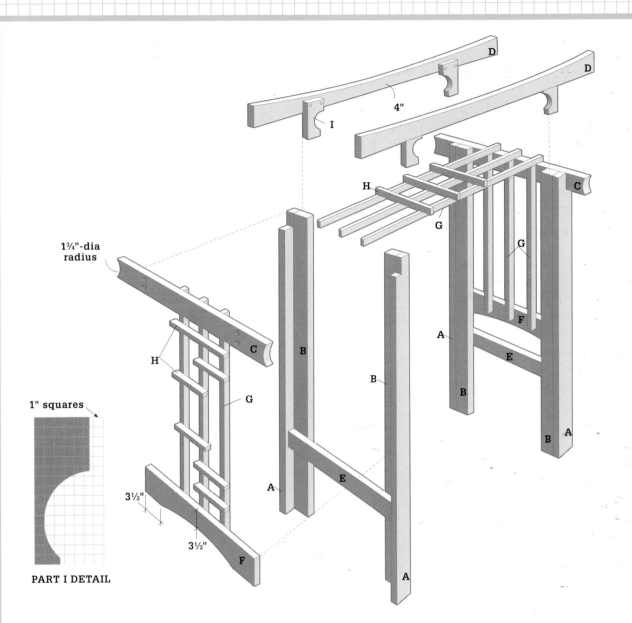

1¾"-dia radius

1" squares

PART I DETAIL

3½"

3½"

4"

Cutting List

Key	Part	Dimension	Pcs.	Material
A	Leg front	1½ × 3½ × 72"	4	Cedar
B	Leg side	1½ × 3½ × 72"	4	Cedar
C	Cross beam	1½ × 3½ × 36"	2	Cedar
D	Top beam	1½ × 5½ × 72"	2	Cedar
E	Side rail	1½ × 3½ × 21"	2	Cedar

Key	Part	Dimension	Pcs.	Material
F	Side spreader	1½ × 5½ × 21"	2	Cedar
G	Trellis strip	⅞ × 1½ × 48"	9	Cedar
H	Cross strip	⅞ × 1½ × *	15	Cedar
I	Brace	1½ × 5½ × 15"	4	Cedar

*Cut to fit

Freestanding Arbor

MAKE THE LEGS

Each of the four arbor legs is made from two 6-foot-long pieces of 2 × 4 cedar fastened at right angles with 3" deck screws. Cut the leg fronts and leg sides to length.

Position the leg sides at right angles to the leg fronts, with top and bottom edges flush. Apply moisture-resistant glue to the joint. Attach the leg fronts to the leg sides by driving evenly spaced screws through the faces of the fronts and into the edges of the sides (**photo 1**). Use a jigsaw to cut a 3½"-long × 2"-wide notch at the top outside corner of each leg front (**photo 2**). These notches cradle the crossbeams when the arbor is assembled.

MAKE THE CROSSBEAMS, RAILS & SPREADERS

Cut the crossbeams to length and then cut a small arc at both ends of each part. Start by using a compass

to draw a 3½"-dia. semicircle at the edge of a strip of cardboard. Cut out the semicircle, and use the strip as a template for marking the arcs (**photo 3**). Cut out the arcs with a jigsaw. Sand the cuts smooth with a drill and drum sander.

Cut two side spreaders to length. The side spreaders fit just above the side rails on each side. Mark a curved cutting line on the bottom of each spreader. To mark the cutting lines, draw starting points 3½" in from each end of a spreader. Make a reference line 2" up from the bottom of the spreader board. Tack a casing nail on the reference line, centered between the ends of the spreader. With the spreader clamped to the work surface, also tack nails into the work surface next to the starting lines on the spreader. Slip a thin strip of metal or plastic between the casing nails so the strip bows out to create a smooth arc. Trace the arc onto the spreader, then cut along the line with a jigsaw. Smooth with a

Create four legs by fastening leg sides to leg fronts at right angles.

Cut a 2 x 4-size notch in the top of each of the four leg pairs to hold the crossbeams.

Lay out profiles on the ends of the crossbeams. A piece of cardboard acts as a template when you trace the outline for the arc.

Lag-screw the crossbeams to the legs, and fasten the spreaders and rails with deck screws to assemble the side frames.

drum sander. Use the first spreader as a template for marking and cutting the second spreader.

Cut the side rails to length. They are fitted between pairs of legs on each side of the arbor, near the bottom, to keep the arbor square.

ASSEMBLE THE SIDE FRAMES

Each side frame consists of a front and back leg joined together by a side rail, a side spreader, and a crossbeam. Lay two leg assemblies parallel on a work surface, with the notched board in each leg facing up. Space the legs so the inside faces of the notched boards are 21" apart. Set a crossbeam into the notches, overhanging each leg by 6". Also set a side spreader and a side rail between the legs for spacing.

Drill ⅜"-dia. pilot holes in the crossbeam. Counterbore the holes to ¼" depth using a counterbore bit. Attach the crossbeam to each leg with glue. Drive two ⅜"-dia. x 2½" lag screws through the crossbeam and into the legs (**photo 4**). Position the side spreader between the legs so the top is 29½" up from the bottoms of the legs. Position the side rail 18" up from the leg bottoms. Drill ⅛" counterbored pilot holes into the spreader and rail

through the leg faces. Keeping the legs parallel, attach the pieces with glue and drive 3" deck screws through the outside faces of the legs and into the side rails and spreaders.

ATTACH THE SIDE TRELLIS PIECES

Each side trellis is made from vertical strips of cedar 1 × 2 that are fastened to the side frames. Horizontal cross strips will be added later to create a decorative cross-hatching effect. Cut three vertical trellis strips to length for each side frame. Space them so they are 2⅜" apart, with the ends flush with the top of the crossbeam (**photo 5**).

Drill pilot holes to attach the trellis strips to the crossbeam and spreader. Counterbore the holes and drive 2½" deck screws. Repeat the procedure for the other side frame.

CUT & SHAPE TOP BEAMS

Cut two top beams to length. Draw 1½"-deep arcs at the top edges of the top beams, starting at the ends of each of the boards. Cut the arcs into the top beams with a jigsaw. Sand smooth—use a drum sander, if you have one.

ASSEMBLE TOP & SIDES

Because the side frames are fairly heavy and bulky, you will need to brace them in an upright position to fasten the top beams between them. A simple way to do this is to use a pair of 1 × 4 braces to connect the tops and bottoms of the side frames (**photo 6**). Clamp the ends of the braces to the side frames so the side frames are 4 ft. apart, and use a level to make sure the side frames are plumb.

Mark a centerpoint for a lag bolt 12¾" from each end of each top beam. Drill a ¼"-dia. counterbored pilot hole through the top edge at the centerpoint. Set the top beams on top of the crossbraces of the side frames. Mark the pilot hole locations onto the crossbeams. Remove the top beams and drill pilot holes into the crossbeams. Secure the top beams to the crossbeams with 6" lag screws.

Cut four braces to length, and transfer the brace cutout pattern from the Diagram on page 183 to each board. Cut the patterns with a jigsaw. Attach the braces at the joints where the leg fronts meet the top beams, using 2½" deck screws. To make sure the arbor assembly stays in position while you complete the project, attach 1 × 2 scraps between the front legs and between the back legs (**photo 7**). Cut and attach three trellis strips between the top beams.

ADD TRELLIS CROSS STRIPS

Cut the cross strips to 7" and 10" lengths. Use wood screws to attach them at 3" intervals in a staggered pattern on the side trellis pieces. You can adjust the sizes and placement of the cross strips but, for best appearance, retain some symmetry of placement. Fasten cross strips to the top trellis in the same manner. Make sure the cross strips that fit across the top trellis are arranged in similar fashion to the side strips (**photo 8**).

APPLY FINISHING TOUCHES

To protect the arbor, coat the cedar wood with clear wood sealer. After the finish dries, the arbor is ready to be placed onto your deck or patio or in a quiet corner of your yard. Because of its sturdy construction, the arbor can simply be set onto a hard, flat surface. If you plan to install a permanent seat in the arbor, you should anchor it to the ground. For decks, try to position the arbor so you can screw the legs to the rim of the deck or toenail the legs into the deck boards. You can buy fabricated metal post stakes, available at most building centers, to use when anchoring the arbor to the ground.

Attach trellis strips to the crossbrace and spreader with deck screws.

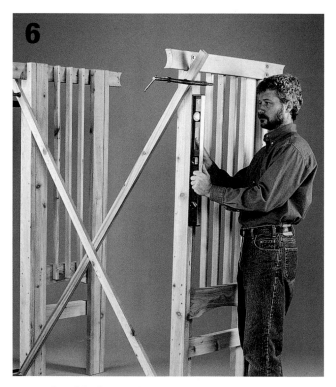

Brace the side frames in an upright, level position with long pieces of 1 x 4 while you attach the top beams.

7

Lock the legs in a square position after assembling the arbor by tacking strips of wood between the front legs and between the back legs.

8

Attach the trellis cross strips to spice up the design and assist climbing plants.

Where to Put Your Arbor ▸

There are no firm rules about arbor placement. It can be positioned to provide a focal point for a porch, patio, or deck. Placed against a wall or at the end of a plain surface, arbors improve the general look of the area. With some thick climbing vines and vegetation added to the arbor, you can also disguise a utility area, such as a trash collection space.

Add a Seat ▸

Create an arbor seat by resting two 2 × 10 cedar boards on the rails in each side frame. Overhang the rails by 6" or so, and drive a few 3" deck screws through the boards and into the rails to secure the seat.

Lattice Arbor

Arbors continue to be popular landscape structures. The sight of this graceful arched arbor, laden with sprays of colorful blossoms, will provide a stunning highlight in your garden and landscape.

Building this arbor requires average carpentry skills, common carpentry tools, and a free weekend. Making the arches at the top is the most difficult part of the job. You need to glue the edges of two pairs of 5-foot-long 2 ×12s to make the 1½ × 22½ × 60" blanks from which the arches are cut. For this job it helps if you have a biscuit joiner or a doweling jig and dowels to reinforce the edge joints and assist with the alignment of the parts.

We built this arbor from clear heart redwood. Dimensional cedar, hemlock, or cypress are good alternatives, too, depending on which wood species are native to your area. If you plan to paint the project you can save money by using treated (or even untreated) pine stock.

The best time to install an arbor is well before planting, even before you pick the specific flowers to grow. Arbors are ideal for climbing, pillar, or rambling roses or perennial climbers such as honeysuckle, clematis, or white jasmine. Even annual climbers such as morning glories will drape themselves elegantly over an arbor; sweet peas will scramble up its sides. For a special, old-fashioned touch, plant mounds of lavender on both sides of the arbor, just in front of the climbers.

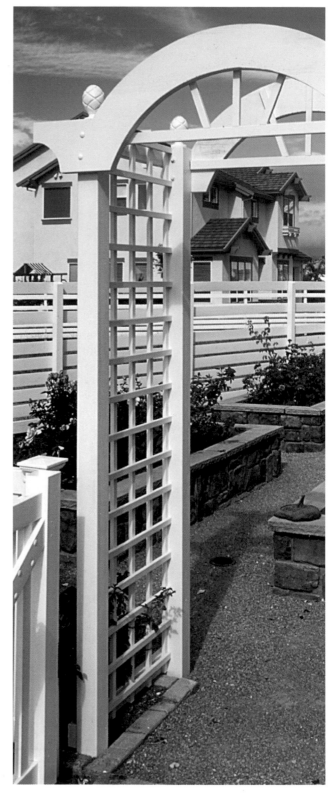

Marking the entry point to a gravel walkway, this lattice arbor defines space and also provides a home for climbing plants.

Materials ▸

4 4 × 4" × 10 ft. redwood	Deck screws (1½", 2½")
2 2 × 4" × 8 ft. redwood	8 ⅜ × 6" carriage bolts with washers and nuts
2 2 × 12" × 10 ft. redwood	Moisture-resistant wood glue
1 2 × 2" × 8 ft. redwood	Gravel
150 lineal ft. ¾ × ¾" redwood	Concrete mix
4 Post finials	Finishing materials
Galvanized finish nails (3d, 6d, 8d)	

Lattice Arbor

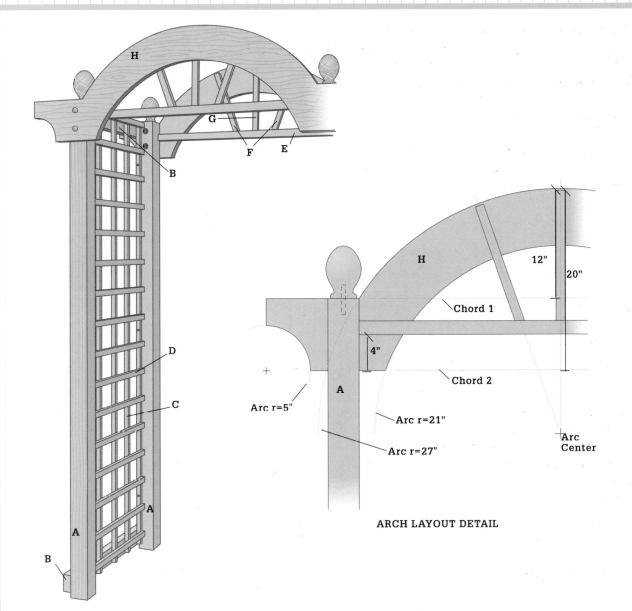

ARCH LAYOUT DETAIL

Cutting List

Key	Part	Dimension	Pcs.	Material
A	Upright	3½ × 3½" × 10 ft.	4	Redwood
B	Cross rail	1½ × 3½ × 36½"	4	Redwood
C	Vertical lattice	¾ × ¾" × 7 ft.	10	Redwood
D	Horiz. lattice	¾ × ¾ × 28"	32	Redwood
E	Mullion crossbars	1½ × 1½ × 41"	2	Redwood
F	Short mullions	¾ × ¾ × 6"	4	Redwood
G	Long mullions	¾ × ¾" × 8"	2	Redwood
H	Arch stock	1½ × 11¼ × 5 ft.	4	Redwood

Lattice Arbor

PREPARE THE STOCK

Before you can cut the parts to length, do a bit of prep work. Each arch is made from two 2 × 12s edge-glued together. When edge-gluing, it is always best to glue fresh-cut edges that have been run through a jointer. But because this is an exterior project (and especially if you plan to paint it) you can probably get away with simply rip-cutting the mating edges on a table saw and sanding them lightly. If you have a biscuit joiner (also called a plate joiner) use biscuits to align the edge-glued boards. Apply glue to the dressed edges and align the boards (**photo 1**). Clamp the workpieces together with bar clamps or pipe clamps and allow to dry for 24 hours.

To make stock for the lattice and mullions, purchase 1× ¾" thick lumber and rip into ¾" wide strips on a table saw. You need at least 150 lineal feet and ten strips that are a full 7 ft. long. Seven 12 ft. boards will maximize yield.

LAY OUT & CUT THE ARCHES

On template paper, draw two concentric arcs with radii of 21" and 27". Draw parallel chord lines 12" and 20" from the outer arc. Mark two points along each side of the top chord: 10½" from the large arc and, along the bottom chord, 8½" from the small arc. Use a framing square to draw a 3" line down from the upper mark (see Arch Layout Detail, page 189). Join the line to the bottom chord with a 5"-radius circle. Transfer the pattern to the laminated arch stock. Use a jigsaw or band saw to cut the arch. For best results, cut slightly outside the cutting lines and then sand up to the lines with a power sander.

FIT THE MULLIONS

The mullions are the wood strips in the tops of the arches that create a sunburst appearance. To install them, mark a line 4" above and parallel to the bottom of the back of each arch. Align the bottom of the crossbar to the line; glue and nail it in place. Mark the centerpoint of the crossbar and measure to the left and right 4½", marking the two points. Mark the centerpoint of the arch top and points 9½" to each side of the curve. Extend lines through the marks.

Center a mullion on each line, flush to the arch top. Trace the crossbar onto the short mullion bases and make bevel cuts along the cutting lines so the bases rest flat on the crossbar. Glue and toenail the mullions to the arches; glue them to the crossbar. Reinforce the joints between the crossbar and the mullions by drilling $\frac{1}{32}$"-dia. pilot holes through the crossbar and into each mullion (**photo 2**); fasten each with an 8d finish nail.

ASSEMBLE THE LATTICE

Cut eight spacers from ¾ x ¾" stock, each one 5⅛" long. On a layout table, use the spacers to position the vertical lattice strips parallel with one another and flush at the top. Tack the lattice to the work surface. Nail the first horizontal lattice piece so it is aligned with the top of the vertical lattice pieces using 3d finish nails. Use two spacer blocks to position and nail each subsequent course (**photo 3**). Repeat to create the lattice for the opposite side of the arbor.

Set the uprights at the edges of the lattice and position the cross rails flush with the ends of the

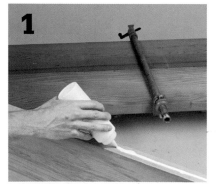

Edge-glue pieces of 2 × 12 to create workpieces large enough to be made into the arches. Use pipe clamps or bar clamps to secure the workpieces while the glue sets.

TIP: Reinforce joints in the arc after cutting it from the laminated blank. Drive screws through pilot holes for reinforcement.

Custom-fit the mullions to the arch, making bevel cuts at the bottoms so they rest flat on the crossbar. Fasten them to the arch and crossbar.

Assemble the lattice. Lay out the vertical lattice pieces and nail the horizontal lattice pieces to them.

Drive deck screws in pre-drilled holes to fasten the lattice cross rails to the upright posts.

Position the lattice frames and mark the postholes. Set the uprights into the postholes and adjust their positions as necessary. Tack them together with temporary braces.

Attach the arches. First, clamp the arch assemblies in position. Then, drill holes and use carriage bolts to fasten the arch to the sides of the arbor.

uprights, checking the assembly for square. Drill four ⅛"-dia. pilot holes in each corner joint and fasten the cross rails to the uprights using 2½" deck screws (**photo 4**). Turn the assembly over and fasten the lattice frame to the uprights using 1½" deck screws. Fasten the lattice frame to the cross rails with 6d finish nails. Repeat this procedure for the other lattice assembly. Drill a pilot hole on top of each upright and add a finial.

ERECT THE SIDES OF THE ARBOR

At the site, position the lattice frames and mark the location of each upright. Dig four 22"-deep postholes and backfill each with 4" of pea gravel. Stand the lattice frames upright in the postholes; set the final

height, and shim, level, and square the frames to one another. Secure the assembly by tacking temporary diagonal braces between the lattice frames (**photo 5**).

Fill each posthole with concrete mix and add water according to the manufacturer's instructions. Allow the concrete to cure for 24 hours.

INSTALL THE ARCHES

With an assistant, align the arch assemblies with the tops of the uprights. Using the mullion crossbar as a spacer, square and level the arched assemblies; clamp them in place. Drill two ⅜"-dia. guide holes through each joint. Bolt the arch assemblies in place using carriage bolts (**photo 6**). Install the finials and, if desired, putty, prime, and paint the entire arbor.

Trash Can Corral

Few household items can ruin a view like trash cans, especially as garbage-collection day draws near. With this trash can corral positioned strategically within your sightlines, you see an attractive, freestanding cedar fence instead of unsightly cans.

This corral offers the convenience of portability because it is freestanding. The two fence panels support one another, so you don't need to set fence posts in the ground or in concrete. And because the collars at the bases of the posts can be adjusted, you can position the can corral on uneven or slightly sloping ground. The staggered panel slats hide the cans completely, but still allow air to pass through to allow some ventilation and reduce the chances of the corral blowing over.

Trash can sizes and numbers vary widely. These days, many homeowners have small dumpsters issued by their waste collection service. This corral

is custom built with cedar infill boards, as opposed to prefabricated fence panels, so it is very easy to modify the dimensions to fit your needs. But do make sure the corral does not obstruct access by the waste collection truck.

Materials ▸

3	2 × 4" × 6 ft. cedar	7	1 × 6" × 10 ft. cedar
2	2 × 2" × 10 ft. cedar	8	1 × 4" × 8 ft. cedar
1	1 × 8" × 2 ft. cedar		Deck screws (1½", 2")
			Finishing materials

This two-sided structure keeps trash cans out of sight from the street without making them difficult to access.

Trash Can Corral

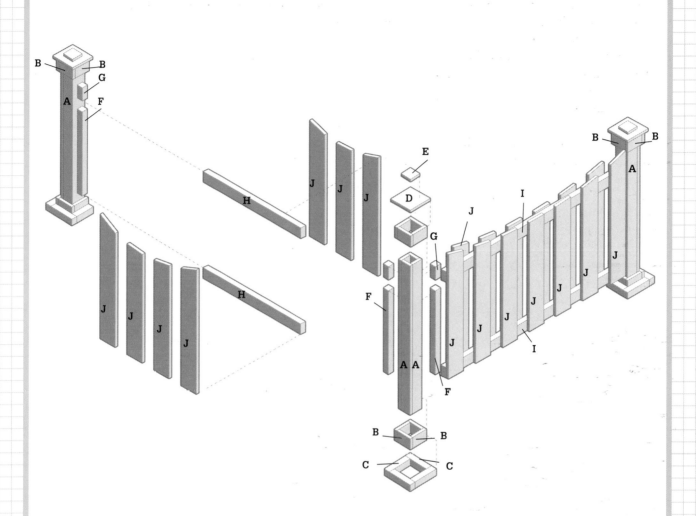

Cutting List

Key	Part	Dimension	Pcs.	Material
A	Post board	⅞ × 3½ × 48"	12	Cedar
B	Collar strip	⅞ × 3½ × 5¼"	24	Cedar
C	Foot strip	1½ × 1½ × 7⅝"	12	Cedar
D	Collar top	⅞ × 7¼ × 7¼"	3	Cedar
E	Collar cap	⅛ × 3½ × 3½"	3	Cedar

Key	Part	Dimension	Pcs.	Material
F	Long post cleat	1½ × 1½ × 26⅞"	4	Cedar
G	Short post cleat	1½ × 1½ × 4"	4	Cedar
H	Short stringer	1½ × 3½ × 35½"	2	Cedar
I	Long stringer	1½ × 3½ × 65½"	2	Cedar
J	Slat	⅞ × 5½ × 39½"	20	Cedar

Trash Can Corral

BUILD THE POSTS

Each post is made of four boards butted together to form a square. Cut the post boards to length and sand them smooth. Clamp one post board to your work surface. Then, butt another post board against it at a right angle. With the ends flush, drill ⅛"-dia. pilot holes at 8" intervals and counterbore the holes to ¼" depth. Connect the boards by driving 2" deck screws through the pilot holes (**photo 1**). Repeat the step until the post boards are fastened together in pairs. Then, fasten the pairs together to form the three posts.

MAKE & ATTACH THE COLLARS

Each post is wrapped at the top and bottom by a four-piece collar. The top collars have two-piece flat caps, and the base collars are wrapped with 2 × 2 strips for stability. Cut the collar strips, collar tops, and collar caps to size. Join the collar strips together to form square frames using 1½" deck screws. Center each collar cap on top of a collar top, and attach the caps to the tops with 1½" deck screws. To center the tops on the frames, mark lines on the bottoms of the top pieces 1⅛" in from the edges. Then, drill pilot holes ½" in from the lines, and counterbore the holes.

Use the lines to center a frame under each top. Then, drive 1½" deck screws through the holes and into the frames. Slip a top collar assembly over one end of each post (**photo 2**), and drill centered pilot holes on each side of the collar. Counterbore the holes and drive 1½" deck screws into the posts. Attach the remaining bottom collar assemblies to the other ends of the posts, with the bottom edges flush.

Cut the foot strips to length. Lay them around the bottoms of the base collars, and screw them together with 2" deck screws. Make sure the bottoms of the frames are flush with the bottoms of the collars. Then, attach the frames to the collars with 2" deck screws.

ATTACH THE CLEATS & SUPPORTS

The long and short post cleats attach to the posts between and above the stringers. Cut the post cleats to length. Center a long post cleat on one face of each post and attach it with 2" deck screws so the bottom is 4" above the top of the base collar on each post. For the corner post, fasten a second long post cleat on an adjacent post face, 4" up from the bottom collar. Center the short post cleats on the same post faces, 3⅝" up from the tops of the long post cleats. Attach the short post cleats to the posts, with 2" deck screws, making sure the short cleats are aligned with the long cleats (**photo 3**).

Create the posts by fastening cedar 1 × 4s into groups of four with the rough faces out.

Fit the top collar assemblies onto each post and attach them. Drill pilot holes for all fasteners in the collar assemblies so they don't split apart when you drive screws.

Attach the short post cleats 3⅝" up from the tops of the long post cleats. The top stringers on the panels fit between the cleats when installed.

Use 4½"-wide spacers to set the gaps between panel slats. This will create gaps that are about an inch narrower than the board on the opposite side of the stringer.

Lay out the panel profiles. Use a flexible guide to mark the top contours.

Set the completed fence panels between the cleats on the faces of the posts and attach.

BUILD THE FENCE PANELS

Cut the short stringers, long stringers, and slats. Position the short stringers on your work surface so they are parallel and separated by a 26⅞" gap. Attach a slat at each end of the stringers, so the ends of the stringers are flush with the outside edges of the slats. Drive a 1½" deck screw through each slat and into the face of each stringer.

Measure diagonally from corner to corner to make sure the fence panel is square. If the measurements are equal, the fence is square. If not, apply pressure to one side of the assembly until it is square. Drive another screw through each slat and into each stringer.

Cut 4½" spacers to set the gaps between panel slats, and attach the remaining slats on the same side of the stringers by driving two 1½" deck screws at each end. Check that the bottoms of the slats are flush with the stringer (**photo 4**).

Turn the panel over and attach slats to the other side, starting 4½" from the ends so slats on opposite sides are staggered—there will only be three slats on this side. Build the long panel the same way.

CONTOUR THE PANEL TOPS

To lay out the curve at the top of each fence panel, first make a marking guide. Cut a thin, flexible strip of wood at least 6" longer than the long fence panel. On each panel, tack nails at the top outside corner of each end slat and midway across each panel, ½" above the top stringer. Form a smooth curve by positioning the guide with the ends above the outside nails, and the midpoint below the nail in the center. Trace the contour onto the slats (**photo 5**), and cut along the line with a jigsaw. Use a short blade to avoid striking the slats on the other side. Use the same procedure on the other side of each panel. Sand the cuts smooth.

Position the fence panels between the posts so the top stringer in each panel fits in the gap between the long and short post cleats (**photo 6**). Drive 2" deck screws through the slats and into the cleats.

APPLY FINISHING TOUCHES

Apply exterior wood stain to protect the wood. You can increase the height of any of the posts slightly by detaching the base collar, lifting the post and reattaching the collar.

Firewood Shelter

This handsome firewood shelter combines rustic ranch styling with ample sheltered storage that keeps firewood off the ground and obscured from sight. Clad on the sides and roof with beveled cedar lap siding, the shelter has the look and feel of a permanent structure. But because it's freestanding, you can move it around as needed. It requires no time-consuming foundation work. As long as it's loaded up with firewood it is very stable, even in high winds. But if it has high exposure to the elements and is frequently empty, secure it with a pair of wood stakes.

This firewood shelter is large enough to hold an entire face cord of firewood. (A face cord, also called a rick, is 4 ft. high, 8 ft. wide, and one log-length deep— typically 16".) Since the storage area is sheltered and raised to avoid ground contact and allow airflow, wood dries quickly and is ready to use when you need it. Raising the firewood above the ground also makes the woodpile a much less attractive nesting area for rodents.

Materials ▸

10 2 × 4" × 8 ft. cedar	8 ⅜ × 4" lag screws
5 2 × 6" × 8 ft. cedar	1½" spiral siding nails
10 ⅝ × 8" × 8 ft. cedar lap siding	Deck screws (2½", 3")
24 ⅜ × 3½" lag screws	Finishing materials

Stacks of firewood will stay drier and be less of an eyesore if you build this rustic firewood shelter.

Firewood Shelter

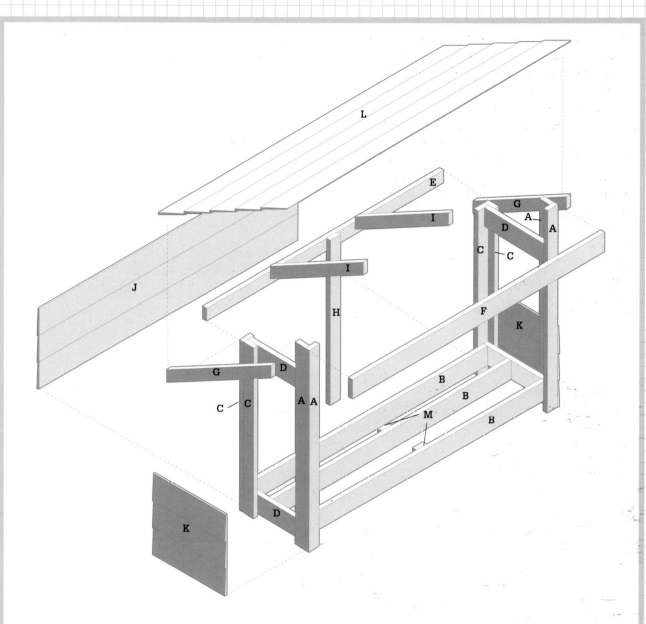

Cutting List

Key	Part	Dimension	Pcs.	Material
A	Front post	$1\frac{1}{2} \times 3\frac{1}{2} \times 59"$	4	Cedar
B	Bottom rail	$1\frac{1}{2} \times 5\frac{1}{2} \times 82\frac{1}{2}"$	3	Cedar
C	Rear post	$1\frac{1}{2} \times 3\frac{1}{2} \times 50"$	4	Cedar
D	End rail	$1\frac{1}{2} \times 5\frac{1}{2} \times 21"$	4	Cedar
E	Back rail	$1\frac{1}{2} \times 3\frac{1}{2} \times 88\frac{1}{2}"$	1	Cedar
F	Front rail	$1\frac{1}{2} \times 5\frac{1}{2} \times 88\frac{1}{2}"$	1	Cedar
G	Roof support	$1\frac{1}{2} \times 3\frac{1}{2} \times 33\frac{3}{4}"$	2	Cedar

Key	Part	Dimension	Pcs.	Material
H	Middle post	$1\frac{1}{2} \times 3\frac{1}{2} \times 50"$	1	Cedar
I	Middle support	$1\frac{1}{2} \times 3\frac{1}{2} \times 28"$	2	Cedar
J	Back siding	$\frac{5}{8} \times 8 \times 88\frac{1}{2}"$	3	Cedar siding
K	End siding	$\frac{5}{8} \times 8 \times 24"$	6	Cedar siding
L	Roof strip	$\frac{5}{8} \times 8 \times 96"$	5	Cedar siding
M	Prop	$1\frac{1}{2} \times 3\frac{1}{2} \times 7\frac{1}{2}"$	2	Cedar

Firewood Shelter

BUILD THE FRAME

Cut the front posts and rear posts to length. Butt the edges of the front posts together in pairs to form the corner posts. Drill ⅛"-dia. pilot holes at 8" intervals. Counterbore the holes ¼" deep using a counterbore bit. Join the post pairs with 2½" deck screws. Follow the same procedure to join the rear posts in pairs.

Cut the bottom rails and end rails. Assemble two bottom rails and two end rails into a rectangular frame, with the end rails covering the ends of the bottom rails. Set the third bottom rail between the end rails, centered between the other bottom rails. Mark the ends of the bottom rails on the outside faces of the end rails. Drill two ⅜"-dia. pilot holes for lag screws through the end rails at each bottom rail position—do not drill into the bottom rails. Drill a ¾"-dia. counterbore for each pilot hole, deep enough to recess the screw heads. Drill a smaller, ¼"-dia. pilot hole through each pilot hole in the end rails, into the ends of the bottom rails (**photo 1**). Drive a ⅜ × 3½" lag screw fitted with a washer at each pilot hole, using a socket wrench.

Draw reference lines across the inside faces of the corner posts, 2" up from the bottom. With the corner posts upright and about 82" apart, set 2"-high spacers next to each corner post to support the frame. Position the bottom rail frame between the corner posts, and attach the frame to the corner posts by driving two 2½" deck screws through the corner posts and into the outer faces of the bottom rails. Drill counterbored pilot holes in the sides of the corner posts. Drive a pair of ⅜ × 4" lag screws, fitted with washers, through the sides of the corner posts and into the bottom rails. The lag screws must go through the post and the end rail, and into the end of the bottom rail. Avoid hitting the lag screws that have already been driven through the end rails.

Complete the frame by installing end rails at the tops of the corner posts. Drill counterbored pilot holes in the end rails. Drive 2½" deck screws through the end rails and into the posts. Make sure the tops of the end rails are flush with the tops of the rear posts (**photo 2**).

MAKE THE ROOF FRAME

Cut the back rail, front rail, roof supports, middle post, and middle supports to length. The roof supports and middle supports are mitered at the ends. To make the miter cutting lines, mark a point 1½" in from each end,

Drill pilot holes through ¾"-dia. counterbores when preparing to drive the lag screws into the ends of the bottom rails.

Attach the end rails between the front and rear corner posts.

Miter-cut the middle supports and roof supports with a circular saw or with a power miter saw.

Attach the front rail by driving screws through the outer roof supports, making sure the top of the rail is flush with the tops of the supports.

Attach the middle roof supports by driving screws through the front and back rails.

Attach the roof strips with siding nails, starting at the back edge and working your way forward.

along the edge of the board. Draw diagonal lines from each point to the opposing corner. Cut along the lines with a circular saw (**photo 3**) or power miter saw.

Drill counterbored pilot holes in the back rail. Use 3" deck screws to fasten the back rail to the backs of the rear corner posts, flush with their tops and sides. Use the same procedure to fasten a roof support to the outsides of the corner posts. Make sure the top of each support is flush with the high point of each post end. The supports should overhang the posts equally in the front and rear.

Drill counterbored pilot holes in the roof supports and drive deck screws to attach the front rail between the roof supports (**photo 4**). The top of the rail should be flush with the tops of the roof supports. Attach the middle supports between the front rail and back rail, 30" in from each rail end. Drive 3" deck screws through the front and back rails into the ends of the middle supports (**photo 5**). Use a pipe clamp to hold the supports in place as you attach them.

Drill counterbored pilot holes in the middle post. Position the middle post so it fits against the outside of the rear bottom rail and the inside of the top back rail. Make sure the middle post is perpendicular and

extends past the bottom rail by 2". Attach it with 2½" deck screws. Cut a pair of props to length. Attach them to the front two bottom rails, aligned with the middle post. Make sure the tops of the props are flush with the tops of the bottom rails.

ATTACH SIDING & ROOF

Cut pieces of 8"-wide beveled cedar lap siding to length to make the siding strips and the roof strips. Starting 2" up from the bottoms of the rear posts, fasten the back siding strips with two 1½" siding nails driven through each strip and into the posts, near the top and bottom edge of the strip. Work your way up, overlapping each piece of siding by ½", making sure the thicker edges of the siding face down. Attach the end siding to the corner posts, with the seams aligned with the seams in the back siding.

Attach the roof strips to the roof supports, starting at the back edge. Drive two nails into each roof support. Make sure the wide edge of the siding faces down. Attach the rest of the roof strips, overlapping the strip below by about ½" (**photo 6**), until you reach the front edges of the roof supports. You can leave the cedar wood untreated or apply an exterior wood stain to keep it from turning gray as it weathers.

Picket Fence

For generations, the idyllic dream home has been a vine-covered cottage surrounded by a white picket fence. These days, the diversity in designs and styles of this classic American fence have expanded the range of possibilities, making the picket fence easy to adapt to any home, from an elaborate Victorian "Painted Lady" to a modest rambler. Although prefab panels are common, making your own pickets from lumber is a fun and rewarding outdoor carpentry project.

The charm of a picket fence lies in its open and inviting appearance. The repetitive structure and spacing create a pleasing rhythm that welcomes family and friends while maintaining a fixed property division. Traditionally, picket fences are 36" to 48" tall. The version shown here is 48" tall, with posts spaced 96" apart on-center and pickets spaced 1⅝" apart—a fairly open arrangement. It's important that the spacing appear consistent. Using a spacer to set the pickets simplifies that process.

Picket fences are usually white; however, matching your house's trim color or stain can be an eye-catching alternative. Painting the fence black or another dark color makes it look more substantial and with certain types it can even suggest a fancy wrought-iron fence. If you prime and paint all the materials before construction, apply the second coat of paint after the fence is completed to cover any marks, smudges, and nail or screw heads.

Materials (Per Panel) ▶

9 1 × 4" × 8 ft.	16d corrosion-
2 2 × 4" × 8 ft.	resistant nails
2 4 × 4" × 8 ft.	1½" deck screws
Paint, stain, or sealer	Fence post finials

This classic picket fence is simple to build and instantly recognizable even when the pickets are redesigned for a bit of unique character, as with the eyehole tops seen here.

Picket Fence

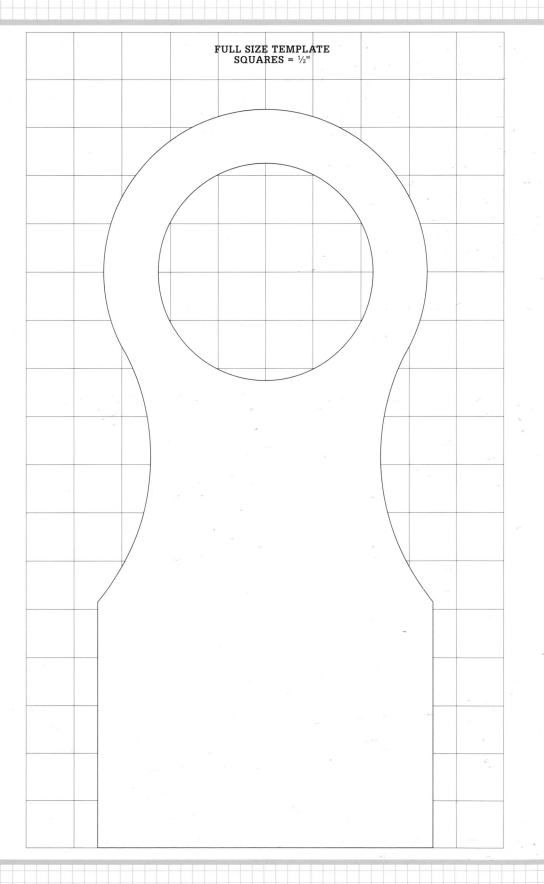

FULL SIZE TEMPLATE
SQUARES = ½"

Picket Fence

PLAN THE PROJECT

On the building site, lay out the fence line with batter boards and mason's string. Space the post locations every 96" on-center. Count the 4 × 4 posts and estimate the number of pickets needed to complete the project. For example:

- 18 (pickets) × 3½" (picket width) = 63" (total width of run of pickets)
- 92½" (space between posts) − 63" = 29½" (unoccupied space)
- 29½" ÷ 19 (18 pickets + 1) = 1⅝" (space between pickets)

Not all calculations will work out evenly. If your figures come out uneven, make slight adjustments across the entire fence section. Since it's common to make a cutting error or two, add 10 percent to your total.

If you are installing your fence on ground that slopes more than a couple of inches over 8 feet, make a design decision up front. You can allow the fence to follow the slope, which means that the rail ends will need to be cut at angles so they fit flat against the posts. The pickets themselves should be vertical. Another way to accommodate the slope is to vary the post heights and the heights of the pickets so the line formed by the picket tops is level and the distance between the picket bottoms and ground stays constant (this means individual pickets will be different lengths). See page 205, Stepped panels vs. Racking a panel.

MAKE THE PICKETS

If you're creating your own pickets, cut 1 × 4s to length (46" as shown). The pickets should be a couple of inches shorter than the overall fence height. Pine or treated pine are good wood choices, but you may also use cedar or other exterior lumbers if you are not planning to paint the fence.

Trim simple pointed pickets with a power miter saw. For more elaborate designs like the one shown here, make a template (see page 201), then use a jigsaw or other appropriate cutting tool to cut the outline of the round picket top shapes. Mark a centerpoint for the mandrel of a 2¼" hole saw and drill out the eyehole opening (**photo 1**).

Make all of your pickets and then apply a first coat of primer and paint, stain, or sealer to all surfaces of each picket. Also prime or seal the posts and post caps or finials, as well as the stringer stock. A sprayer, such as an HVLP paint sprayer, will make quick work of this job.

SET THE POSTS

Dig postholes at least 24" deep and set the posts in concrete. Make sure the posts are level and plumb and aligned correctly and that the spacing is exactly 96" on-center. Refer to additional information on installing fences if you are unsure how to go about this.

Allow the concrete to dry for two days. Measure up 48" from ground level at each post and mark

Make the pickets by cutting the outline shape at the top with a jigsaw and then removing a round waste piece in the center of each top with a hole saw.

Install and trim the posts. Set them in concrete, then trim them to height after the concrete has dried for at least two days.

Set the stringer stock in position against the posts, then mark a trim line and cut the stringer to length.

Toenail the stringers to the posts with 16d galvanized finish nails. Drill pilot holes for the nails to prevent splitting. Or, you can use deck screws or fence panel hangers.

Install the pickets by hanging your spacer next to each picket and screwing the next one in line to the stringers. Keep the tops aligned.

Install post caps or finials (or both). Determine the centers of the post tops, drill pilot holes, and then attach caps or finials (many come with a mounting screw preattached on the bottom).

cutting lines, or set varying cutting lines in sloped situations (see Plan the Project). Trim the posts along the cutting lines **(photo 2)** using a circular saw, reciprocating saw, or handsaw.

INSTALL THE STRINGERS
Mark a line 6" down from the top of each post to indicate the upper stringer position, and mark another line 36½" down from each post top to indicate the lower stringer. At the upper stringer marks on the first two posts, clamp an 8-foot long 2 × 4 that's oriented so the top edge of the 2 × 4 is flush with the mark. Scribe the post outline on the back of the stringer at each end **(photo 3)**. Remove and cut the upper stringer to length. Position the upper stringer between the two posts, set back ¾" from the faces of the posts. Toe-nail the stringer into place with 16d corrosion-resistant nails **(photo 4)**. Or, you can use galvanized fence stringer hanger hardware. Install all the upper and lower stringers.

INSTALL THE PICKETS
Make a spacer by rip-cutting a 30"-long 1 × 4 to the spacing width size—1⅝" in this project. Mount a

pair of L-brackets to one face of the spacer so they will hang on the upper and lower stringers.

Draw a reference mark on each picket 6" down from the peak. Place a picket flat against the stringers and adjust the picket until the reference line is flush with the top edge of the upper stringer. The distance from the picket to a post should equal your spacing distance. Drill pilot holes and attach the picket, using 1½" deck screws. Hang the spacer on the upper stringer and hold it flush against the attached picket. Position a new picket flush against the jig and attach it. Reposition the spacer and continue along the fence line **(photo 5)**. *TIP: To ensure even picket tops you can also run a mason's string between post tops and use it as a reference.*

APPLY FINISHING TOUCHES
Attach fence post caps or finials. These improve post appearance and, more importantly, extend the life of the post by protecting the exposed end grain from water. Use a straightedge to draw lines from corner to corner on the top of the post to determine the center. Drill a pilot hole where the lines intersect **(photo 6)** and attach a finial or post cap at the center of each post. On painted fences, apply the second coat of paint.

Wood Panel Fence

Prefabricated fence panels take much of the work out of putting up a fence, and, surprisingly, using them is often less expensive than building a board-and-stringer fence from scratch. They are best suited for relatively flat yards, but may be stepped down on slopes that aren't too steep.

Fence panels come in many styles, ranging from privacy to picket. Most tend to be built lighter than fences made from scratch, with thinner wood for the stringers and siding. When shopping for panels, compare quality and heft of lumber and fasteners as well as cost.

Purchase panels, gate hardware, and gate (if you're not building yours) before setting and trimming your posts. Determine also if panels can be trimmed or reproduced from scratch for short sections.

The most exacting task when building a panel fence involves insetting the panels between the posts. This requires that preset posts be precisely spaced and perfectly plumb. In our inset panel sequence, we set one post at a time as the fence was built, so the attached panel position can determine the spacing, not the preset posts.

An alternative installation to setting panels between posts is to attach them to the post faces. Face-mounted panels are more forgiving of preset posts, since the attachment point of stringers doesn't need to be dead center on the posts.

Wood fence panels usually are constructed in either 6- or 8-foot lengths. Cedar and pressure-treated pine are the most common wood types used in making fence panels, though you may also find redwood in some areas. Generally, the cedar panels cost half-again to twice as much for similar styles.

When selecting wood fence panels, inspect every board in each panel carefully (and be sure to check both sides of the panel). These products are fairly susceptible to damage during shipping.

Building with wood fence panels is a great time saver and allows you to create a more elaborate fence than you may be able to building the parts yourself from scratch.

Materials (Per Panel) ▸

2 4 × 4" × 8 ft. posts (subtract for shared posts)	1¼" deck screws
	Gate hardware
	Post caps
1 Prefabricated panel (varies from 4 to 8 ft. long)	Wood sealer/ protectant or paint
1 Gate (optional)	
Corrosion-resistant fence brackets (6 per panel)	

Building with wood fence panels is a great time saver and allows you to create a more elaborate fence than you may be able to building the parts yourself from scratch.

Preassembled fence panels are an attractive, timesaving option when building a fence. The entire panel is attached to the posts, eliminating the need to individually cut and attach stringers. Some popular styles of wood panels include: (A) lattice panels; (B) solid panels with lattice tops; (C) staggered board; (D) horizontal board; (E) modified picket; (F) dog-eared board.

Stepped panels are horizontal, maintaining an even height between posts. A good strategy for pre-built panel systems, stepping fences is the only way to handle slope when working with prefabricated panels that cannot be trimmed or altered.

Racking a panel involves manipulating a simple fence panel by racking or twisting it out of square so the stringers follow a low slope while the siding remains vertical. Picket-style panels are good candidates for this trick, but the degree to which you can rack the panels is limited. If the siding is connected to stringers with more than one fastener at each joint, remove some fasteners and replace them after racking the panel.

Wood Panel Fence

DIG HOLES & BRACE END POST

Lay out the fence line and mark the posthole locations using batter boards and mason's string (**photo 1**). Space the holes to fit the purchased panels, adding the actual post diameter (3½" for 4" nominal posts) plus ¼" for brackets to the length of a panel. Measure spacing for stepped fences on a level line, not along the slope. Transfer the locations down from the level line to the ground using a plumb bob and mark by pinning a piece of bright-colored plastic to the turf (**photo 2**).

Dig the first two holes of a run with a post-hole digger, starting at an end or corner (**photo 3**). Use a 2 × 4 cut to the length of the panels as a spacing guide for locating the second hole (**photo 4**). Tamp gravel into the hole bottoms for drainage. Position, plumb, and stake the end post, adding a forming tube at the top of the hole if needed. Set your bracing so it won't interfere with the first fence panel. If you're renting an auger, you may want to dig all your holes at once, otherwise, digging as you go leaves room for spacing adjustment if needed. Use a stake to hold your alignment line out of the way while digging. Fill your first posthole with concrete and tamp it into the posthole with the end of a 2 × 4 (**photo 5**).

SET THE FIRST PANEL

Attach fence brackets to the first post with deck screws (**photo 6**). The bottom of the fence panel needs to be at least 2" off the ground. Transfer your bracket spacing to a 1 × 4 gauge board using a marker. Bend down the bottom tabs on the top two brackets.

Level the panel in the brackets, supporting the loose end against the ground with blocking. For extremely gradual slopes, you may follow a mason's line that follows the actual grade instead of trying to establish true level. Attach the brackets to the panel with deck screws (**photo 7**). *TIP: Using screws has the advantage of reversibility: if, for example, you need to get a piece of large equipment into your yard you can easily remove and replace a fence panel.*

Set the second post in its hole, and mark the position of the bottom bracket (**photo 8**). Remove the post and use your gauge board to mark the locations of the other brackets and post tops. Unless your fence needs to step up or down a slope, trace your marks

Lay out the fence line using a batter board at the end of each run. Tie a mason's string to a crosspiece on the batter board and level it. Measure along the string and mark the posthole locations.

around the post with a speed square and mark the locations of the brackets for the next section as well. Attach the brackets (**photo 9**). Set the post in the hole, and insert the stringers in the brackets. Plumb and brace the post (**photo 10**), making sure the panel is level and then attach the brackets to the fence panel with deck screws.

ATTACH REMAINING POSTS & PANEL SECTIONS

Continue installing posts and panels in sequence. For a stepped fence, establish a consistent step height or determine the step-up or step-down height one panel at a time. Fill post holes with concrete if they have not been filled already (**photo 11**). Allow two or three days for the concrete to cure before removing braces. Trim the posts to height with a circular saw or reciprocating saw. Attach the post caps or finials to the post tops with galvanized casing nails or deck screws (**photo 12**). Paint, stain, or seal the fence. Hang the gate (see pages 212 to 225 for more information on selecting and installing gates).

Transfer post locations from the string to the ground and mark them with pieces of plastic pinned to the turf.

Dig a posthole at a corner or an end post location. A clam-shell-type posthole digger is a good choice for holes up to 30" deep. Make a depth gauge from scrap wood to measure the hole depth as you dig.

Set, plumb, and brace the first post, then lay a 2 × 4 the same length as the panel width along the fence line as a reference for digging the next posthole.

Fill your first posthole with concrete unless you are setting posts in gravel or sand. Tamp the wet concrete with a scrap 2 × 4 to pack it into the posthole.

Attach fence brackets to align with your stringer locations, to the first post, centered side to side.

Set the first fence panel into the brackets, level it, and attach the end of the panel to the brackets with deck screws or joist hanger nails.

Position a post in the next posthole in line and clamp the unattached end of the fence panel to the post (you may need to attach a clamping block to the post rail first). Mark the positions of the rails onto the post. Unclamp the fence panel and remove the post from the hole.

Attach the fence brackets using a story pole as a gauge for marking consistent bracket locations.

Plumb the post perpendicular to the fence line, making sure the panel is level. Brace the post, recheck for plumb and level, and then set the post the same way you set the first one.

Fill the holes with concrete one at a time as you work, or wait and fill them all once the posts are all positioned and braced.

Attach post caps or finials to protect the post tops, and then seal, stain, or paint your new fence.

VARIATION: Overlaid Fence Panels

SET & TRIM THE POSTS

Some types of fence panels (generally not privacy fence styles) look better and are easier to install if you attach the open stringer ends directly to the fence post faces, instead of hanging them between posts.

Lay out the fence line with batter boards and string (see photo 1, page 206). Mark post locations, dig postholes, and then level, plumb, and brace the posts. Once posts are all in place, set them in concrete (**photo 1**). Posts should be spaced so the distance between them (on-center) equals one panel length plus ¼"

For level or nearly level fences, mark the desired post height on the end posts. Be sure to allow for at least 2" panel clearance at ground level. Stretch a mason's string between marked end posts to establish cutoff heights for line posts. Trim all posts with a reciprocating saw or circular saw (**photo 2**).

ATTACH THE PANELS

Pull a mason's line from end post to end post to establish the top line for the fence panels (the position should allow a minimum 2" clearance of panel bottoms above the ground). Lean the first fence panel against the posts in position, with blocking underneath so it is at least 2" above the ground (**photo 3**).

Lap stringers across the full width of end posts and half the width of line posts. Attach with two deck screws per stringer end, sized to penetrate at least 2" into the post (**photo 4**). It's always a good idea to drill pilot holes before driving the screws. Continue installing panels until the fence is complete (**photo 5**). Add a gate and post caps or finials as desired.

Set the posts for your project. Spacing is less critical when you're attaching panels to the post faces than when you're hanging panels between posts.

Trim posts to a consistent height once they are all installed. Use a circular saw or reciprocating saw.

String a mason's line across all the posts to set the height for the stringers. Check with a line level. Position one of the panels against the posts it will attach to, resting on spacer blocks that are at least 2" high.

Attach the first panel by driving deck screws through the ends of the stringers and into the posts. At corners and end posts, the stringers should run all the way across the post faces.

Install the remaining panels, attach post caps or finials, and apply your finish of choice.

Attach Panels to Posts & Auxiliary Stringers ▸

Auxiliary stringers are boards the same width and thickness as the panel stringer (often 2 × 4) that are attached to the posts to provide support for the actual panel stringers that rest on and are attached to the auxiliary stringers. Set and trim posts as described in photo 1, then temporarily attach your first panel with a 2" minimum ground clearance. Mark the stringer bottoms on the posts. Remove the fence panels.

Set the top edges of the auxiliary stringers to the marks. Stringers should fully overlap end posts and overlap line posts by half. Attach each stringer with a single deck screw per post, sized to penetrate at least 2" into the post. Attach the remaining auxiliary stringers.

Rest the stringers that are pre-attached to the fence panels on top of the auxiliary stringers. Attach the fence panels to the posts with deck screws set flush with the surface of the panel stringers. If a panel stringer doesn't reach all the way to a post, attach one of the panel siding boards near the post to the auxiliary stringer.

Attach auxiliary stringers directly to the posts so you can rest the panel stringers on top of them. This adds strength to the fence and also gives you some ability to compensate if the posts are a little too far apart.

Two Simple Gates

If you understand the basic elements of gate construction, you can build a sturdy gate to suit almost any situation. The gates shown here illustrate the fundamental elements of a well-built gate. To begin with, adequate distribution of the gate's weight is critical to its operation. Because the posts bear most of a gate's weight, they're set at least 12" deeper into the ground than fence posts and should always be anchored in concrete. Depending on building codes in your area, they may even need to be set in concrete footings that extend below the frost line.

No matter how the gatepost is anchored, it must be plumb. A sagging post can be reinforced by attaching a sag rod at the top of the post and running it diagonally to the lower end of the next post. Tighten the knuckle in the middle until the post is properly aligned. A caster can be used with heavy gates over smooth surfaces to assist with the weight load.

The frame also plays an important part in properly distributing the gate's weight. The two basic gate frames featured here are the foundation for many gate designs. A Z-frame gate is ideal for a light, simple gate. This frame consists of a pair of horizontal braces with a diagonal brace running between them. A perimeter-frame gate is necessary for a heavier or more elaborate gate. It employs a solid, four-cornered frame with a diagonal brace attached at opposite corners. In both styles, the diagonal brace must run from the bottom of the hinge side to the top of the latch side, to provide support and keep the gate square.

There is a multitude of hinge, latch, and handle styles available. Whichever you choose, purchase the largest hinges available that are in proportion with your gate, and a latch or handle appropriate for the gate's purpose.

Materials ▶

Pressure-treated, cedar, or redwood lumber (1 × 2, 1 × 4, 2 × 4)	Hinge hardware Deck screws (2", 2½")
4 × 4 gatepost	
Gate handle or latch	

A Z-frame gate is one solution for gate construction that couldn't be easier to build.

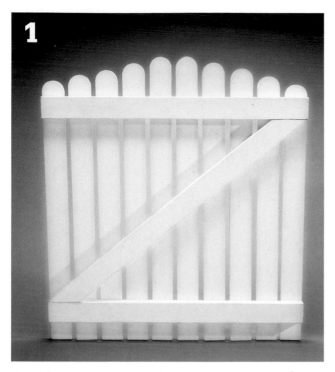

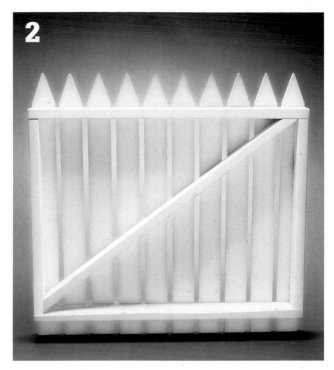

The Z-frame gate consists of a 3-board frame that is hung with hinges to a gatepost. The gate siding (the vertical pickets) are attached directly to the frame.

A perimeter frame gate has a sturdier 5-board frame that consists of a square 2 × 4 box with a diagonal crossbrace.

Another Option: Prefab Gates ▸

With some fence panels, it's possible to disassemble the frame, trim it down to width (3 ft. to 4 ft.) and then reassemble it into a gate that matches the panels. Some manufacturers offer prefabricated gates that match their panel styles.

Stronger Joints ▸

A gate frame can be strengthened by using woodworking joinery instead of simple butt joints. Here, a ¾"-wide × 1½"-deep rabbet joint is cut to make a stronger 2 x 4 frame. Deck screws and exterior wood glue reinforce the joints.

Z-frame Gate

CALCULATE THE WIDTH & CUT BRACES

Check both gateposts on adjacent sides for plumb using a level. If a post is not plumb, reinforce it with a sag rod. When both posts are plumb, measure the opening between them. Consult the packaging on your hinge and latch hardware, if provided, for the clearance necessary between the frame and gate posts. Subtract this figure from the measurement of the opening. The result will be the finished width of the gate. Cut two 2 × 4s to this length for the frame's horizontal braces.

ATTACH THE DIAGONAL BRACE

On the fence, measure the distance from the bottom of the upper stringer to the top of the lower stringer. Cut two pieces of scrap 2 × 4 to this length to use as temporary spacers. On a flat work surface, lay out the frame, placing the temporary spacers between the braces. Square the corners of the frame, using a framing square.

Place a 2 × 4 diagonally from one end of the lower brace across to the opposite end of the upper brace. Mark cutting lines on the diagonal so it will fit between the braces (**photo 1**). Cut the diagonal brace along the cutting lines with a power miter saw or circular saw. Remove the temporary spacers and test the fit of the diagonal brace. Attach the diagonal brace to the horizontal braces with exterior glue and 2½" deck screws driven through pilot holes.

INSTALL THE SIDING

Position the frame so the diagonal brace runs from the bottom of the hinge side to the top of the latch side, then plan the layout of the siding to match the position and spacing of the fence siding. If the final board needs to be trimmed, divide the difference and trim two boards instead. Use these equally trimmed boards as the two end pieces of siding. Cut the siding pieces and then prime and paint all wood parts before assembling the gate.

Clamp a scrap 2 × 4 flush against the bottom brace as a placement guide. Align the first and last boards flush with the ends of the braces. Attach these two boards to the horizontal braces using pairs of 2" deck screws versus nails to cinced fasteners (**photo 2**). Attach the rest of the siding, using spacers as necessary.

HANG THE GATE

Shim the gate into position with spacers below and make sure it has enough side-to-side clearance to swing freely. Remove the gate. Measure and mark the hinge positions on the gate. Drill pilot holes, and secure the hinges to the gate using the screws provided with the hardware or other exterior fasteners as indicated. If your latch hardware doesn't include a catch, add a stop on the latch-side post. Clamp a 1 × 2 in place, then shim the gate back into position, centered within the opening. Use a level to make sure the gate is level and plumb, and the stop is properly positioned. Drill pilot holes and secure the stop to the post, using 2" deck screws.

With the gate shimmed into position, mark the hinge-side post to indicate the hinge screw locations, then drill pilot holes. Fasten the hinges to the post (**photo 3**) using the screws provided with the hardware. Install the latch hardware to the opposite gatepost and the catch to the gate, according to the manufacturer's instructions.

Mark the diagonal for cutting. Place a 2 x 4 diagonally across the temporary frame, from the lower corner of the hinge side, to the upper latch-side corner, and mark the cutting lines.

Attach the siding boards. Align the end boards so they are flush with the edges of the frame. Using spacers, attach all siding boards to the frame with deck screws.

Install the gate. Shim the gate into place with blocking below and mark the position of the hardware on the gate and gateposts. Attach the hardware.

Perimeter Frame Gate

BUILD THE GATE FRAME

Determine the gate width and cut the horizontal braces, as for a Z-frame gate (**photo 1**). On the fence line, measure the distance from the bottom of the upper stringer to the top of the lower stringer. Cut two pieces of 2 × 4 to this length for the vertical braces. Paint, stain, or seal the lumber for the gate and siding, then let it dry thoroughly.

Position the pieces of the frame and measure from one corner to the diagonally opposite corner. Repeat at the opposite corners. Adjust the pieces until these measurements are equal, which indicates that the frame is square. Secure each joint using exterior glue and 2½" deck screws.

ATTACH THE DIAGONAL BRACE

Position the frame on a painted 2 × 4 set on edge, running diagonally from the lower corner of the hinge side to the opposite latch-side corner. Support the frame with 2 × 4 scraps underneath the opposing corners. Make sure the frame is square, and scribe the corners of the frame onto the board (**photo 2**).

Transfer the cut marks to the face of the 2 × 4 using a combination square. Cut with a circular saw or power miter saw, making sure to set the saw blade to the appropriate bevel angle. Attach the brace with glue and 2½" deck screws driven through the frame and into the beveled ends of the diagonal brace.

ATTACH THE SIDING

Lay out the siding on the frame, making sure that the diagonal brace runs up from the bottom hinge-side corner to the opposite top latch-side corner. Use wood scraps the same width as the gaps between the pickets in the fence line for spacing. If a board must be ripped to fit, rip the first and last boards to the same width.

Clamp a scrap 2 × 4 flush against the bottom brace as a placement guide. Align the first and last boards, flush with the ends of the braces. Attach these two boards to the horizontal braces using pairs of 2" deck screws. Attach the rest of the siding using spacers as necessary (**photo 3**).

Mount the hardware and hang the gate as you would a Z-frame gate (opposite page).

Make the frame. Determine the lengths of the horizontal and vertical braces of the frame then lay out the boards, check them for square, and secure the joints with 2½" deck screws.

Trace the opposite corners of the frame onto the 2 × 4 diagonal brace to make cutting lines. Cut the brace using a circular saw with the blade adjusted for the appropriate bevel angle.

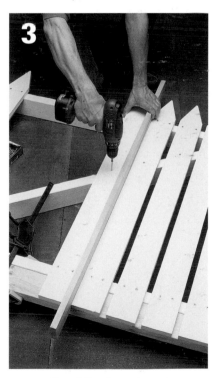

Secure the siding boards to the frame with deck screws using scrap wood as spacers.

Arched Gate

With its height and strategically placed opening, this gate is a great choice for maintaining privacy and enhancing security without sacrificing style. No ordinary "peephole," the decorative cast iron insert provides a stunning accent and gives you the opportunity to see who's heading your way or passing by. The arch of the gate also adds contrast to the fence line and draws attention to the entryway.

We built this gate from cedar and gave it a clear finish to match the cedar fence. You could use any other exterior wood you like, keeping in mind that wood that is not treated for exterior application or naturally resistant should be painted.

Shaping the top of the arch is a simple matter: Just plot the profile provided on page 217 onto the siding. Then, cut out the shape with a jigsaw.

This piece of cast iron came from a banister we found at a salvage yard. We used a reciprocating saw with a metal-cutting blade to cut it to a usable size. You can use just about any decorative grid you can find for your gate, or leave it out if you prefer.

Materials ▸

3 2 × 4" × 8 ft. exterior wood	Piece of ornamental metal (8" high and 30" long as shown here)	16d nails; deck screws (1¼", 2")	Hinges
1 2 × 4" × 10 ft. exterior wood		6 1½" mending plates	Latch hardware
13 1 × 4" × 8 ft. exterior wood	Construction adhesive	6 ¼ x 2½" bolts with nuts and washers	3d galvanized finish nails
			Paint, stain, or sealer

An elegantly arching top distinguishes this gate from the matching fence siding surrounding it. The insert is an attractive accent that gives the gate some enhanced visual appeal.

Arched Gate

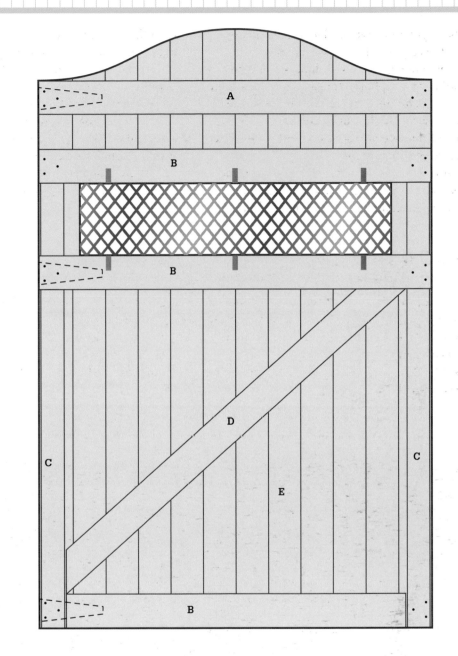

Cutting List

Key	Part	Dimension	Pcs.	Material
A	Siding brace	⅞ × 3½ × 42¾"	1	Cedar
B	Horizontal brace	1½ × 3½ × 42¾"	3	Cedar
C	Vertical braces	1½ × 3½ × 63"	2	Cedar
D	Diagonal brace	1½ × 3½ × 72"	1	Cedar
E	Siding	⅞ × 3½ × 96*"	12	Cedar

* Pre-trimming dimension

Arched Gate

PREPARE THE LUMBER

Measure the opening between the gateposts and determine the finished size of your gate. The dimensions shown here are for a gate that is 42¾" wide, which should fit into gate openings between 43 and 44" depending on the hinges and latch you choose. (Check the packaging of your hinge and latch hardware, if any, for clearance allowances.) Cut the lumber for the gate.

BUILD THE FRAME

Lay out the parts of the frame and mark the cutting lines for the half-lap joints (see page 217). *NOTE: The layout seen here will frame an 8"-high insert; if your insert is a different size, adjust the brace locations accordingly.* To make a half-lap joint, set the depth of a circular saw to ¾" and cut along the marked line; make a cut approximately every ⅛ to ¼", working from the end of the board or joint area back toward that first cut. Remove the waste material and smooth the cut surface using a mallet and chisel (**photo 1**). Repeat with each of the marked joints.

Position the pieces of the frame and measure from one corner to the diagonally opposite corner. Repeat at the opposite corners. Adjust the pieces until these measurements are equal, which indicates the frame is square. Secure each joint using 1¼" deck screws and glue. Position a 2 × 4 so it runs from the bottom of the hinge side of the frame to the first horizontal brace on the latch side. Trace the angle of the points of intersection to create cutting lines (**photo 2**), then cut the brace to fit, using a circular saw or power miter saw. Screw the diagonal brace to the vertical braces with 2½" deck screws driven through pilot holes near the ends of the diagonal brace.

ADD SIDING & CUT THE INSERT OPENING

Clamp a 2 × 4 across the bottom of the frame to act as a stop-block guide for installing the siding. Position the 1 × 4s for the siding even with the lower edge of the clamped 2 × 4; use 16d nails as spacers between siding boards. For each siding piece, drive three 2" deck screws at each horizontal brace. Flip the frame over.

Working from the back side, mark a line across the siding, 9" up from the top of the top brace, indicating the location for the bottom of the siding brace. Run a bead of construction adhesive on the backs of the

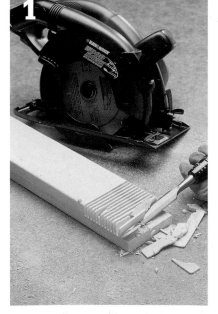

Remove waste wood in the half-lap areas. Make ¾"-deep kerf cuts first with a circular saw and then chisel out the remaining waste wood.

Position a diagonal brace from the bottom of the hinge side to the top of the first horizontal brace of the frame. Mark and cut the brace, then fasten it into the frame..

Add the siding brace above the frame after the siding boards are installed. Apply a bead of construction adhesive to set the brace into.

Plunge cut with a circular saw to make the cutout for the insert. Finish the corners of the cutout with a jig saw or hand saw.

Make a template and transfer the arch shape to the tops of the siding. Cut along the marked lines with a jig saw..

Install the insert piece by drilling holes through the cast iron and the lumber, and then bolting the cast iron into place.

siding in the brace location. Set the siding brace into the adhesive (**photo 3**). Carefully flip the frame back over and drive deck screws through the fronts of the siding and into the siding brace.

Mark the edges of the insert opening (the top and bottom should be flush with the edges of the horizontal braces that frame the opening). Set the cutting depth on a circular saw to ¾" (the thickness of the siding), and cut along the marked lines (**photo 4**). Finish the cuts at the corners with a hand saw or jigsaw. Remove the siding in the cutout area.

PROFILE THE GATE TOP
Draw the top profile seen on page 217 on some poster board or cardboard and then cut a template to match the profile. Trace it onto the top of the gate. Cut the profile into the siding tops, using a jigsaw (**photo 5**).

INSTALL THE INSERT
Drill three equally spaced holes across the top and bottom of the ornamental insert piece. To drill into cast iron, start with a small bit and move through increasingly larger bits up to ¼"-dia. Use lubricating

oil, drill slowly, and wear safety goggles. Set the cast iron into place and mark the corresponding holes onto the horizontal braces at the top and bottom of the cutout. Remove the cast iron and drill a hole at each mark, drilling all the way through the frame. Attach it to the gate (**photo 6**).

HANG THE GATE
Mount the hinges on the gate. Measure and mark the hinge positions. Drill pilot holes and drive screws to secure the hinges to the gate. Shim the gate into position with blocking from below, centered within the opening. Use a level to make sure the gate is level and plumb. Mark the post to indicate the hinge screw positions, then drill pilot holes. Fasten the hinges to the post using the screws provided with the hinge hardware. Position the latch hardware on the opposite post. Mark the screw positions and drill pilot holes; drive screws to secure the latch in place. Mark the catch positions on the gate. Drill pilot holes and secure the catch, using the screws provided with the hardware. Install a gate handle according to manufacturer's instructions.

Trellis/Gate Combination

This trellis/gate combination is a grand welcome to any yard. But don't let its ornate appearance fool you—the simple components create an impression far beyond the skills and materials involved in its construction.

This gate is best suited to a location where it will receive plenty of sunlight to ensure an abundant canopy of foliage. It's best to choose perennials rather than annuals, since they will produce more luxurious growth over time. Heirloom roses are a good choice, providing a charming complement to the gate's old-fashioned look and air of elegance.

Larger-scale, traditional styles of hardware that showcase well against the painted wood also will enhance the gate's impressive appearance. The hardware and the millwork that we used are available at most building centers, but you might want to check architectural salvage shops. They may have unique pieces that add another touch of character to the piece.

As with just about any project, you can alter the dimensions of this trellis/gate to fit an existing opening. Just recalculate the materials and cutting lists, and make sure you have enough lumber to accommodate the changes.

Materials ▸

8 2 × 2" × 8 ft.	6d galvanized finish
9 2 × 4" × 8 ft.	nails
4 1 × 4" × 8 ft.	Hinges
1 1 × 6" × 8 ft.	Gate handle
1 1 × 2" × 4 ft.	PVC pipe
2 4 × 4" × 8 ft.	Paint, stain, or sealer
⅜ × 3" lag screws	2 Victorian
2 24" treated wood	millwork brackets
stakes	(optional)
Deck screws (1½",	Concrete
2", 2½")	

This lovely trellis and gate combination makes a perfect home for climbing flowers and vines, resulting in a breathtaking entrance to your home.

Trellis/Gate Combination

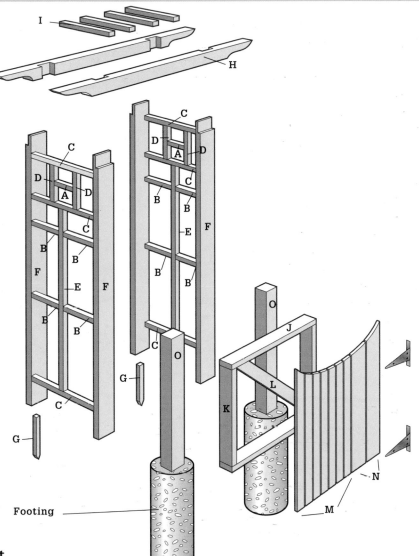

Footing

Cutting List

Frames

Key	Part	Dimension	Pcs.	Material
A	Horizontal brace	2 × 2 × 12"	2	Cedar
B	Horizontal brace	2 × 2 × 15¾"	8	Cedar
C	Horizontal brace	2 × 2 × 33"	6	Cedar
D	Vertical brace	2 × 2 × 17"	4	Cedar
E	Vertical brace	2 × 2 × 54½"	2	Cedar
F	Vertical brace	2 × 4 × 87½"	4	Cedar
G	Stake	1 × 2 × 46½"	2	Cedar

Top

Key	Part	Dimension	Pcs.	Material
H	Tie beams	2 × 4 × 72¾"	2	Cedar
I	Rafters	2 × 2 × 33"	4	Cedar

Gate

Key	Part	Dimension	Pcs.	Material
J	Horizontal brace	2 × 4 × 40½"	2	Cedar
K	Vertical brace	2 × 4 × 32¾"	2	Cedar
L	Diagonal brace	2 × 4 × 49½"	1	Cedar
M	Siding	1 × 4 × 45¼"	7	Cedar
N	Siding	1 × 6 × 45¼"	2	Cedar
O	Gate posts	4 × 4" × 10 ft.	2	Cedar

Trellis/Gate Combination

ASSEMBLE THE TRELLIS FRAMES

Measure the opening between the gateposts and determine the finished size of your gate and trellis. Compare your dimensions to the ones in the list on page 221, then check the cutting list and make any necessary adjustments. The tie beams for the trellis should be about 32" longer than the width of the gate. Cut the lumber for the trellis and gate. Paint, stain, or seal the pieces on all sides and edges. Let them dry.

Lay out one side of the trellis, following the diagram. Mark the cutting lines and cut the lap joints, then set the frame back together. When you're satisfied with the layout and sure the frame is square, secure the joints using two 2½" deck screws in each joint (**photo 1**). Build the other trellis frame.

ANCHOR THE FRAME TO THE GATEPOSTS

Referring to the diagram and to your own gate measurements, mark the positions of the trellis frame on the ground using stakes and string. Make sure the layout is square by measuring from corner to corner and adjusting the stakes until these diagonal measurements are equal. Set one trellis frame into position, with the inside face of the frame flush with the inside face of the gatepost. Drive a 24" pressure-treated stake behind the opposite side of the frame to hold the trellis in position. Drill three evenly spaced guide holes through the frame and into the gatepost and attach the frame to the post using 3" lag screws (**photo 2**). Attach the other trellis frame to the opposite post.

SECURE THE FREE SIDES OF THE FRAMES

Check the position of the free sides of the frames and measure the diagonals to ensure the layout is square. Clamp each frame to its stake and check the frame for level. Adjust as necessary. When the trellis frame is level, drill pilot holes and attach the frames to the stakes using lag screws (**photo 3**).

INSTALL THE TIE BEAMS

Make a template using the drawings on page 221 as guide and mark the cutting profiles onto the ends of each 2 × 4 tie beam. Cut the profiles, using a jigsaw.

Lay out the pieces for each side of the trellis frame, then secure each joint with 2½" deck screws.

Position the trellis frames, clamping them against the gateposts. Attach the frame to the posts with 3" lag screws.

Secure the free end of each frame to stakes using lag screws or deck screws.

Make the half-lap joints securing the tie beams to the trellis frame post tops and fasten with four 1¼" deck screws at each joint.

Attach four evenly spaced 2 × 2s between the tie beams for rafters using 2½" deck screws.

Mark and cut the lap joints. Sand the cut surfaces, then touch them up with paint, stain, or sealer and let them dry.

Position a tie beam flush with the top of the posts. Clamp the beam into place and drill pilot holes through it and into each post. Drive four 1¼" deck screws into each joint to attach the tie beam to the posts at the half-lap joints (**photo 4**). Install both tie beams.

ATTACH THE RAFTERS

Hold a 2 × 2 in position between the tie beams, flush with the top of the beams. Drill pilot holes through the tie beams, one into each end of the rafter; secure the rafter with 2½" deck screws. Repeat, placing a total of four evenly spaced rafters across the span of the tie beams (**photo 5**).

ADD THE TRIM

OPTIONAL: *Set a millwork bracket into place at each of the corners between the tie beams and the trellis*

frame posts (**photo 6**). Drill pilot holes and secure the brackets using finish nails.

BUILD THE GATE FRAME

Lay out the parts of the gate frame and measure from one corner to the diagonally opposite corner. Repeat at the opposite corners. Adjust the pieces until these measurements are equal and the frame is square. Secure each joint using 2½" deck screws. Position a 2 × 4 so it runs from the bottom of the hinge side of the frame to the first horizontal brace on the latch side. Mark the angle of the cutting lines (**photo 7**), then cut the brace to fit using a circular saw. Use 2½" deck screws to secure the brace into position.

ADD THE SIDING

Clamp a 2 × 4 across the bottom of the frame to act as a reference for the length of the pickets. Position the siding flush with the lower edge of the clamped 2 × 4. Align the right edge of a 1 × 6 flush with the right edge of the frame. Drill pilot holes and attach the siding to the frame using 1½" deck screws. Set scraps of ⅝"-thick plywood in place as spacers, then add a second 1 × 6. Continuing to use the ⅝" plywood as spacers, cover the remainder of the frame with 1 × 4 siding (**photo 8**).

HANG THE GATE

Measure and mark the hinge positions on the gate. Drill pilot holes and drive screws to secure the hinges to the gate. On the handle-side post, clamp a 1 × 2 in place to act as a stop for the gate. Shim the gate into position, centered within the opening. Use a carpenter's level to make sure the gate is level and plumb and the stop is properly positioned. Mark the position of the stop and set the gate aside. Drill pilot holes and secure the stop to the post using 2½" deck screws (**photo 9**).

With the gate shimmed back into position, mark the hinge-side post to indicate the hinge screw locations, then drill pilot holes. Fasten the hinge to the post using the screws provided with the hinge hardware.

SHAPE THE SIDING & ADD THE GATE HANDLE

Cut a piece of flexible ½"-dia. PVC pipe that's 52½" long (or 12" longer than the width of your gate). Clamp the PVC at the top of the outside edges of the last piece of siding on each side of the gate. Tack a nail just above the first horizontal brace of the frame at the center of the gate. If this happens to be between two pieces of siding, set a scrap behind the siding to hold the nail. Adjust the PVC until it fits just below the nail and creates a pleasing curve. Trace the curve of the PVC onto the face of the siding (**photo 10**). Remove the pipe and cut along the marked line using a jig saw. Sand the tops of the siding and repair the finish as necessary.

Mark the handle location on the gate. Drill pilot holes and secure the handle using the screws provided by the manufacturer.

Add millwork brackets at each corner where the tie beams and the trellis frame posts meet. Secure with finish nails.

Mark and cut the diagonal brace, and then screw it in place using 2-½" deck screws.

Attach the siding. Clamp a 2 × 4 across the bottom of the gate frame as a guide. Begin with two 1 × 6s on the hinge side, then finish with 1 × 4s. Use scraps of ⅝"-thick plywood as spacers.

Attach a 1 × 2 to the latch-side gatepost as a stop, using 1½" deck screws.

Draw the curved gate profile. Clamp the ends of a length of PVC pipe at each end of the gate top. Deflect the pipe down to create the curve, and trace. Cut to shape using a jig saw.

Classical Pergola

Tall and stately, the columned pergola is perhaps the grandest of garden structures. Its minimal design defines an area without enclosing it and makes it easy to place anywhere—from out in the open yard to right up against your house. Vines and flowers clinging to the stout framework create an eye-catching statement of strength and beauty.

In our selected project, Tuscan-style columns supporting shaped beams mimic the column-and-entablature construction used throughout classical architecture. Painting the columns white or adding faux marbling enhances the classical styling. The columns used here are made of structural fiberglass designed for outdoor use. They even adhere to the ancient practice of tapering the top two-thirds of the shaft.

Structural fiberglass columns, like the ones used in this project, are available from architectural products dealers (see Resources, page 236). You can order them over the phone and have them shipped to your door. This type of column is weather-resistant, but most manufacturers recommend painting them for appearance and longevity. Whatever columns you use, be sure to follow the manufacturer's instructions for installation and maintenance.

Materials ▸

6 8"-dia. by 8 ft. columns	6 ½"-dia. × 99" threaded rod and coupling nuts
6 16"-dia. concrete tube forms	Exterior construction adhesive or waterproof wood glue
4 2 × 8" × 16 ft. treated pine	
7 2 × 6" × 8 ft. treated pine	16d galvanized common nails
1 4 × 4" × 8 ft. treated post	6 Corrosion-resistant bearing plates
Compactable gravel	Deck screws (2½")
Concrete (3,000 PSI)	Coupling nuts
6 ½" × 6" J-bolts	Paintable caulk
6 ½"-dia. × 48" threaded rod and coupling nuts	Paint

Building a pergola is a fairly major carpentry project, but it is also a very rewarding way to put your skills to work and create a beautiful structure in your yard.

Classical Pergola

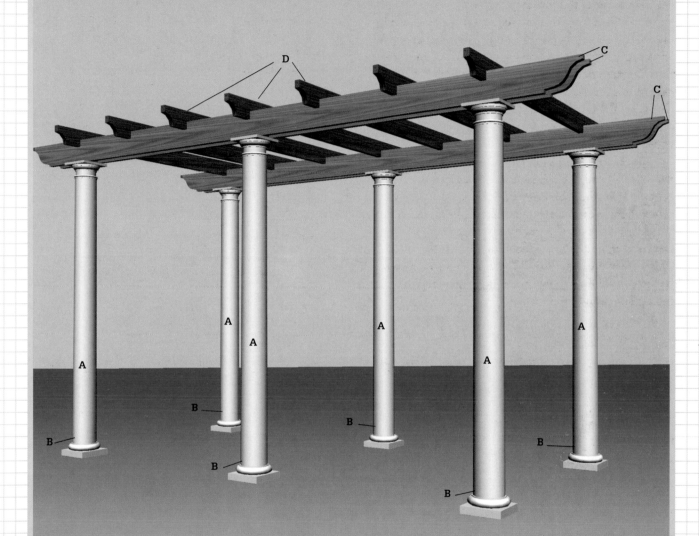

Key	Part	Dimension	Pcs.	Material
A	Columns	8" dia x 8 ft.	6	Structural fiberglass
B	Concrete Piers	16" dia.	6	Concrete & tube forms
C	Main beams	$1\frac{1}{2} \times 7\frac{1}{4}" \times 16$ ft.	4	Treated pine
D	Crossbeams	$1\frac{1}{2} \times 5\frac{1}{2}" \times 8$ ft.	7	Treated pine
E	Blocks*	$3\frac{1}{2} \times 3\frac{1}{2} \times 8"$	6	Treated pine

*See Classical Pergola Side Elevation

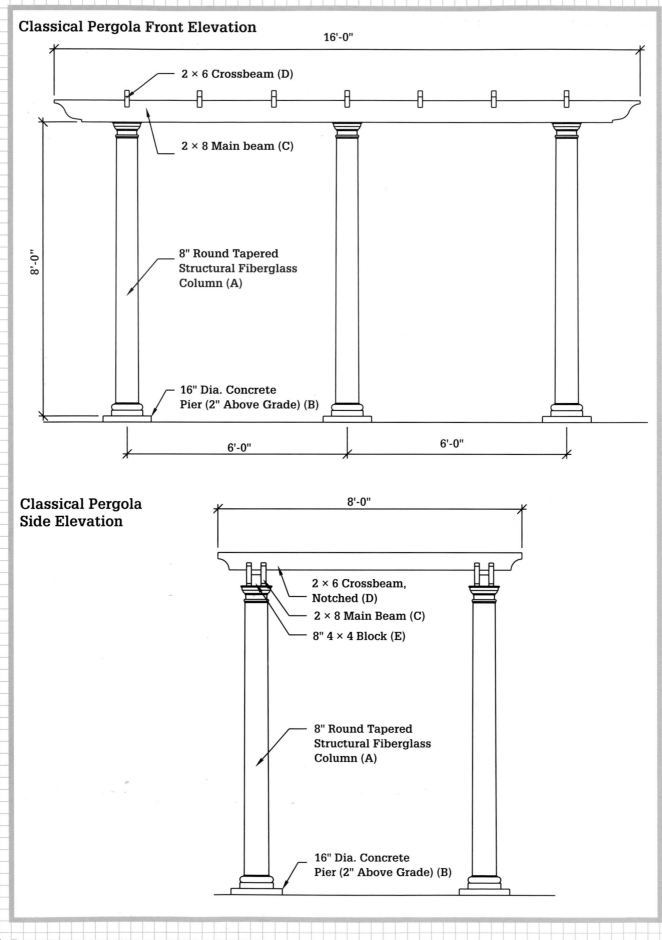

Classical Pergola Front Elevation

16'-0"

2 × 6 Crossbeam (D)

2 × 8 Main beam (C)

8'-0"

8" Round Tapered
Structural Fiberglass
Column (A)

16" Dia. Concrete
Pier (2" Above Grade) (B)

6'-0"

6'-0"

Classical Pergola
Side Elevation

8'-0"

2 × 6 Crossbeam,
Notched (D)

2 × 8 Main Beam (C)

8" 4 × 4 Block (E)

8" Round Tapered
Structural Fiberglass
Column (A)

16" Dia. Concrete
Pier (2" Above Grade) (B)

Classical Pergola Foundation Plan

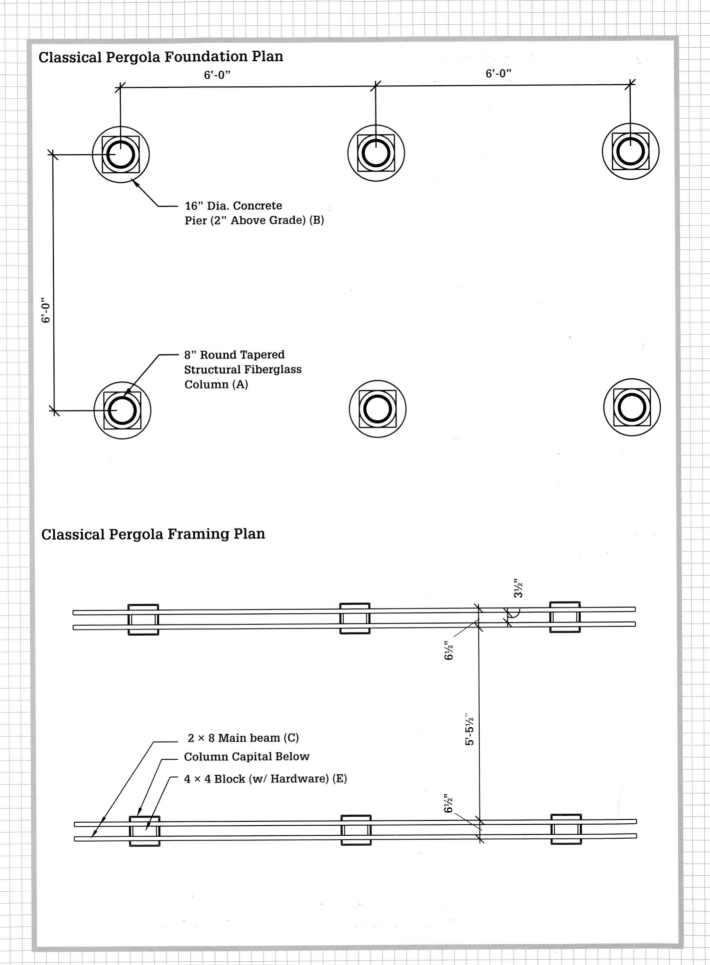

6'-0"   6'-0"

6'-0"

16" Dia. Concrete
Pier (2" Above Grade) (B)

8" Round Tapered
Structural Fiberglass
Column (A)

Classical Pergola Framing Plan

3½"

6½"

5'-5½"

6½"

2 × 8 Main beam (C)

Column Capital Below

4 × 4 Block (w/ Hardware) (E)

Classical Pergola Roof Framing Plan

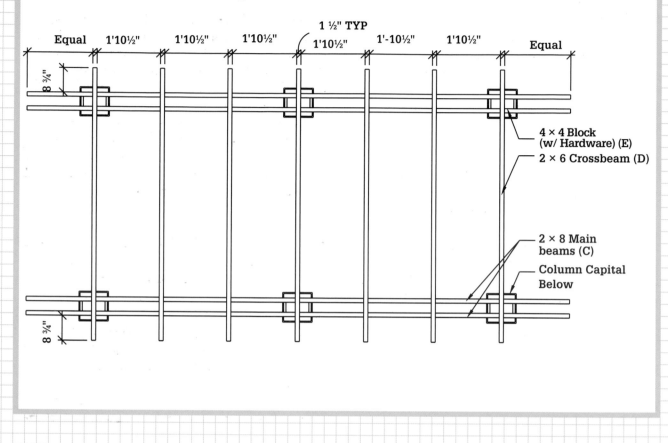

Equal 1'10½" 1'10½" 1'10½" 1 ½" TYP 1'-10½" 1'10½" Equal
1'10½"

8 ¾"

8 ¾"

4 × 4 Block (w/ Hardware) (E)
2 × 6 Crossbeam (D)
2 × 8 Main beams (C)
Column Capital Below

Classical Pergola Beam End Templates

1" × 1" GRID SHOWN

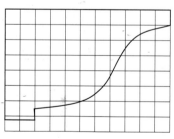

2 × 8 Main beams

2 × 6 Crossbeams

Classical Pergola Column Connection

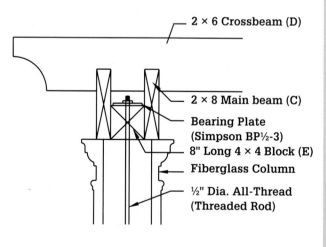

2 × 6 Crossbeam (D)
2 × 8 Main beam (C)
Bearing Plate (Simpson BP½-3)
8" Long 4 × 4 Block (E)
Fiberglass Column
½" Dia. All-Thread (Threaded Rod)

Classical Pergola

POUR THE FOOTINGS

Set up batter boards and mason's lines to lay out the pergola columns following the Foundation Plan on page 229. Dig the six holes for the concrete forms. Add a layer of gravel, then set and brace the forms. Make sure the pier depth and gravel layer meet the requirements of the local building code. For this project, the piers are 16" in diameter and extend at least 2" above the ground. You may have to adjust the height of some piers so that all of them are in the same level plane; measure against your level mason's lines to compensate for any unevenness of the ground.

Pour the concrete for each form, and set a ½ × 6" J-bolt in the center of the wet concrete. Make sure the bolt is perfectly plumb and extends 1¾ to 2" above the surface of the concrete. Following the concrete manufacturer's instructions, finish the tops of the piers to create a smooth, attractive surface (**photo 1**). When painted, the piers become part of the finished project.

CUT & SHAPE THE BEAMS

Cut the four main beams to length at 192". Cut the seven crossbeams to length at 96". Check all of the beams for crowning—a slight arching shape that's apparent when the board is set on edge. Hold each board flat and sight along its narrow edges. If the board arches, mark the top (convex) side of the arch. This is the crowned edge and should always be installed facing up.

Make cardboard patterns for shaping the ends of the main beams and crossbeams; follow the Beam End Templates on page 230. Use the patterns to mark the shapes onto the beam ends. Shape the beam ends using a jigsaw, coping saw, or bandsaw, and then sand the cuts smooth.

CONSTRUCT THE MAIN BEAM ASSEMBLIES

Cut six 4 × 4 blocks at 8". Lay each block flat, and drill a ⁹⁄₁₆"-dia. hole through the center of one side. Coat the ends of the blocks and the insides of the holes with wood preservative, following the manufacturer's instructions. The blocks are the main structural connecting points for the pergola, and the preservative helps prevent rotting that may occur over the years.

Make a mark 20" in from the end of each main beam. These marks represent the outside ends of the

Finish the tops of the concrete piers using a concrete float after making sure the J-bolt is perpendicular and no more than 2" above the surface.

Sandwich the blocks between the main beams, and fasten the assemblies with exterior adhesive and 16d nails.

blocks. Construct the main beam assemblies by applying construction adhesive or waterproof wood glue to the side faces of the blocks and sandwiching the beams over the blocks. Make sure the blocks are flush with the bottoms of the beams and their ends are on the reference marks. The holes are face up (vertical). Clamp the assembly, and then fasten the beams to the blocks with 16d common nails (**photo 2**). Drive four nails on each side, making sure to avoid the center hole in the blocks. Let the glue dry completely.

Mark the crossbeam layout on to the top edges of main beams, following the Roof Framing Plan on page 230.

PREPARE & SET THE COLUMNS

You'll need at least two helpers for this step and the following step. Once you set the columns for one side, continue to the next step to install the main beam. Then, repeat the two steps for the other side of the pergola.

Cut the threaded rods to length at 99". Add a corrosion-resistant coupler nut to each J-bolt (threaded anchor rod for patio installation). Lay the columns down next to their respective piers. Slip the base and capital over the ends of the column shafts; these will stay loose so you can slide them out of the way until you secure them.

Run the threaded rod through the center of each column. Tip up each column and center it on top of a pier. Check the joint where the column meets the pier; it should make even contact all the way around the column. If necessary, use a rasp to shave the end of the column to ensure even contact.

While one person holds the column out of the way, thread the rod into the coupling nut (**photo 3**). Adjust the nut so the rod and J-bolt have equal penetration into the nut, and tighten the nut following the manufacturer's instructions. Temporarily brace the column if necessary or have a helper hold it upright. Set up the remaining two columns.

SET THE MAIN BEAMS

Using stepladders set up next to the columns, place one of the main beams onto the columns, inserting the rod ends through the blocks. Check for even contact of the beam on all three columns. If necessary, you can trim a column: Cut from the bottom end only using a sharp handsaw. *Note: If there's a slight gap above the center column due to a crowning beam, it will most likely be gone once the beam is anchored.*

Install the columns. Have one person lift up the column while another tightens the coupler nut to the J-bolt and threaded rod.

Center the column at both ends, then tighten the nut over the bearing plate to secure the entire assembly.

Make the notch cuts. Set a circular saw to cut kerfs just above the notch seat; clean up the notch with a chisel and mallet.

Seal the columns. After fastening the base and capital, caulk all of the joints to hide any gaps and create a watertight barrier.

Add bearing plates and nuts to the end of each threaded rod, loosely threading the nuts. Working on one column at a time, make sure the column shaft is centered on the pier and is centered under the beam block at the top end. Place a 2-ft. level along the bottom, untapered section of the column shaft and check the column for plumb. Hold the column plumb while a helper tightens the nut on the rod (**photo 4**). Repeat to adjust and secure the remaining columns. Repeat the procedure to install the columns and beam on the other side of the pergola.

NOTCH & INSTALL THE CROSSBEAMS

Place each crossbeam onto the layout marks on top of the main beams so the crossbeam overhangs equally at both ends. Mark each edge where the main beam pieces meet the crossbeam. This ensures that the notches will be accurate for each crossbeam. Number the crossbeams so you can install them in the same order. On your workbench, mark the notches for cutting at 2½" deep.

To cut the notches, you can save time by clamping two beams together and cutting both at once. Using a circular saw or handsaw, first cut the outside edges of the notches. Next, make a series of interior cuts at ⅛" intervals (**photo 5**). Use a mallet and chisel to remove the waste and smooth the seats of the notches.

Set the crossbeams onto the main beams following the marked layout. Drill angled pilot holes through the sides of the crossbeams and into the main beams; drill one hole on each side, offsetting the holes so the screws won't hit each other. Fasten the crossbeams with 2½" deck screws.

FINISH THE COLUMNS

Secure the base to the pier with masonry screws: First, drill pilot holes slightly larger than the screws through the base. Using a masonry bit, drill pilot holes into the pier. Fasten the base with the screws. Fit each capital against the main beam, drill pilot holes, and fasten the capital with deck screws.

Caulk the joints around the capital and base with high quality, paintable caulk (**photo 6**). Paint the columns—and beams, if desired— using a primer and paint recommended by the column manufacturer.

Reference Charts

Metric Conversions

To Convert:	To:	Multiply by:
Inches	Millimeters	25.4
Inches	Centimeters	2.54
Feet	Meters	0.305
Yards	Meters	0.914
Square inches	Square centimeters	6.45
Square feet	Square meters	0.093
Square yards	Square meters	0.836
Ounces	Milliliters	30.0
Pints (U.S.)	Liters	0.473 (Imp. 0.568)
Quarts (U.S.)	Liters	0.946 (Imp. 1.136)
Gallons (U.S.)	Liters	3.785 (Imp. 4.546)
Ounces	Grams	28.4
Pounds	Kilograms	0.454

To Convert:	To:	Multiply by:
Millimeters	Inches	0.039
Centimeters	Inches	0.394
Meters	Feet	3.28
Meters	Yards	1.09
Square centimeters	Square inches	0.155
Square meters	Square feet	10.8
Square meters	Square yards	1.2
Milliliters	Ounces	.033
Liters	Pints (U.S.)	2.114 (Imp. 1.76)
Liters	Quarts (U.S.)	1.057 (Imp. 0.88)
Liters	Gallons (U.S.)	0.264 (Imp. 0.22)
Grams	Ounces	0.035
Kilograms	Pounds	2.2

Converting Temperatures

Convert degrees Fahrenheit (F) to degrees Celsius (C) by following this simple formula: Subtract 32 from the Fahrenheit temperature reading. Then, multiply that number by $5/9$. For example, $77°F - 32 = 45$. $45 \times 5/9 = 25°C$.

To convert degrees Celsius to degrees Fahrenheit, multiply the Celsius temperature reading by $9/5$. Then, add 32. For example, $25°C \times 9/5 = 45$. $45 + 32 = 77°F$.

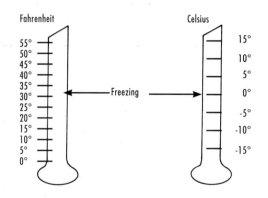

Metric Plywood Panels

Metric plywood panels are commonly available in two sizes: 1,200 mm × 2,400 mm and 1,220 mm × 2,400 mm, which is roughly equivalent to a 4 × 8-ft. sheet. Standard and Select sheathing panels come in standard thicknesses, while Sanded grade panels are available in special thicknesses.

Standard Sheathing Grade		Sanded Grade	
7.5 mm	(5/16 in.)	6 mm	(4/17 in.)
9.5 mm	(3/8 in.)	8 mm	(5/16 in.)
12.5 mm	(1/2 in.)	11 mm	(7/16 in.)
15.5 mm	(5/8 in.)	14 mm	(9/16 in.)
18.5 mm	(3/4 in.)	17 mm	(2/3 in.)
20.5 mm	(13/16 in.)	19 mm	(3/4 in.)
22.5 mm	(7/8 in.)	21 mm	(13/16 in.)
25.5 mm	(1 in.)	24 mm	(15/16 in.)

Lumber Dimensions

Nominal - U.S.	Actual - U.S. (in inches)	Metric
1 × 2	3/4 × 1 1/2	19 × 38 mm
1 × 3	3/4 × 2 1/2	19 × 64 mm
1 × 4	3/4 × 3 1/2	19 × 89 mm
1 × 5	3/4 × 4 1/2	19 × 114 mm
1 × 6	3/4 × 5 1/2	19 × 140 mm
1 × 7	3/4 × 6 1/4	19 × 159 mm
1 × 8	3/4 × 7 1/4	19 × 184 mm
1 × 10	3/4 × 9 1/4	19 × 235 mm
1 × 12	3/4 × 11 1/4	19 × 286 mm
1 1/4 × 4	1 × 3 1/2	25 × 89 mm
1 1/4 × 6	1 × 5 1/2	25 × 140 mm
1 1/4 × 8	1 × 7 1/4	25 × 184 mm
1 1/4 × 10	1 × 9 1/4	25 × 235 mm
1 1/4 × 12	1 × 11 1/4	25 × 286 mm
1 1/2 × 4	1 1/4 × 3 1/2	32 × 89 mm
1 1/2 × 6	1 1/4 × 5 1/2	32 × 140 mm
1 1/2 × 8	1 1/4 × 7 1/4	32 × 184 mm
1 1/2 × 10	1 1/4 × 9 1/4	32 × 235 mm
1 1/2 × 12	1 1/4 × 11 1/4	32 × 286 mm
2 × 4	1 1/2 × 3 1/2	38 × 89 mm
2 × 6	1 1/2 × 5 1/2	38 × 140 mm
2 × 8	1 1/2 × 7 1/4	38 × 184 mm
2 × 10	1 1/2 × 9 1/4	38 × 235 mm
2 × 12	1 1/2 × 11 1/4	38 × 286 mm
3 × 6	2 1/2 × 5 1/2	64 × 140 mm
4 × 4	3 1/2 × 3 1/2	89 × 89 mm
4 × 6	3 1/2 × 5 1/2	89 × 140 mm

Liquid Measurement Equivalents

1 Pint	= 16 Fluid Ounces	= 2 Cups
1 Quart	= 32 Fluid Ounces	= 2 Pints
1 Gallon	= 128 Fluid Ounces	= 4 Quarts

Drill Bit Guide

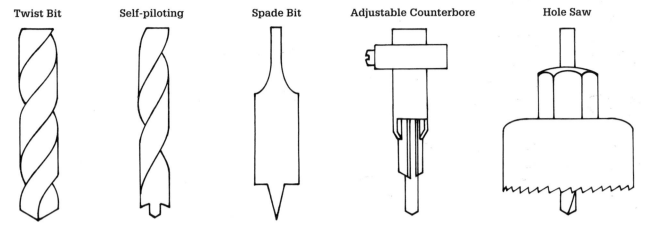

Twist Bit   Self-piloting   Spade Bit   Adjustable Counterbore   Hole Saw

Counterbore, Shank & Pilot Hole Diameters

Screw Size	Counterbore Diameter for Screw Head	Clearance Hole for Screw Shank	Pilot Hole Diameter	
			Hard Wood	Soft Wood
#1	.146 9/64	5/64	3/64	1/32
#2	1/4	3/32	3/64	1/32
#3	1/4	7/64	1/16	3/64
#4	1/4	1/8	1/16	3/64
#5	1/4	9/64	5/64	1/16
#6	5/16	5/32	3/32	5/64
#7	5/16	5/32	3/32	5/64
#8	3/8	11/64	1/8	3/32
#9	3/8	11/64	1/8	3/32
#10	3/8	3/16	1/8	7/64
#11	1/2	3/16	5/32	9/64
#12	1/2	7/32	9/64	1/8

Abrasive Paper Grits - (Aluminum Oxide)

Very Coarse	Coarse	Medium	Fine	Very Fine
12 - 36	40 - 60	80 - 120	150 - 180	220 - 600

Credits

© Lorraine Kourafas
p. 7 iStockphoto

Simon McBride
p. 77 Photolibrary

Lynn Keddie
p. 121 Photolibrary

Nora Frei
p. 181 Photolibrary

© Brian Vanden Brink
p. 226

Resources

Airless bicycle wheels
865-644-0494
www.airfreetires.com
p. 174

Aluminum angle
859-745-2650
www.metalsdepot.com
p. 112

Axle push cap (½")
888-713-2880
www.sportsmith.net
p. 75

Decorative Washers
(finish washers)
800-279-4441
www.rockler.com
p. 20

Dek-Block Piers
Precast concrete piers
800-664-2705
www.deckplans.com
p. 14

Power tools & accessories
Black & Decker Corp.
800-544-6986
www.blackanddecker.com

Stainless steel lag screws
(and other stainless steel fasteners)
McFeely's
800-443-7937
www.mcfeelys.com
p. 40

Structural Fiberglass Columns
Pacific Columns Inc.
800-294-1098
www.enduracolumns.com
p. 226

Index

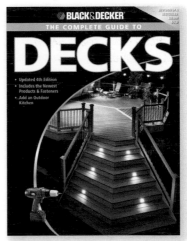
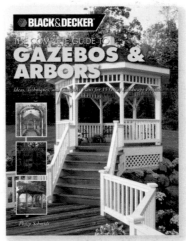
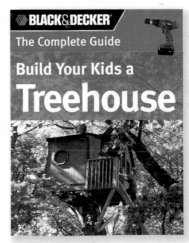